JANE AUSTEN: *Emma* (Revised) David Lodge
JANE AUSTEN: *'Northanger Abbey'* & *'Persuasion'* B. C. Southam
JANE AUSTEN: *'Sense and Sensibility'*, *'Pride and Prejudice'* & *'Mansfield Park'*
  B. C. Southam
BECKETT: *Waiting for Godot* Ruby Cohn
WILLIAM BLAKE: *Songs of Innocence and Experience* Margaret Bottrall
CHARLOTTE BRONTE: *'Jane Eyre'* & *'Villette'* Miriam Allott
EMILY BRONTE: *Wuthering Heights* (Revised) Miriam Allott
BROWNING: *'Men and Women'* & *Other Poems* J. R. Watson
CHAUCER: *The Canterbury Tales* J. J. Anderson
COLERIDGE: *'The Ancient Mariner'* & *Other Poems* Alun R. Jones & W. Tydeman
CONRAD: *'Heart of Darkness'*, *'Nostromo'* & *'Under Western Eyes'* C. B. Cox
CONRAD: *The Secret Agent* Ian Watt
DICKENS: *Bleak House* A. E. Dyson
DICKENS: *'Hard Times'*, *'Great Expectations'* & *'Our Mutual Friend'* Norman Page
DICKENS: *'Dombey and Son'* & *'Little Dorrit'* Alan Shelston
DONNE: *Songs and Sonets* Julian Lovelock
GEORGE ELIOT: *Middlemarch* Patrick Swinden
GEORGE ELIOT: *'The Mill on the Floss'* & *'Silas Marner'* R. P. Draper
T. S. ELIOT: *'Prufrock'*, *'Gerontion'* & *'Ash Wednesday'* B. C. Southam
T. S. ELIOT: *The Waste Land* C. B. Cox & Arnold P. Hinchliffe
T. S. ELIOT: *Plays* Arnold P. Hinchliffe
HENRY FIELDING: *Tom Jones* Neil Compton
E.M. FORSTER: *A Passage to India* Malcolm Bradbury
WILLIAM GOLDING: *Novels 1954–64* Norman Page
HARDY: *The Tragic Novels* (Revised) R. P. Draper
HARDY: *Poems* James Gibson & Trevor Johnson
HARDY: *Three Pastoral Novels* R. P. Draper
GERARD MANLEY HOPKINS: *Poems* Margaret Bottrall
HENRY JAMES: *'Washington Square'* & *'The Portrait of a Lady'* Alan Shelton
JONSON: *Volpone* Jonas A. Barish
JONSON: *'Every Man in his Humour'* & *'The Alchemist'* R. V. Holdsworth
JAMES JOYCE: *'Dubliners'* & *'A Portrait of the Artist as a Young Man'* Morris Beja
KEATS: *Odes* G.S. Fraser
KEATS: *Narrative Poems* John Spencer Hill
D.H. LAWRENCE: *Sons and Lovers* Gamini Salgado
D.H. LAWRENCE: *'The Rainbow'* & *'Women in Love'* Colin Clarke
LOWRY: *Under the Volcano* Gordon Bowker
MARLOWE: *Doctor Faustus* John Jump
MARLOWE: *'Tamburlaine the Great'*, *'Edward II'* & *'The Jew of Malta'* J. R. Brown
MARLOWE: *Poems* Arthur Pollard
MAUPASSANT: *In the Hall of Mirrors* T. Harris
MILTON: *Paradise Lost* A. E. Dyson & Julian Lovelock
O'CASEY: *'Juno and the Paycock'*, *'The Plough and the Stars'* & *'The Shadow of a Gunman'* Ronald Ayling
EUGENE O'NEILL: *Three Plays* Normand Berlin
JOHN OSBORNE: *Look Back in Anger* John Russell Taylor
PINTER: *'The Birthday Party'* & *Other Plays* Michael Scott
POPE: *The Rape of the Lock* John Dixon Hunt
SHAKESPEARE: *A Midsummer Night's Dream* Antony Price
SHAKESPEARE: *Antony and Cleopatra* (Revised) John Russell Brown
SHAKESPEARE: *Coriolanus* B. A. Brockman

Jane Austen

Northanger Abbey and *Persuasion*

A CASEBOOK

EDITED BY

B. C. SOUTHAM

MACMILLAN

First published 1976 by
THE MACMILLAN PRESS LTD
Houndmills, Basingstoke, Hampshire RG21 2XS
and London
Companies and representatives
throughout the world

ISBN 0–333–19208–7

A catalogue record for this book is available
from the British Library.

15 14 13 12 11 10 9 8 7
03 02 01 00 99 98 97 96 95

Printed in Hong Kong

CONTENTS

Part Two: *Persuasion*

1. *Contemporary and Victorian Opinions*

2. *Twentieth-century Studies*

ACKNOWLEDGEMENTS

The editor and publishers wish to thank the following, who have kindly given permission for the use of copyright material: Elizabeth Bowen, *'Persuasion'*, by permission of Curtis Brown Ltd on behalf of the Estate of Elizabeth Bowen; Malcolm Bradbury, *'Persuasion* Again', from *Essays in Criticism*, xviii (1968), by permission of the author and editors of *Essays in Criticism*; Marilyn Butler, 'The Juvenilia and *Northanger Abbey'*, from *Jane Austen and the War of Ideas*, © Oxford University Press 1975, reprinted by permission of the publisher; R. S. Crane, 'Jane Austen: *Persuasion'*, essay in *The Idea of the Humanities and Other Essays, Critical and Historical* (1967), by permission of Mrs Julia Crane and The University of Chicago Press; D. W. Harding, Introduction to 'Jane Austen: *Persuasion'*, © D. W. Harding 1965, reprinted by permission of Penguin Books Ltd; D. W. Harding, extract from 'Regulated Hatred: An Aspect of the Work of Jane Austen', from *Scrutiny*, viii (1940), reprinted by permission of the author and Cambridge University Press; Elizabeth Hardwick, extract from 'Afterword' from New English Library edition of *Northanger Abbey* (1965), by permission of the author; Mary Lascelles, extracts from *Jane Austen and her Art* (1939), published by Oxford University Press and reprinted by permission; A. Walton Litz, *'Persuasion*: Forms of Estrangement', from *Jane Austen: Bicentenary Essays* (1975), by permission of the author and Cambridge University Press; Marvin Mudrick, 'The Literary Pretext Continued: Irony *versus* Gothicism', from *Jane Austen: Irony as Defense and Discovery* (1952), by permission of the author; Virginia Woolf, extract from *The Common Reader* (1925), by permission of the Hogarth Press on behalf of the author's Literary Estate.

GENERAL EDITOR'S PREFACE

The Casebook series, launched in 1968, has become a well-regarded library of critical studies. The central concern of the series remains the 'single-author' volume, but suggestions from the academic community have led to an extension of the original plan, to include occasional volumes on such general themes as literary 'schools' and genres.

Each volume in the central category deals either with one well-known and influential work by an individual author, or with closely related works by one writer. The main section consists of critical readings, mostly modern, collected from books and journals. A selection of reviews and comments by the author's contemporaries is also included, and sometimes comment from the author himself. The Editor's introduction charts the reputation of the work or works from the first appearance to the present time.

Volumes in the 'general themes' category are variable in structure but follow the basic purpose of the series in presenting an integrated selection of readings, with an Introduction which explores the theme and discusses the literary and critical issues involved.

A single volume can represent no more than a small selection of critical opinions. Some critics are excluded for reasons of space, and it is hoped that readers will pursue the suggestions for further reading in the Select Bibliography. Other contributions are severed from their original context, to which some readers may wish to turn. Indeed, if they take a hint from the critics represented here, they certainly will.

A. E. Dyson

VOLUME EDITOR'S FOREWORD

In an earlier Jane Austen Casebook, covering *Sense and Sensibility*, *Pride and Prejudice* and *Mansfield Park* together, a good deal of space in the Introduction and the documents was given to a general discussion of Jane Austen's art – its major characteristics and principles and its contribution to the development of the English novel. There was also a summary account of her life and times, concentrating on the facts of her writing career and the publication and reception of the novels. This range of background information has not been repeated in the present volume, and readers who want to see *Northanger Abbey* and *Persuasion* in a broader biographical and literary-historical context can refer to the appropriate sections in the earlier Casebook.

A note on the text: there are a few odd spellings in the documents collected here. For example, Whately writes about 'Miss Austin', Margaret Oliphant about 'General Tylney', Howells about 'Eliot' and 'Admiral Crofts'. These could be printers' errors; but they look more like the misrememberings of the critics themselves (single 'l' 'Eliot' and 'Austin' are not uncommon in the early reviews and articles). So, for their more than curiosity value, I have let them stand.

B. C. S.

INTRODUCTION

Critics have tended to keep *Persuasion* and *Northanger Abbey* apart, to put *Persuasion* towards the top of the list and *Northanger Abbey* towards the bottom. Of the six novels, *Northanger Abbey* is usually regarded as the youthful work, brisk, high-spirited and unprofound, *Persuasion* as the mature and autumnal novel, a product of the last, reflective phase of the author's life, in which she takes an older heroine, a woman whose experience of love is touched with disappointment and loss. *Northanger Abbey* is seen as the most purely comic, the most detached and, in terms of its narrative technique, the most primitive and undeveloped of the six novels, *Persuasion* as the one in which Jane Austen's personal feelings and experiences were most deeply involved and which displays the originality and inventiveness of her artistry at a highly developed stage.

So, although the pairing of the novels in this Casebook is an unplanned accident of the Series, it is a convenient accident, since it brings together for comparison elements of the early and late Jane Austen (or, as some critics would put it, the 'mature' and 'immature'). The further logic to this pairing is that the two novels were originally published together as a four-volume set in December 1817 (1818 on the title-pages). This was not intended to suggest any special association between them; it was merely that these were the two completed manuscripts that remained unpublished at the time of Jane Austen's death in July 1817. Her brother Henry thought that it would be appropriate to bring them out together (easily managed, since both were on the short side). He also took the occasion to provide a 'Biographical Notice' at the beginning of the set. This revealed the identity of the anonymous 'Lady' whose previous four novels had won for her a keen and devoted following, which even included the Prince Regent, so much an enthusiast that he kept a complete set of the novels in each of the royal residences and invited the dedication of *Emma*.

The publication of *Northanger Abbey* and *Persuasion*, with the biographical sketch, gave the reviewers an opportunity to pay Jane Austen the tribute of an appreciative farewell, to lament that six novels were all too few. This note of regret was echoed memorably a few years later in Sir Walter Scott's diary. After he had finished reading *Pride and Prejudice* for the third time, he jotted down, 'That young lady had a talent for describing the involvement and feelings and characters of ordinary life which is to me the most wonderful I ever met with. The Big Bow-wow strain I can do myself like any now going, but the exquisite touch which renders ordinary commonplace things and characters interesting from the truth of the description and the sentiment is denied to me. What a pity such a gifted creature died so early!'[1]

This entry is worth quoting, not so much for its final note of regret as for its sharp and succinct identification of these central qualities in Jane Austen's art. Scott was writing only for himself so the points are not spelt out. But he was making an important distinction between two types of fiction, his own 'Big Bow-wow' style of the Romantic, historical novel – with its broad canvas, its social panorama, its highly dramatic rendering of great events, its interpretation of momentous political and social processes, its colour and swagger – as against the quiet small-scale effects of Jane Austen's domestic fiction, where the power and scope of the writer's imagination is not measured by the dimensions of the story or the magnitude of its events but by the 'truth' (as Scott puts it) with which 'the involvement and feelings and characters of ordinary life' are drawn. Scott's was the epic fiction of public history, Jane Austen's the domestic fiction of private lives, whose 'truth' lay in its aesthetic and moral realism, its ironic, unsentimental acceptance that 'man's inhumanity to man' can take place between two women in a Regency drawing-room as cruelly and destructively to the human spirit as the actual woundings and cruelties of the man's world of real conflict and aggression. Scott recognised that the miniature truths of Jane Austen's fiction were as penetrating and important to an understanding of life as the large truths of his wide historical compass. This contrast between the Bow-wowism of Romantic literature and Jane Austen's subdued everyday sobriety is also explored in the *Blackwood's Magazine* review, May 1818 (pp. 47–50).

Within Scott's recognition lies part of the answer to the seeming paradox of Jane Austen's art, the reconciliation of the greatness of her achievement with the minuteness of her fictional scene – its tight focus on the middle-class gentry, predominantly the lesser country gentry; its persistent 'commonplaceness', if to write about the everyday facts of everyday life is to be commonplace. Some strands of this argument were first laid out in Scott's famous review of *Emma* (in the *Quarterly Review*, XIV, March 1816), where he drew attention to the artistic feat involved in creating fiction which imitates ordinary, verifiable reality, which succeeds in remaining faithful to the characters, events and situations in 'the current of ordinary life' and where the 'dramatis personae conduct themselves upon the motives and principles which the reader may recognise as ruling their own and most of their acquaintances'. Scott pointed out that this was not a realism and a truth-to-life *in vacuo*, not just a virtuoso feat, an end in itself, but critically directed and providing an implicit commentary upon the unrealities of popular contemporary fiction. Some of this 'trash' (Jane Austen's own word for it) was unreal simply because it was badly written, some of it because the authors were anyway pursuing an 'unreal' purpose in trying to present an improved version of life, idealised and morally inspiring, while another kind of unreality stemmed from romantic melodrama furnished with distressed heroines, heroic heroes and villainous villains. The story of *Emma*, he remarked, has 'cross-purposes enough (were the novel of a more romantic cast) for cutting half the men's throats and breaking all the women's hearts'. It is not that Jane Austen is *un*-romantic but *anti*-romantic: anti-romantic aesthetically, in the fact of her realism, and directly, in satirising the conventions of the popular novel, as, for example, she parodies the rhetoric and behaviour of 'sentimental' fiction in *Sense and Sensibility*, the 'first impressions' convention in *Pride and Prejudice* and the Gothic novel in *Northanger Abbey*.

Scott identified in Jane Austen what he called 'the modern novel'. His line of analysis was continued in the other major essay of this period, the 1821 review of *Northanger Abbey* and *Persuasion* by Whately. The very short sections of the review relating directly to these novels are quoted below (pp. 50–1, 131–5). But Whately's general argument is important in helping us to understand the immediate context of his remarks and the critical-philosophical position from which he was writing. He asked that the novel, until then regarded as a rather inferior literary form, should now be taken seriously because it was capable, in its imitation of life, of giving a 'correct' and instructive view of everyday existence: 'it guides the judgement, and supplies a kind of artificial experience'. Whately is careful to explain what he means by a 'correct' view. It turns on the distinction between the terms 'natural' and 'probable', an Aristotelian premise: the novel is a kind of 'fictitious biography', offering us 'the general, instead of the particular . . . the probable instead of the true', bringing the result of 'wide experience' into 'small compass'.

The early reviews and comments, especially those of Scott and Whately, are still interesting to us for their critical insights. They are also useful historically in helping us to understand how the novels struck their contemporary audience and in illustrating the literary values that the reviewers brought into play. From the very beginning, with the publication of *Sense and Sensibility* in 1811, the critics had no difficulty in recognising this new and distinctive voice in English fiction. This is not surprising. Jane Austen's style is unmistakable and inimitable. Not only that: at this time, English fiction was in the doldrums. Apart from Scott, there was no other novelist worth naming. However strongly historians of the period may contend on behalf of Fanny Burney, Maria Edgeworth and other candidates, Scott and Jane Austen are the only Regency novelists who answer the simple test of survival. They are the only novelists that people continue to read for pleasure. So to reviewers condemned to a diet of mediocre fiction, Jane Austen's cool, ironic humour, her stylish prose, her elegant and beautifully constructed books came as a refreshing and welcome relief. In particular, they appreciated her combination of entertainment and edification. The idea that literature should have an identifiable moral purpose was a crucial issue in eighteenth-century critical theory, that it should 'teach' as well as 'please'. With the rise of the novel, earlier in the century, this became a heated issue, since of all the literary forms the novel was potentially the most influential. It provided easy reading and became extremely popular. In the eyes of reactionary moral commentators and critics, it was a bogey, an instrument of the devil, let loose to corrupt the minds of the young and impressionable. Love-stories were condemned for their immorality, picaresque comedies of low-life for their unedifying vulgarity, sentimental fiction for its excessive emotionalism, Gothic fiction for its sensationalism. Not content with criticising, some moralising educationalists hit back more positively with 'conduct' novels, illustrating the temptations and pitfalls of everyday life and holding up models of exemplary behaviour.

Jane Austen plays with these arguments. The closing lines of *Northanger Abbey* are a joke against those who read novels expecting to find a pat moral lesson; its opening makes fun of the extravagance of popular fiction; while overall, the novel is a critique of the theory of impressionability: we are invited to ask ourselves how far Catherine Morland is really influenced by her Gothic reading and how much her Gothic fantasising isn't rather a self-titillation that she enters upon semi-consciously, self-dramatisingly, partly following a fashion she has picked up in Bath, partly enjoying her role in a private, interior drama. At the same time, while Jane Austen encourages us to question whether a novel can ever possess our minds so powerfully as to be a threat to judgement, and whether it should be used as a vehicle for moral teaching, she insists upon the novel's status as a supreme product of the creative imagination:

> only some work in which the greatest powers of the mind are displayed, in which the most thorough knowledge of human nature, the happiest delineation of its varieties, the liveliest effusions of wit and humour are conveyed to the world in the best chosen language.

This statement is fenced in with a self-deprecating irony. But its force can be seen in the novels themselves and in the essays of Scott and Whately which carry the recognition that fiction was to be taken seriously as a form of literature and that, at its best, criticism of the novel could itself become a serious intellectual activity.

Northanger Abbey

From a note by Cassandra Austen, we know that *Northanger Abbey* was written 'about the years 98 & 99' (and her spelling of 'North-hanger' settles the question of pronunciation: it should be a hard 'g'). But in 1968, Mr C. S. Emden suggested in the *Review of English Studies* (XIX, 1968) that *Northanger Abbey* might really originate in work of an earlier period, going back to the beginning of the 1790s, when Jane Austen was parodying the various styles of current literature. On this supposition, the novel may have been put together from two separate pieces: a burlesque on Fanny Burney's style of social fiction, corresponding to the first part of the book, Catherine's experiences in Bath; the other, a Gothic satire, corresponding to Catherine's stay at the Abbey. There is no direct evidence to support this theory; none the less, it seems tenable. The two parts are very simply, indeed, minimally linked; no one would argue that *Northanger Abbey* is a structural masterpiece; and the connections between the two parts are adequate, and no more, to the needs of the story. Mr Emden's theory is also consistent with the nature of Jane Austen's development in the 1790s. In the juvenilia – the childhood writing collected in the three notebooks 'Volume the First', 'Volume the Second' and 'Volume the Third' – dating from about 1787 to about 1793 – we can trace a clear movement from pure literary burlesque to satire which intermixes literary elements with realistic social comedy of a kind that we find in the later novels. So there is no strain in supposing the existence of an early parody of Fanny Burney's favourite narrative device, where the story is constructed around the experiences of a young lady on her first entry into fashionable society, exactly as Catherine Morland comes to Bath. On this hypothesis, Cassandra's reference to 1798–9 would be to the combination of the two separate pieces rather than to the writing of *Northanger Abbey* at that time as a work entirely new.

Henceforward, its publishing history was rather chequered. In the spring of 1803 it was sold to the publisher Richard Crosby for £10 and was advertised under the title 'Susan' (presumably, at this stage, this was the heroine's name). But Crosby had second thoughts. Himself a publisher of Gothic tales, he may have come to the conclusion that 'Susan' was rocking the boat too much; or he may have been afraid that the market for Gothic satire was declining. Whatever the reason, he simply sat on the manuscript and Jane Austen left it with him, making no enquiry about its fate until April 1809, when a letter went to Crosby (the signature is a nice ironic touch: 'M. A. D.', the initials for 'Mrs Ashton Dennis', Jane Austen's pseudonym for this correspondence). Crosby offered to return the manuscript for the original £10. But Jane Austen let it pass. By then, she may have found herself tied up in the revision of *Sense and Sensibility* and *Pride and Prejudice*, two other manuscripts dating from the late 1790s for which she had publishing ambitions; and from this point onwards, until the autumn of 1816, her time was taken up fully with the writing of the three later novels, *Mansfield Park*, *Emma* and *Persuasion*, and with the proofs of the four novels that reached publication over these years.

'Susan' remained with Crosby until 1816, when Henry Austen bought it back. Jane Austen may have seen the possibility of working on it again as she came towards the end of *Persuasion*, which was finished in August 1816. There was an interval of six months before she began *Sanditon*, the seventh novel, on 27 January 1817, and it was probably during this time that 'Susan' was revised into *Northanger Abbey* as we know it today. To complete the bibliographical chronology: on 13 March 1817, Jane Austen wrote to her niece Fanny Knight that 'Miss Catherine is put upon the Shelve for the present, and I do not know that she will ever come out . . .'.[2]

The interesting point that emerges from this historical record is that although *Northanger Abbey*'s origins may go back as far as the early 1790s, the manuscript was finally revised in the same year that *Persuasion* was being written. It may have begun as a novice work; but this is not how it left the writer's hands; and any theory of development that labels it 'immature', and *Persuasion* 'mature', has to take account of their proximity in 1816. The implied inferiority of one, the superiority of the other (in December 1817, *Northanger Abbey* was first advertised as 'a Romance', *Persuasion* as 'a Novel'), may, in the event, be confirmed in our reading of the novels. But it is not a discrimination that should be taken for granted, and it certainly does less than justice to the literary brilliance and satirical tone – light, sustained and controlling – of *Northanger Abbey*: qualities which make it so different from each of the other novels and create its distinctive individuality, what Reginald Farrer described as its 'sumptuous vintage'.

Some of these questions are brought to our notice in the 'Advertisement' that Jane Austen provided for *Northanger Abbey* in 1816. She refers there to its completion in 1803, when it was meant 'for immediate publication'; to the mystery of its non-appearance (she never did find out why Crosby kept it back); and she asks her readers to remember that if certain parts of the book have become 'obsolete' it is because 'many more' than thirteen years have passed 'since it was begun, and that during this period, places, manners, books and opinions have undergone considerable changes'.

Jane Austen made no attempt whatsoever to bring the story

up to date. Its Bath is Bath of the late 1790s, with the correct period features – in the social usages and customs, the fashions of dress, speech and behaviour, and the character-types. The only anomaly is a single literary reference, to *Belinda*, a novel by Maria Edgeworth, published in 1801. Apart from this trivial detail, the story is set a year or so earlier, at the height of the Gothic fashion, and the Gothic satire remains keyed-in to the leading Gothic novel of the decade, Mrs Radcliffe's *The Mysteries of Udolpho*, published in 1794, which was still in print and well known in 1816. We see in the *British Critic* review (p. 41) that Gothic fiction was still popular as late as 1818.

What, then, was the extent of the 1816 revision? It must have involved more than simply changing the heroine's name from Susan to Catherine (a change which may have been made necessary by the existence of a novel entitled *Susan*, published in 1809). One answer lies in the freedom of the writing from the kind of stiffness and unevenness that crop up occasionally in *Sense and Sensibility* and even in *Pride and Prejudice*. Instead, the writing is remarkable for its sustained brilliance and the consistency and assurance of the comic tone. We can take this to be the polish of the late revision, the process that renders *Northanger Abbey* the most flawless of the early novels. Another 'maturity' of *Northanger Abbey* can be discovered in Catherine Morland. Whereas in *Sense and Sensibility* the presentation of Marianne Dashwood as a literary heroine (within the scheme of satire upon sentimental fiction) sometimes interferes with her role in the story as a young woman passionately in love, in *Northanger Abbey* Jane Austen's handling of the heroine is faultless: the literary satire nowhere clashes with the vivid realism of her portrayal; Margaret Oliphant is surely not alone in feeling that here we have 'the most captivating picture of a very young girl which fiction, perhaps, has ever furnished' (p. 53).

On the biographical and textual side, there is only one outstanding query. What exactly did Jane Austen mean in March 1817 when she told her niece that she had put the manuscript aside and doubted if it would ever be published, a strange doubt in the face of the 'Advertisement' which was clearly designed with the reading public in view? There are no apparent loose ends to the story nor weaknesses in the style, although Douglas Bush has recently suggested that the last three chapters 'composed mainly of narrative summaries of feelings and events, do not altogether restore the dominant tone and easy flow of the earlier, much larger, and much better part of the novel'.[3]

While each of the other novels has attracted a substantial body of critical writing and possesses its own individual critical tradition, *Northanger Abbey* has inspired rather little, the un-stated implication being that this of the six novels is the most lightweight, the least in need of commentary, interpretatively the least rewarding, technically the least accomplished, artis-tically the least achieved. Certainly, none of the characters belongs to the gallery of Jane Austen's greatest creations. Its emotional range is the most curtailed, the most strictly confined by the comic tone. Of the novels, it engages our feelings least of all. There is nothing to match the passion and bitterness of *Sense and Sensibility*, the Beatrice and Benedict Shakespearianism of Elizabeth Bennet and Darcy, the dense reverberation of *Mansfield Park*'s sombre comedy, the artistic perfection and complexity of *Emma* (the so-called 'Book of Books'), the gravity, tenderness and pathos of *Persuasion*. Judged alongside these other novels, as *Northanger Abbey* is all too often judged, it comes off badly; and (with the notable exception of Reginald Farrer) critics have tended to define its success in rather limited terms, as a youthful *jeu d'esprit*. All this is reflected in the rather insubstantial group of critical documents collected here, with only one considerable essay, the chapter by Marvin Mudrick, and a small quantity of scraps and extracts.

Following the contemporary reviews, the earliest Victorian comments worth quoting are taken from critical works by Julia Kavanagh and Margaret Oliphant, both of whom were very productive novelists who admired Jane Austen, indeed championed her at a time when she was rather lost from public view, yet who none the less wrote about her objectively and analytically: Mrs Oliphant remarking that she is unsurprised that books 'so calm and cold and keen' should fail to stir the general public; Mrs Kavanagh acknowledging 'that powers so great should fail somewhere', 'she is too calm, too dispassionate, too self-possessed to be bitter or eloquent'. Mrs Kavanagh judged *Northanger Abbey* the least good of the novels and she confines herself to illustrating Jane Austen's satirical method in the portrayal of Catherine Morland and the Thorpes. Mrs Oliphant belongs to that small but eloquent group of critics captivated by Catherine Morland. She thought 'the machinery of the story was wonderfully bad, but the novel as a whole saved by its heroine'.

The line of Catherine's admirers is continued by the American critic W. D. Howells who makes the interesting point that 'our delight' in the heroine – her character and her adventures – is so strong as to distract our attention from the Gothic satire; and his descriptive analysis of her encounters with the Thorpes and the Tilneys is warmly affectionate, just as Mrs Oliphant was motherly. The treatment of fictional characters as human beings and the open expression of love and affection may seem inappropriate, sentimental and uncritical. But it is worth remembering that these writers did not see themselves as professional critics writing for an academic audience; neither did they feel any embarrassment in saying what they felt. A. C. Bradley, the great Shakespearian critic, spoke of Elizabeth Bennet as a girl we are meant to fall in love with, as he said he did.[4] This is the 'character' approach to literature, nowadays rather unfashionable. More important, it is a testimony to the power of Jane Austen's character-portrayal, to the fact that readers can experience them as if they are flesh and blood. Of course, this is a question that relates to all Jane Austen's novels and it is touched upon again here in the discussion of *Persuasion* (see pp. 24–38).

Reginald Farrer's *Quarterly Review* essay of 1917 is a minor masterpiece, perhaps *the* minor masterpiece of Jane Austen criticism; his two paragraphs on *Northanger Abbey* are brim-full of ideas. His view of the novel is totally original. He places it above *Sense and Sensibility* and *Pride and Prejudice* and locates it, in Jane Austen's development, as the transitional work, bridging the early and late periods. He also draws our attention to the evidence here of Jane Austen's 'taste for technical problems', her daring and skill in attempting to combine parody and serious comedy. We can only regret that Farrer's *magnum opus* was an exhaustive two-volume study of rock-plants, not a full-scale study of Jane Austen.

To move from this group of writers to Mary Lascelles is a jump that carries us from the carefree pre-critical era to the age of methodology and critical scholarship. The book from which this extract is taken, *Jane Austen and her Art* (1939), is a most subtle and skilful analysis of the novelist's 'art' (in the Jamesian sense of 'the art of the novel'), the first to approach Jane Austen from such a serious technical standpoint. Miss Lascelles' focus, in the chapter 'Reading and Response', is upon the patterns of burlesque that run throughout Jane Austen's work; and in these pages she is concerned with the burlesque method in *Northanger Abbey*, its elaboration and ingenuity, also its imperfection, the evidence for which Miss Lascelles finds in General Tilney's treatment of Catherine at the end of the story and its disassociation from the burlesque structure.

Like Miss Lascelles, D. W. Harding also brings out the weakness of *Northanger Abbey* in relation to the other novels, although from an altogether different point of view. Professor Harding contends that Jane Austen has been persistently mis-read as 'a delicate satirist', as an urbane and comfortable refuge from the pressures and unpleasantnesses of everyday life; and that this misreading is 'an essential part of her complex inten-tion as a writer: her books are, as she meant them to be, read and enjoyed by precisely the sort of people whom she disliked'. Professor Harding takes his first 'misreading' illustration from *Northanger Abbey*; and I have continued the extract to include a second illustration, from *Persuasion*, in order to indicate the direction of the argument for the earlier novel's inferiority (although, of course, this is not his main contention).

One of the most important accounts of *Northanger Abbey* is the chapter taken from Marvin Mudrick's *Jane Austen: Irony as Defense and Discovery* (1952); and anyone coming fresh to the novel might well begin with this as an introduction, since it provides an excellent historical account of the burlesque tradition in the juvenilia and of the literary fashions that Jane Austen was ridiculing there. Professor Mudrick's chronological thesis is that *Northanger Abbey* is the earliest of the novels and that it displays Jane Austen's prime and characteristic response of *irony* at its post-juvenilia stage, at times working against the novel's artistic life. This is a challenging and controversial interpretation. Whether or not its conclusions are accepted, the argument is conducted with close, alert attention to the text and with the assumption that within it we can discover a writer of high intelligence, grappling with a writer's problems in the arrangement and presentation of her material and in her authorial relationship towards it.

Elizabeth Hardwick (1965) takes the Harding–Mudrick line in rejecting the sentimental notion of Jane Austen as a delightful entertainer, the genteel and 'Gentle Jane' of nineteenth-century mythology. Her Jane Austen is a 'serious' writer of 'superb intelligence' and *Northanger Abbey* 'an engaging story of human beings in pursuit of love, money and pleasure', a 'pursuit' 'not always lighthearted and innocently romantic'. Miss Hardwick's piece suggests some worthwhile comparisons with earlier critics: she mentions Professor Mudrick's view of Jane Austen's irony; and her appraisal of Catherine Morland can be usefully considered alongside Julia Kavanagh, Margaret Oliphant and Howells.

The piece by Marilyn Butler is chapter 7 of her recent study, *Jane Austen and the War of Ideas* (1975), an important contribution to literary history and to our understanding of the context of thought in which Jane Austen was writing, in particular, to the ideological debate between the jacobin and sentimental advocates of individualism and revolution, and the conservative voices of traditional morality and social order. This debate was going on in the novels of the period, as well as in straight

polemical writing; and part of Dr Butler's purpose is to draw
our attention to this hitherto neglected and unsuspected ideological element in Jane Austen and to show that although
'ideologically', *Northanger Abbey* 'is a very clear statement of the
anti-jacobin position', the novel preserves its integrity as a work
of art and is quite free from the kind of propagandising and
partisanship that burdened so much contemporary fiction. This
analysis leads Dr Butler to the striking conclusion that in
Northanger Abbey, as in *Sense and Sensibility*, 'Jane Austen's
achievement, the feat of the subtlest technician among the
English novelists, is to rethink the material of the conservative
novel in terms that are at once naturalistic and intellectually
consistent'.

Finally, I have included a short piece of my own. This goes
a stage further than Dr Butler in taking a much more severely
historical approach which is relatively new. Until very recently,
the historical approach has tended to be almost exclusively
literary-historical; and the consequence for *Northanger Abbey* in
particular has been a serious disbalance, for while there has
been no shortage of commentary on the Gothic satire involving
The Mysteries of Udolpho, the novel's contemporary historical
reference has been either ignored or assumed to be non-existent.

Persuasion

Persuasion was Jane Austen's last completed novel, written in
twelve months between 8 August 1815 and 6 August 1816, and
finished eleven months before her death. As I suggested at the
beginning of this Introduction, the fact that it was a last novel,
written at the end of Jane Austen's life, together with the
particular qualities of the work itself – its older heroine, its
deeper emotional tones, its story of love reawakened – have
encouraged its critics to treat *Persuasion* as a crowning achievement. Whately, writing in 1821, thought it the best of the novels,
with the 'superiority' that comes 'from the more mature age at
which it was written'. He particularly mentions its 'tender'
character, an aspect taken up by Julia Kavanagh in 1862. She

read in it 'the tender and sad' side of the author's 'literary personality', a 'melancholy cast' which set it apart from the other novels. In 1870, Richard Simpson called it 'the most charming' (meaning affecting, rather than delightful) of the novels and interpreted its argument as a retraction of Jane Austen's earlier position, where 'the heart and the head, intellect and passion' were separated: in Anne Elliot the two are joined. For Margaret Oliphant in 1882, *Persuasion* 'stands by itself . . . as a story with one sustained and serious interest of a graver kind' and she connects this with the figure of Anne Elliot, 'pensive and overcast with the shadow of disappointment and wistful uncertainty', a character who holds our attention 'with a sentimental interest which is not to be found in any other of Miss Austen's works'.

The American critic W. D. Howells, writing at the turn of the century, like Mrs Oliphant, connects the individuality of *Persuasion* with the individuality of its heroine – 'yet never was there a heroine so little self-assertive, so far from forth-putting' (a suggestive and disputable assertion). Howells accepted that his reading was very personal and equally he accepts that other people would read the novel differently: 'People will prefer Anne Eliot to Elizabeth Bennet according as they prefer a gentle sufferance in women more than a lively rebellion'. Left at this point, the question remains one of individual response, about which there can be no argument. But Howells takes the issue a stage further, continues the comparison, and draws our attention to the originality of *Persuasion*, a work 'imagined with as great novelty and daring as *Pride and Prejudice*, and . . . Anne . . . as genuinely a heroine as Elizabeth'. Virginia Woolf also found new elements in *Persuasion*, 'a peculiar beauty and a peculiar dullness': the 'beauty' connected with the author's discovery, at this late period of her life, 'that the world is larger, more mysterious, and more romantic than she had supposed'; the 'dullness' coming from her boredom, her over-familiarity 'with the ways of her world'. A novelist herself, Virginia Woolf felt qualified to diagnose these contraries as marking a stage of 'transition' as Jane Austen moved away from the novels

already written to a new phase of novels yet to come, the works
which would have established her as the 'forerunner' of Henry
James and Proust.

In this Casebook, Virginia Woolf is followed closely by
another woman novelist, Elizabeth Bowen, who also writes
with the confidence and insight of a fellow-practitioner. In
Persuasion, 'a masterpiece of delicate strength', she detects a
'note unheard hitherto' and she identifies the novel to be about
'restraint' and 'maturity'. The words 'mature' and 'maturity'
occur several times at the beginning of D. W. Harding's 1965
essay, in the paragraphs analysing the Cinderella motif repeated
from novel to novel, with Anne Elliot as 'the most mature and
profound of Cinderellas' and the novel itself 'a more mature
interpretation of the theme', its inherent problems of fictional
presentation solved 'by the dexterity of a practised writer' and
'through more mature understanding of the basic situation and
the forms it may take'. The essays by R. S. Crane (1957) and
Malcolm Bradbury (1968), for all their differences (and these
are quite considerable), both analyse the narrative structure
and fictional technique of *Persuasion* as procedures which Jane
Austen deployed in this novel in answering the special demands
of its subject; and in the extracts from Mary Lascelles (1939)
we see this more technical, 'art of the novel', approach used to
show how much Jane Austen's narrative technique in the
novel owes to her experience as a writer.

About the artistic and emotional maturity of *Persuasion* there
is fairly general agreement, although, of course, between
individual critics there are considerable variations and differences of opinion, and wide divergences of critical method
and approach, as, for example, between the rigorous scientific
criticism of R. S. Crane, the founder of the so-called Chicago
school, with its disciplined technical analysis and its tight focus
upon the novel as an autonomous literary object, and, at the
other extreme, the subjective, impressionistic free-wheeling
criticism of the novelist-critics, a line running from Julia
Kavanagh to Elizabeth Bowen. While the emphasis of the
professional critics has tended to fall upon more purely aesthetic

issues, relating to the structure and organisation of *Persuasion*, writer-critics have fastened upon the novel's human qualities and have explored their feeling that in telling the story of Anne's suffering in love, her endurance, disappointment and resignation, Jane Austen was drawing upon experiences of her own. In this light, of the six novels, *Persuasion* is seen as the most intensely personal and the one closest to the author's inner world of emotion.

The most extravagant and fanciful biographicalism is in Rudyard Kipling's poem 'Jane's Marriage', which has the novelist transported to Paradise and offered a single wish. When she asks for 'Love', Wentworth is summoned up from 'a private limbo', where he has been engrossed in a copy of *Persuasion* which 'told the plain/Story of love between/Him and Jane'. This is the simplest one-for-one correlation between life and art, a remarkable Janeite example of poetic licence. Fortunately, the best of the writer-critics are less bald in their speculations. When Julia Kavanagh detects a special sadness in *Persuasion*, 'the result, perhaps, of some secret personal disappointment', she attaches the idea of sadness and disappointment to Jane Austen's portrayal of love in general – that it was not her 'forte' to 'paint happy love. Did she believe in it? If we look under the shrewdness and quiet satire of her stories, we shall find a much keener sense of disappointment than of joy fulfilled. Sometimes we find more than disappointment.' Virginia Woolf puts the biographical issue within the context of Jane Austen's literary development. As we have already seen, she regarded *Persuasion* as a transitional work, a stepping away from her established style of fiction, and also a movement away personally from her former stance of reticence: 'There is an expressed emotion in the scene at the concert and in the famous talk about woman's constancy which proves not merely the biographical fact that Jane Austen had loved, but the aesthetic fact that she was no longer afraid to say so.' Elizabeth Bowen provides the historical connection by concluding her essay with a reference to what she calls the 'one mystery' of Jane Austen's 'otherwise open life': 'her love affair', without which, she suggests, *Persuasion* would not have been written. Elizabeth Bowen rightly called this area of Jane Austen's life a 'mystery'. If we try to substantiate the speculations about *Persuasion*, there is no hard evidence. All we have to go on is a confused medley of facts and hearsay rumours collected in the family memoirs and biographies, while the prime source, Jane Austen herself, is silent. If she ever wrote love-letters, these have disappeared; and whatever confidences she may have entrusted to correspondence within the family have also disappeared, not accidentally, but as a result of Cassandra's protective guardianship of her sister's private affairs; and amongst the family at large there persisted an attitude of possessive jealousy; so letters were censored, cut up, or burnt. What we are left with is anecdotage: that there was a mild flirtation with an Irishman early in 1796; that in 1798 or 99 she may have turned down a Fellow of Emmanuel College, Cambridge, staying in the locality of Steventon; that one evening in November 1802 she agreed to marry a Hampshire landowner but that the next morning she changed her mind. Then, closest to Mrs Kavanagh's idea of 'disappointment', are a number of stories, collectively irreconcilable, associating her with a naval officer/army officer/clergyman who died before their love could develop.

So, unless a batch of intimate and revealing letters comes to light, the mystery of Jane Austen's innermost emotional experience remains and the novels are our sole insight into that hidden area of her life – not, of course, into its facts and circumstances, but into its qualities of feeling and experience.

In the penultimate paragraph of her essay, Elizabeth Bowen also touches upon the question of Anne's persuasion by Lady Russell, the ghostly event from which the heroine's present situation in the story derives. Is it, she asks, a 'fundamental improbability', as some people have suggested? In examining this question, she reminds us that 'long ago' 'girls deferred, instinctively, to adult authority' (although Elizabeth Bennet's dealings with Lady Catherine and Fanny Price's defiance of

Sir Thomas show us that for Jane Austen this was not an invariable rule). Whately also goes into the pros and cons of the 'persuasion' issue, weighing the case finely. As a theologian moral-philosopher, he was obviously attracted by the prominence of the 'persuasion' theme, which is discussed and analysed by Jane Austen, dramatically through the characters and action, and directly, both through the authorial commentary and by Anne Elliot herself. The theme of 'persuasion' is closely linked with the ideas of 'duty' and of the woman's proper role in life. We can feel the pressure of these ideas throughout the novels, although it is in this last work that they are most explicitly and searchingly analysed. The 'persuasion' theme again takes us towards Jane Austen's life. One of her nieces, Fanny Knight, who, like Anne Elliot, was motherless, turned to her aunt, whom she loved and respected, for advice. This was in November 1814, when Fanny was twenty-one, uncertain whether or not to enter into a long engagement which would have continued until her fiancé had money enough to set up home. Jane Austen tried to leave the decision to her niece, tried not to offer advice which would be obediently followed, tried not to play a Lady Russell. But her own firm views broke through, her passionate, persuasive conviction that 'Nothing can be compared to the misery of being bound *without* Love, bound to one, & preferring another. *That* is a punishment which you do *not* deserve.' Leading up to this conclusion, Jane Austen puts the case for freedom: '. . . I dare not say, "Determine to accept him". The risk is too great for *you*, unless your own Sentiments prompt it . . . When I consider how few young Men you have yet seen much of – how capable you are (yes, I do still think you *very* capable) of being really in love – and how full of temptation the next 6 or 7 years of your Life will probably be – (it is the very period of Life for the *strongest* attachments to be formed) – I cannot wish you with your very cool feelings to devote yourself in honour to him . . . Years may pass, before he is Independant. – You like him well enough to marry, but not well enough to wait.'[5] In the event, Fanny followed her aunt's advice and gave the young man up. Two and a half years later, in March 1817, Jane Austen wrote to her about *Persuasion*: 'You will not like it, so you need not be impatient. You may *perhaps* like the Heroine, as she is almost too good for me.'[6] In reading of Anne Elliot and Lady Russell, Fanny would have recalled her own experience of 'persuasion' and have recognised the theme of love's endurance in waiting. But why should her aunt suppose that she would not like it? Because she chose *not* to wait? Or was Jane Austen alluding to some other cryptic joke between them? And the heroine 'too good' – in waiting, or in obeying Lady Russell? These ironies we are left to resolve.

D. W. Harding's essay provides the most extensive modern examination of the 'persuasion' theme and the mother-and-daughter relationship between Anne Elliot and Lady Russell. Professor Harding also raises the question of the so-called cancelled chapter. *Persuasion* was originally completed on 16 July 1816. Then Jane Austen added an additional paragraph to the ending, re-dating it 18 July. Then she had more extensive second thoughts and scrapped the penultimate chapter in which she had brought Anne and Wentworth together in rather comic circumstances. She incorporated about a quarter of that old material in a new chapter, sober in tone and more appropriate to the novel as a whole. She also took the opportunity to make some minor verbal changes to the final chapter. We are able to follow these alterations because the manuscript of the original draft of the last two chapters has survived. These thirty-two pages are unique as the only piece of manuscript from the writing of the novels, the rest having completely disappeared. This makes these chapters of *Persuasion* very precious. They tell a great deal about Jane Austen's methods of composition, her meticulous attention to verbal detail, to nuances of rhythm, to shades of irony, to creating the effect of a highly selective realism; and they highlight the particular problems that she faced in constructing a setting and a course of action which would bring Wentworth and Anne Elliot together in a dramatic climax that would also effect a resolution to the emotional and thematic levels of meaning. In full detail, these are specialised questions and anyone who wishes to pursue them can do so in chapter 6 of *Jane Austen's Literary Manuscripts* (Oxford, 1963), which analyses the differences between the original draft and the final printed text and suggests why, at such a very late stage, Jane Austen undertook this considerable alteration to the book's design.

The issues arising from the cancelled chapter are not narrowly bibliographical, as Professor Harding's discussion indicates, and they lead on to the 'slight' but 'fascinating' puzzle of what he terms a 'creative work not quite completed'. He questions, as Mary Lascelles does, the presentation of Mr Elliot and Mrs Clay; although he is also careful to quote Jane Austen's words in a letter to Fanny Knight, where, in March 1817, she writes of the novel as 'a something ready for Publication'. Professor Harding wonders if Jane Austen, 'given her earlier resources of physical energy', would not have handled Mr Elliot more 'enterprisingly'. This is only a side-issue. But readers who are interested in the circumstances of *Persuasion*'s composition will be able to reconstruct the course of events from the two family biographies – the *Memoir* (1870) and the *Life and Letters* (1913) – and from the collected *Letters*. From these sources, we know that the first signs of Addison's disease, from which she died in July 1817, were already evident early in 1816. So at this period her writing could have been a race against time. It was certainly a brisk pace to finish a novel in twelve months, as *Persuasion* was. *Persuasion* seems to have been followed by the revision of *Northanger Abbey*, an early work which she wanted to make presentable for publication. Then, in January 1817, she began a seventh novel, *Sanditon*, abandoned in March when she was too weak to write on. Given all this, it is feasible to suppose that with more time and better health Jane Austen might have worked further on *Persuasion*. Of course, this is fanciful speculation and should not distract our reading of the novel. But it is worth remembering that as far as Jane Austen was concerned, *Persuasion* was not her last word. Virginia Woolf's speculation about the novels unwritten may also be a fanciful distraction. But it is salutary fantasy if it reminds us that Jane Austen hurried on to *Sanditon*, that her creative energies were set on the future. To celebrate *Persuasion* as a swan-song, a final statement, is unhistorical and untrue to the sequence of events as we know it.

Apart from the section of Whately's review-article, there was very little contemporary comment on *Persuasion*. Only three reviews are recorded: a trifling notice in the *Gentleman's Review*, LXXXVIII (July 1818), really an obituary, with the merest reference to *Persuasion* and *Northanger Abbey*: 'The characters in both are principally taken from the middle ranks of life, and are well supported. *Northanger Abbey*, however, is decidedly preferable to the second Novel, not only in the incidents, but even in its moral tendency.' The *British Critic* (March 1818) (pp. 41–7) treated *Northanger Abbey* at some length and also attempted an appraisal of Jane Austen's overall achievement. But, like the *Gentleman's Review*, it found *Persuasion* inferior to the other novel and objected to the 'moral' of the story. There is another general appraisal in *Blackwood's Magazine*, May 1818 (pp. 47–50), in which *Northanger Abbey* is designated 'the more lively' and *Persuasion* 'the more pathetic'. Apart from these public comments, there are also a few lines in a letter (dated 21 February 1818) from a contemporary novelist, Maria Edgeworth:

excepting the tangled, useless histories of the family in the first 50 pages – appears to me, especially in all that relates to poor Anne and her lover, to be exceedingly interesting and natural. The love and lover admirably well-drawn: don't you see Captain Wentworth, or rather don't you in her place feel him taking the boistrous child off her back as she kneels by the sick boy on the sofa? And is not the first meeting after their long separation admirably well done? And the overheard conversation about the nut? But I must stop, we have got no further than the disaster of Miss Musgrove's jumping off the steps.[7]

Although Mrs Edgeworth had not got far into *Persuasion*, her comments are worth quoting, firstly, because she was the only contemporary novelist, apart from Scott, that Jane Austen seems to have admired (and she sent her a copy of *Mansfield Park*). Unfortunately, we don't have Mrs Edgeworth's reply, although it is recorded that she found the story 'like real life and very interesting'[8] and that her family was 'much entertained'[9] by it. Secondly, Mrs Edgeworth's letter gives us her response to specific episodes in the early part of the novel, particularly to the scene in chapter 9 where Wentworth takes little Walter Musgrove off the heroine's back. Howells also refers to this episode, commenting in the same spirit 'that this simple, homely scene, is very pretty, and is very like things that happen in life where there is reason to think love is oftener shown in quality than quantity, and does its effect as perfectly in the little as the great events'.

Richard Whately's *Quarterly Review* article, January 1821, has been referred to earlier in this Introduction as one of the most important contemporary statements about Jane Austen's art in general; and his remarks on *Persuasion* are particularly valuable for the commentary they provide on the morality of 'prudence' which Anne Elliot followed in allowing herself to be advised by Lady Russell. His analysis of this point helps us to understand what the reviewers were objecting to in the novel's 'moral tendency' and it also provides us with an impression of the seriousness and intelligence with which Jane Austen might expect to be read. Whately was certainly not a typical reader in his philosophical and theological training; and, towards the end, his review begins to take on a sermonising air. None the less, *Persuasion* assumes an audience prepared to attend closely to its (sometimes allusive) moral logic. We have to weigh carefully the direct arguments put forward by Anne Elliot, and be alert to the implicit lines of argument conveyed in the narration of the story, in the tones of sympathy and irony, and in the author's commentary.

The later nineteenth-century view of *Persuasion* is represented by brief extracts from the writing of three very fine critics – the novelists Julia Kavanagh and Margaret Oliphant and the Shakespearian critic, Richard Simpson. Both Mrs Kavanagh and Mrs Oliphant have been mentioned previously in this Introduction, in the *Northanger Abbey* section (pp. 20–1) and in the review of the biographical approach to *Persuasion*. Mrs Kavanagh reads a 'sorrowful' novel and draws attention to the portrait of Anne Elliot, not just as an individual, but as a type – 'an unloved woman, condemned to suffer thus because she is a woman and must not speak'. Mrs Oliphant also focuses upon Anne Elliot as a suffering heroine and represents the novel as 'the least amusing' of the six, yet balances this with the claim that it is 'perhaps the most interesting' for its motif of love. For Simpson, *Persuasion* is 'the most charming of the novels'; and his Shakespearian predilections are revealed in his suggestion that it was based pretty directly upon *Twelfth Night*. I have also quoted Simpson's account of Sir Walter Elliot, illustrating one direction in Jane Austen's increasing mastery in the presentation of her fools. Another aspect of her development, according to Simpson, is the later and more mature treatment of themes originally stated in the three early novels. In this perspective, he presents *Mansfield Park* as 'a kind of supplement' to *Pride and Prejudice*, *Emma* as 'the complement' to *Northanger Abbey* and *Sense and Sensibility*, and *Persuasion* in the same relationship to *Sense and Sensibility* – and it is at this point in his thesis that the extract opens.

The nineteenth-century tradition of character-criticism is continued in the extract from the American W. D. Howells whose writing also seems slightly old-fashioned in its strongly personal flavour and its reliance upon story-telling quotations. But this quaintness is deceptive. Howells is a very shrewd critic; the extensive quotations take their place in a relaxed and understated argument; and his attention to the method and artistry of the novel is distinctly modern, for example, in his observation that 'the final understanding of the lovers' is not brought about by the activity of the other characters but accomplished largely 'subjectively through the nature of Anne and Wentworth'. To this, he makes one exception: Louisa Musgrove's accident at the Cobb. Howells' account of this scene can be compared with Mary Lascelles' analysis and that in turn with Herbert Read's famous comment that the Cobb episode is an example of Jane Austen's style collapsing, becoming 'almost ludicrous . . . under the strain of dramatic action'.[10] Reginald Farrer has already been mentioned for his few masterly sentences on *Northanger Abbey*; and there is the same distinction and originality to his view of *Persuasion*, in his appraisal of its uncertainties and weaknesses, and in his grasp of its 'new note of glacial contempt' for the characters disliked and its 'intensified tenderness' for those Jane Austen does like. Above all, Farrer sees Anne Elliot as the dominant, dominating figure: '*Persuasion* is primarily Anne Elliot'; 'her feelings consume the book'. It is useful to compare Farrer's opinion of the novel's shortcomings with the views of Virginia Woolf and Mary Lascelles; and his opinion of Wentworth ('delightful jolly fellow that he is'), fading out of our interest, with R. S. Crane's ('one of the best of her heroes').

Some readers may find Virginia Woolf's playfulness rather difficult to take; also her fantasy that had Jane Austen lived a few years longer, she would have emerged from the quiet rural retreat of Chawton Cottage and 'would have stayed in London, dined out, lunched out, met famous people, made new friends', in short, have become an early Bloomsburyite in the same mould as Virginia Woolf herself. But this self-indulgence is worth having for the sake of her extremely challenging comments on *Persuasion*'s 'peculiar dullness'. Obviously, she is writing out of her own experience as a novelist; and we have to ask ourselves if it rings true; but we need to be as open to the comment that *Persuasion*'s 'satire is harsh, and the comedy crude', that 'The writer is a little bored', as to the much more readily acceptable suggestion of its 'peculiar beauty'.

The work of Mary Lascelles is introduced on page 22. The first extract is taken from the chapter 'Reading and Response' and alerts us to the levels of irony and the comedy of self-deception that are to be found in *Persuasion*. Miss Lascelles touches upon two *causes célèbres*, the Cobb accident (already mentioned) and the death of Richard Musgrove (which from time to time is cited as an example of Jane Austen's callous-

ness). Miss Lascelles also questions the place of Mr Elliot and
Mrs Clay, an element of 'crude farce . . . thrust into this
delicate comedy', an enquiry continued in the second extract
(taken from the chapter on 'Narrative Art'), where the principal concern is with the heroine's point of view and Anne's
observation of the incidents which mark the change in Wentworth's feelings towards her. This is another point on which
Howells comments helpfully.

Elizabeth Bowen's essay of 1957 is the most recent contribution to the line of novelists who have felt drawn to *Persuasion*.
Like Virginia Woolf, she sensed that a change was taking place
and that while in the earlier novels some 'compelling personal
reason' led Jane Austen to choose 'restraint', in this last work
she broke 'with her self-set limitations', not to reject restraint
but to study 'its hard cost' and its 'painful causes'. This is a
very individual essay, biographical in inclination and constantly
asking us to examine our own experience of life alongside the
vision of life presented in the novel; Miss Bowen calls *Persuasion*
Jane Austen's testimony 'to the valour, the enduringness of
human spirit . . . that love for another can be the light of a life –
can rise above egotism, accept hardship, outlive hope of reward'.
Perhaps we could guess that this essay was itself written out of
such a powerful and sustaining experience.

The four remaining items in this part of the Casebook
represent the work of professional academic critics – R. S.
Crane, D. W. Harding, A. Walton Litz and Malcolm Bradbury,
who is also a novelist in his own right. Crane employs a highly
analytical approach. Observing the large cast of characters and
the simple sequence of events, he sets out to understand these
phenomena in relation to the essential nature of *Persuasion* as a
serious comedy of personal relations, within which he identifies
the novelist's tasks as the presentation of Anne as a likable
heroine; the rightness, for both Anne and Wentworth, of their
marriage; the compatibility of Wentworth's early misunderstanding of Anne with the eventual revival of his love. Crane
points out the difficulties that faced Jane Austen in achieving
these ends with a heroine so passive and self-effacing and with

a hero whose mind can never be as fully entered and who is required by the plot to act coolly towards her and to be often away. The body of his essay points to some of the methods Jane Austen deployed in achieving her aims; and his consideration of Wentworth ('one of the best of her heroes') is the most extensive and rewarding in all the criticism of *Persuasion*.

D. W. Harding's essay provides the most complete discussion of the novel, looking at it in relation to the earlier novels, examining the cancelled chapter and the inadequate treatment of the Mr Elliot–Mrs Clay intrigue, explaining the combination of 'tough rationality' and 'fine discrimination' in the passage about Robert Musgrove's death and locating the comi-tragic tones of the Cobb accident. These, we might say, are the classical cruces of critical discussion. The most distinctive and individual note that Professor Harding brings to this essay is the psychological insight which informs his elucidation of both the Cinderella theme and the mother–child relationship in *Persuasion*. Like Professor Crane, he looks at the writer's problem in creating a heroine 'unappreciated and neglected by a credible social world', and examines the fictional techniques used in its solution.

Malcolm Bradbury's essay rehearses some of the principal criticisms made against *Persuasion* and offers the interesting comment that 'Undergraduates generally seem not to like the novel in comparison with Jane Austen's other books'. His response, like Crane's, is to make the case for *Persuasion* as a novel in which Jane Austen was seeking to achieve new effects by new methods; and he sees her main purpose here to lie in revealing the intimate connection between 'the life of the classes' (i.e. the traditional land-owning aristocracy and the naval families) and 'the moral life'. This line of social-historical interpretation is becoming increasingly prominent in the most recent criticism of Jane Austen. *Persuasion* seems to answer this approach very well. The action of the story is located very precisely in the period of Napoleon's defeat, at a time when the naval officers were returning to society, as Wentworth does, with the recommendation of wealth (from prize-money) and a new heroic status as the saviours of the nation. It is worth comparing Bradbury's argument with Howells' slight aside about Jane Austen's partiality for the navy as the Austen family profession and with Crane's serious and important contention that the two worlds of the novel are 'moral', rather than 'social', in their 'contrariety', and that Jane Austen's drama is there rather than in the dynamics of change within 'a decaying feudal class' and a rising middle class. Finally, the recent essay by A. Walton Litz returns us to Virginia Woolf's comment on *Persuasion*'s 'peculiar beauty and a peculiar dullness'. Professor Litz advances the discussion of the 'qualities of Romantic poetry reflected in Jane Austen's new attitudes towards nature and "feeling"', and remarks on the way in which these 'new attitudes' belong, in their depth and maturity, specifically to this late novel. This line of analysis also enables Professor Litz to connect the novel's 'beauty' and 'dullness' with its two-part structure; and, widening the argument, to explain the novel's particular fascination for modern readers and to observe that *Persuasion* 'is marked by a peculiar terror as well as a peculiar beauty'.

NOTES

1. *Journal of Walter Scott, 1825–26*, ed. J. G. Tait (1939) p. 135: entry for 14 March 1826.
2. *Jane Austen's Letters*, ed. R. W. Chapman (1952) p. 484.
3. Douglas Bush, *Jane Austen* (New York, 1975) p. 70.
4. A. C. Bradley, *Jane Austen* (1911) p. 3.
5. *Letters*, pp. 417–18.
6. Ibid. 487.
7. F. A. Edgeworth, *Memoir of Maria Edgeworth* (1867) II pp. 5–6.
8. E. I. Jones, *The Great Maria* (1959) p. 124.
9. *Memoir of Maria Edgeworth*, vol. I, p. 310: letter of 26 December 1814.
10. Herbert Read, *English Prose Style* (1928) p. 119.

PART ONE
Northanger Abbey

1. CONTEMPORARY AND VICTORIAN OPINIONS

ANONYMOUS (1818): (*British Critic* review)

In order to impart some degree of variety to our journal, and select matter suited to all tastes, we have generally made it a point to notice one or two of the better sort of novels; but, did our fair readers know, what a vast quantity of useful spirits and patience, we are for this purpose generally forced to exhaust, before we are able to stumble upon any thing that we can at all recommend to their approbation; what innumerable letters we are compelled to read from the witty Lady Harriet F—— to the pathetic Miss Lucretia G——, through what an endless series of gloomy caverns, long and winding passages, secret trap doors, we are forced to pass – now in the Inquisition, now in a gay modern assembly – this moment in the east wing of an old castle in the Pyrenees; in the next, among banditti; and so on, through all the changes and chances of this transitory life, acquiescing in every thing, with an imperturbable confidence, that he or she, who has brought us into all these difficulties, will, in their own good time, release us from them: sure we are, that even the most resolute foes to all the solid parts of learning, will agree with us in admitting, that the sound and orthodox divinity with which so considerable a portion of our pages is usually filled, and of which we have so often had the mortification to hear many sensible young ladies complain, is nevertheless very far from being quite so dull and exhausting, as are their own favourite studies, when indiscriminately pursued. In return for this concession on their part, we on our's will frankly allow, that a good novel, such, for example, as that at present before us, is, perhaps, among the most fascinating productions of modern literature, though we cannot say, that it is quite so improving as some others.

Northanger Abbey and *Persuasion*, are the productions of a pen, from which our readers have already received several admired productions; and it is with most unfeigned regret, that we are forced to add, they will be the last. [Provides a biographical sketch derived and quoting from the *Biographical Notice* (see p. 11).]

With respect to the talents of Jane Austen, they need no other voucher, than the works which she has left behind her; which in some of the best qualities of the best sort of novels, display a degree of excellence that has not been often surpassed. In imagination, of all kinds, she appears to have been extremely deficient; not only her stories are utterly and entirely devoid of invention, but her characters, her incidents, her sentiments, are obviously all drawn exclusively from experience. The sentiments which she puts into the mouths of her actors, are the sentiments, which we are every day in the habit of hearing; and as to her actors themselves, we are persuaded that fancy, strictly so called, has had much less to do with them, than with the characters of Julius Cæsar, Hannibal, or Alexander, as represented to us by historians. At description she seldom aims; at that vivid and poetical sort of description, which we have of late been accustomed to (in the novels of a celebrated anonymous writer) never; she seems to have no other object in view, than simply to paint some of those scenes which she has herself seen, and which every one, indeed, may witness daily. Not only her characters are all of them belonging to the middle size, and with a tendency, in fact, rather to fall below, than to rise above the common standard, but even the incidents of her novels, are of the same description. Her heroes and heroines, make love and are married, just as her readers make love, and were or will be, married; no unexpected ill fortune occurs to prevent, nor any unexpected good fortune, to bring about the events on which her novels hinge. She seems to be describing such people as meet together every night, in every respectable house in London; and to relate such incidents as have probably happened, one time or other, to half the families in the United Kingdom. And yet, by a singular good judgment, almost every individual represents a class; not a class of humourists, or of any of the rarer specimens of our species, but one of those classes to which we ourselves, and every acquaintance we have, in all probability belong. The fidelity with which these are distinguished is often admirable. It would have been impossible to discriminate the characters of the common-place people, whom she employs as the instruments of her novels, by any set and formal descriptions; for the greater part of them, are such as we generally describe by saying that they are persons of 'no characters at all'. Accordingly our authoress gives no definitions; but she makes her *dramatis personæ* talk; and the sentiments which she places in their mouths, the little phrases which she makes them use, strike so familiarly upon our memory as soon as we hear them repeated, that we instantly recognize among some of our acquaintance, the sort of persons she intends to signify, as accurately as if we had heard their voices. This is the forte of our authoress; as soon as ever she leaves the shore of her own experience, and attempts to delineate fancy characters, or such as she may perhaps have often heard of, but possibly never seen, she falls at once to the level of mere ordinary novellists. Her merit consists altogether in her remarkable talent for observation; no ridiculous phrase, no affected sentiment, no foolish pretension seems to escape her notice. It is scarcely possible to read her novels, without meeting with some of one's own absurdities reflected back upon one's conscience; and this, just in the light in which they ought to appear. For in recording the customs and manners of commonplace people in the commonplace intercourse of life, our authoress never dips her pen in satire; the follies which she holds up to us, are, for the most part, mere follies, or else natural imperfections; and she treats them, as such, with good-humoured pleasantry; mimicking them so exactly, that we always laugh at the ridiculous truth of the imitation, but without ever being incited to indulge in feelings, that might tend to render us ill-natured, and intolerant in society. This is the result of that good sense which seems ever to keep complete possession over all the other qualities of the mind of our authoress; she sees every thing just as it is; even her want of imagination (which is the principal defect of her writings) is useful to her in this respect, that it enables her to keep clear of all exaggeration, in a mode of writing where the least exaggeration would be fatal; for if the people and the scenes which she has chosen, as the subjects of her composition, be not painted with perfect truth, with exact and striking resemblance, the whole effect ceases; her characters have no kind of merit in themselves, and whatever interest they excite in the mind of the reader, results almost entirely, from the unaccountable pleasure, which, by a peculiarity in our nature, we derive from a simple imitation of any object, without any reference to the abstract value or importance of the object itself. This fact is notorious in painting; and the novels of Miss Austen alone, would be sufficient to prove, were proof required, that the same is true in the department of literature, which she has adorned. For our readers will perceive (from the instance which we are now about to present, in the case of the novels before us,) that be their merit what it may, it is not founded upon the interest of a narrative. In fact, so little narrative is there in either of the two novels of which the publication before us consists, that it is difficult to give any thing like an abstract of their contents. *Northanger Abbey*, which is the name of the first novel, is simply, the history of a young girl, the daughter of a country clergyman of respectability, educated at home, under the care of her parents; good kind of people, who taught their large family all that it was necessary for them to know, without apparently troubling themselves about accomplishments in learning of any kind, beyond what our fathers and mothers were instructed in. Our heroine is just such a person, as an education under such circumstances, would lead us to expect; with respect to the hero of the tale, (for every heroine must have a hero) that which fortunately threw one in the way of Catherine, was a journey to Bath which she happily made, in company with the lady of the manor, who was ordered to that place of fashionable resort, for the benefit of her health. The first evening of Catherine's acquaintance with the gaiety of the Bath balls, was unpromising, from the circumstance that neither she, nor Mrs. Allen, her chaperon, had any knowledge of a single individual in the room; and the manner in which our authoress paints the effects of this circumstance upon the feelings and conversation of both, is sufficiently entertaining; but our heroine's second visit, was more favourable; for she was then introduced to a young clergyman, who is the other wheel upon which the interest of the narrative is made to run. The young clergyman's name was Tilney.

The description of our heroine's residence at Bath, is chiefly taken up with an account of her intimacy with a family of the name of Thorpe, consisting of a foolish mother, a foolish son, and four or five foolish daughters; the eldest of whom is a fine handsome girl, thinking of nothing but finery and flirting, and an exact representation of that large class of young women, in the form they assume among the gayer part of the middling ranks of society; for flirts, like all other parts of the animal kingdom, may be divided into two or three species. The character is pourtrayed with admirable spirit and humour; but the impression conveyed by it, is the result of so many touches, that it would be difficult to place it before our readers by means of extracts. During the time of our heroine's intimacy with this family, the acquaintance with Mr. Tilney goes on; he proves to be the son of a General Tilney, a proud rich man; but who, in consequence of misinformation respecting the circumstances and family of Catherine, acquiesces in Miss Tilney's request of inviting Catherine to pass a few weeks with them, at their family seat of Northanger Abbey. This visit forms the next and only remaining incident in the novel; the result of it was the marriage of Catherine with the son. The circumstance which principally renders the history of our heroine's residence at Northanger Abbey amusing, arises from the mistakes which she makes, in consequence of her imagination, (which had just come fresh from the *Mysteries of Udolpho,*) leading her to anticipate, that the Abbey which she was on the point of adorning by her presence, was to be of the same class and character, as those which Mrs. Radcliffe paints. On her arrival, she was, as may be supposed, a little disappointed, by the unexpected elegance, convenience, and other advantages of General Tilney's abode; but her prepossession was incurable. [Quotes ch. 20 'An abbey!' to 'very distressing', and ch. 21 'The night was stormy' to '"to alarm one."']

Catherine, in a few days, was forced to resign all her hopes of discovering subterraneous passages, mysterious pictures, or old parchments; but, however, she still hoped to be able to detect a hidden secret, in the instance of the General, who having been an unkind husband to his late wife, and being, moreover, of a haughty and supercilious temper, she naturally concluded must have the weight of his wife's untimely end upon his conscience. A thousand little circumstances combined to give strength to her suspicions. But we have no room for extracts; if our readers wish to be entertained with the whole history of our heroine's mistakes in this way, we can safely recommend the work to their perusal. *Northanger Abbey*, is one of the very best of Miss Austen's productions, and will every way repay the time and trouble of perusing it. Some of the incidents in it are rather improbable, and the character of General Tilney seems to have been drawn from imagination, for it is not a very probable character, and is not pourtrayed with our authoress's usual taste and judgment. There is also a considerable want of delicacy in all the circumstances of Catherine's visit to the Abbey; but it is useless to point them out; the interest of the novel, is so little founded upon the ingenuity or probability of the story, that any criticism upon the management of it, falls with no weight upon that which constitutes its appropriate praise, considered as a literary product. With respect to the second of the novels, which the present publication contains, it will be necessary to say but little. It is in every respect a much less fortunate performance than that which we have just been considering. It is manifestly the work of the same mind, and contains parts of very great merit; among them, however, we certainly should not number its *moral*, which seems to be, that young people should always marry according to their own inclinations and upon their own judgment; for that if in consequence of listening to grave counsels, they defer their marriage, till they have wherewith to live upon, they will be laying the foundation for years of misery, such as only the heroes and heroines of novels can reasonably hope ever to see the end of.

SOURCE: review in *British Critic*, new series, IX (March 1818) 293–301.

ANONYMOUS (1818): (*Blackwood's Magazine* review)

We are happy to receive two other novels from the pen of this amiable and agreeable authoress, though our satisfaction is much alloyed, from the feeling, that they must be the last. We have always regarded her works as possessing a higher claim to public estimation than perhaps they have yet attained. They have fallen, indeed, upon an age whose taste can only be gratified with the highest seasoned food. This, as we have already hinted, may be partly owing to the wonderful realities which it has been our lot to witness. We have been spoiled for the tranquil enjoyment of common interests, and nothing now will satisfy us in fiction, any more than in real life, but grand movements and striking characters. A singular union has, accordingly, been attempted between history, and poetry. The periods of great events have been seized on as a ground work for the display of powerful or fantastic characters: correct and instructive pictures of national peculiarities have been exhibited; and even in those fictions which are altogether wild and monstrous, some insight has been given into the passions and theories which have convulsed and bewildered this our 'age of Reason'. In the poetry of Mr Scott and Lord Byron, in the novels of Miss Edgeworth, Mr Godwin, and the author of *Waverley*, we see exemplified in different forms this influence of the spirit of the times, – the prevailing love of historical, and at the same time romantic incident, – dark and high-wrought passions, – the delineations, chiefly of national character, – the pursuit of some substance, in short, yet of an existence more fanciful often than absolute fiction, – the dislike of a cloud, yet the form which is embraced, nothing short of a Juno. In this raised state of our imaginations, we cannot, it may be supposed, all at once descend to the simple representations of common life, to incidents which have no truth, except that of universal nature, and have nothing of fiction except in not having really happened, – yet the time, probably, will return, when we shall take a more permanent delight in those familiar cabinet pictures, than even in the great historical pieces of our more eminent modern masters; when our sons and daughters will deign once more to laugh over the Partridges and the Trullibers, and to weep over the Clementinas and Clarissas of past times, as we have some distant recollection of having been able to do ourselves, before we were so entirely engrossed with the Napoleons of real life, or the Corsairs of poetry; and while we could enjoy a work that was all written in pure English, without ever dreaming how great would be the embellishment to have at least one half of it in the dialect of Scotland or of Ireland.

When this period arrives, we have no hesitation in saying, that the delightful writer of the works now before us, will be one of the most popular of English novelists, and if, indeed, we could point out the individual who, within a certain limited range, has attained the highest perfection of the art of novel writing, we should have little scruple in fixing upon her. She has confined herself, no doubt, to a narrow walk. She never operates among deep interests, uncommon characters, or vehement passions. The singular merit of her writings is, that we could conceive, without the slightest strain of imagination, any one of her fictions to be realized in any town or village in England, (for it is only English manners that she paints,) that we think we are reading the history of people whom we have seen thousands of times, and that with all this perfect commonness, both of incident and character, perhaps not one of her characters is to be found in any other book, portrayed at least in so lively and interesting a manner. She has much observation,

– much fine sense, – much delicate humour, – many pathetic touches, – and throughout all her works, a most charitable view of human nature, and a tone of gentleness and purity that are almost unequalled. It is unnecessary to give a particular account of the stories here presented to us. They have quite the same kind of merit with the preceding works of their author. As stories they are nothing in themselves, though beautiful and simple in their combination with the characters. The first is the more lively, and the second the more pathetic; but such is the facility and the seemingly exhaustless invention of this lady, that, we think, like a complete mistress of a musical instrument, she could have gone on in the same strain for ever, and her happy talent of seeing something to interest in the most common scenes of life, could evidently never have been without a field to work upon. But death has deprived us of this most fascinating companion, and the few prefatory pages which contain a sketch of her life, almost come upon us like the melancholy invitation to the funeral of one whom we had long known and loved.

She was the daughter of a clergyman of the name of Austen, 'a scholar and a ripe one', whose care of her education was soon rewarded by the early promise which she displayed. It was not, however, till after his death that she published any of her works; 'for though in composition she was equally rapid and correct, yet an invincible distrust of her own judgment induced her to withhold her writings from the public till time and many perusals had satisfied her that the charm of recent composition was dissolved'. She lived a quiet and retired life with her mother and sister, in the neighbourhood of Southampton, when early in 1816 she was attacked by the disease which carried her off. It was a decline, at first deceitfully slow, and which her natural good constitution and regular habits, had given little room to dread. 'She supported all the varying pain, irksomeness and tedium attendant on decaying nature, with more than resignation, – with a truly elastic cheerfulness. She retained her faculties, her memory, her fancy, her temper, and her affections warm, clear, and unimpaired to the last. Neither her love of God nor of her fellow creatures flagged for a moment. The following passages from a letter written a few weeks before her death, are the best representation of her happy state of mind.

My attendant is encouraging, and talks of making me quite well. I live chiefly on the sofa, but am allowed to walk from one room to another. I have been out once in a sedan chair, and am to repeat it, and be promoted to a wheel chair as the weather serves. On this subject I will only say further, that my dearest sister, my tender, watchful, indefatigable nurse, has not been made ill by her exertions. As to what I owe to her, and to the anxious affection of all my beloved family on this occasion, I can only cry over it, and pray to God to bless them more and more.

She then turns off in her lively way to another subject. 'You will find Captain —— a very respectable, well meaning man, without much manners, – his wife and sister all good humour and obligingness, and, I hope, (since the fashion allows it,) with rather longer petticoats than last year.'

Such was this admirable person, the character of whose life fully corresponds with that of her writings. There is the same good sense, happiness, and purity in both. Yet they will appear very defective to that class of readers who are constantly hunting after the broad display of religious sentiments and opinions. It has been left for this age to discover that Mr Addison himself was scarcely a Christian: but we are very certain, that neither the temper of his writings, nor even that of Miss Austen's, (novels as they are, and filled with accounts of balls and plays, and such abominations,) could well have been formed without a feeling of the spirit of Christianity.

SOURCE: review in *Blackwood's Magazine*, new series, II (May 1818) 453–5.

RICHARD WHATELY (1821): Decidedly inferior

. . . We must proceed to the publication of which the title is prefixed to this article [*Northanger Abbey* and *Persuasion*]. It contains, it seems, the earliest and the latest productions of the author; the first of them having been purchased, we are told, many years back by a bookseller, who, for some reason unexplained, thought proper to alter his mind and withhold it. We do not much applaud his taste; for though it is decidedly inferior to her other works, having less plot, and what there is, less artificially wrought up, and also less exquisite nicety of moral painting; yet the same kind of excellences which characterise the other novels may be perceived in this, in a degree which would have been highly creditable to most other writers of the same school, and which would have entitled the author to considerable praise, had she written nothing better.

We already begin to fear, that we have indulged too much in extracts, and we must save some room for *Persuasion*, or we could not resist giving a specimen of John Thorpe, with his horse that *cannot* go less than 10 miles an hour, his refusal to drive his sister 'because she has such thick ankles', and his sober consumption of five pints of port a day; altogether the best portrait of a species, which, though almost extinct cannot yet be quite classed among the Palæotheria, the Bang-up Oxonian. Miss Thorpe, the jilt of middling life, is, in her way, quite as good, though she has not the advantage of being the representative of a rare or a diminishing species. We fear few of our readers, however they may admire the naiveté, will admit the truth of poor James Morland's postscript, 'I can never expect to know such another woman.'. . .

SOURCE: extract from unsigned article in *Quarterly Review*, XXIV (January 1821) 352–76.

JULIA KAVANAGH (1862): Food for satire

. . . The impression life produced on Miss Austen was peculiar. She seems to have been struck especially with its small vanities and small falsehoods, equally remote from the ridiculous or the tragic. She refused to build herself, or to help to build for others, any romantic ideal of love, virtue, or sorrow. She laughed at her first heroine, Catherine Morland, in *Northanger Abbey*, and described her by negatives. Her irony, though gentle, was a fault, and the parent of much coldness. She learned to check it, but she never conquered it entirely. Catherine, though she makes us smile, is amiable and innocent, and she contrasts pleasantly with Isabella Thorpe. The selfish enthusiasm, the foolish ardour, of this girl were fit food for satire – for such satire especially as Miss Austen loved; for to deceit, assumption, and mere simple silliness she was inexorable. Isabella introduces Catherine to Mrs. Radcliffe's romances, and she promises her plenty more.

'But are you sure they are all horrid?' anxiously asks Catherine.

'Yes, quite sure; for a particular friend of mine, a Miss Andrews, a sweet girl, one of the sweetest creatures in the world, has read every one of them. I wish you knew Miss Andrews; you would be delighted with her. She is netting herself the sweetest cloak you can conceive.'

The connexion between the Radcliffe school of fiction and one of the sweetest creatures in the world, and between being delighted with her and the sweet cloak she is netting, are irresistibly absurd. Over such instances of folly Miss Austen exulted – not ill-naturedly, but with the keen enjoyment of humour and sense, and, to complete her triumph over the hollow Isabella, she makes her conclude her praise of 'the sweetest girl' by the acknowledgment that 'there is something amazingly insipid about her'.

Isabella's brother, Mr. Thorpe, is a masculine variety of the same species of hollow, selfish talkers. But he is a boaster, which partly redeems him, for boasters have a sort of breadth and imagination – and he, for one, has talked himself into a half belief of his horse's spirit and vivacity. There is really an air of good faith about him which cannot be all assumed. We really do think that he believes in the speed and wickedness of that slow horse of his, and that, when he entreats Catherine not to be frightened if she sees him dance and plunge a little at first setting off, he expects that exhibition of liveliness and vigour. There is a sort of tenderness, too, in his declaration – 'He will soon know his master. He is full of spirits, playful as can be, but there is no vice in him.'

None, indeed – and exquisite, therefore, is the servant standing at the head of the quiet animal, and whom, in an important voice, Mr. Thorpe requests to 'let him go'. With more geniality, but not with more finesse, did Goldsmith paint this class of self-deceivers. We love and pity the immortal Beau Tibbs. Mr. Thorpe's vivacity in all that relates to horse-flesh is almost a good point in his character; he has a heart, even though it is but a jockey's heart. Say anything, or speak of anyone to him, and immediately comes the question – 'Does he want a horse? Here is a friend of mine, Sam Fletcher, has got one to sell that would suit anybody. A famous clever animal for the road,' &c.

Catherine Morland herself is led away in the same natural manner by her favourite subject: Mrs. Radcliffe's romances. She talks quite learnedly about the south of France, for she has been there with Emily and Valancourt, and, by the same power of association, a fine English evening becomes just such another as that on which St. Aubin died. . . .

SOURCE: extract from *English Women of Letters* (1862).

MARGARET OLIPHANT (1882): The most captivating . . . girl

. . . *Northanger Abbey* is once more on the higher level. Such a picture of delightful youth, simplicity, absurdity, and natural sweetness, it is scarcely possible to parallel. Catherine Morland, with all her enthusiasm and her mistakes, her modest tenderness and right feeling, and the fine instinct which runs through her simplicity, is the most captivating picture of a very young girl which fiction, perhaps, has ever furnished. Her biographer informs us that when Miss Austen was very young she amused herself with writing burlesques, 'ridiculing the improbable events and exaggerated sentiments which she had met with in sundry silly romances'. It is to be hoped that he did not rank the *Mysteries of Udolpho* among these silly romances; for certainly it is with no ungenial criticism that the young author describes the effect upon her Catherine's ingenuous mind of the mysterious situations and thrilling incidents in the books she loves. It is, on a small scale, like the raid of Cervantes upon the books of chivalry which were so dear to him, and which the simple reader believes, and the heavy critic assures him, that great romancer wrote *Don Quixote* to overthrow. Miss Austen makes her laughing assault upon Mrs. Radcliffe with all the affectionate banter of which she was mistress – the genial fun and tender ridicule of a mind which in its day had wondered and worshipped like Catherine. And she makes that innocent creature ridiculous, but how lovable all through! – letting us laugh at her indeed, but tenderly, as we do at the follies of our favourite child. All her guileless thoughts are open before us – her half childish love, her unconscious candour, her simplicity and transparent truth. The gentle fun is of the most exquisite description, fine and keen, yet as soft as the touch of a dove. The machinery of the story is wonderfully bad, and General Tylney an incredible monster; but all the scenes in Bath – the vulgar Thorpes, the goodhumoured Mrs. Allen – are clear and vivid as the daylight, and Catherine herself throughout always the most delightful little gentlewoman, never wrong in instinct and feeling, notwithstanding all her amusing foolishness. . . .

SOURCE: extract from *The Literary History of the Nineteenth Century* (1882) pp. 228–9.

2. TWENTIETH-CENTURY STUDIES

W. D. Howells

A VERY ENGAGING GOOSE (1901)

... From the beginning we know that it is a comedy the author has in hand; and we lose sight of her obvious purpose of satirizing the Radcliffe school of romance in our delight with the character of the heroine and her adventures in Bath and at Northanger Abbey. Catharine Morland is a goose, but a very engaging goose, and a goose you must respect for her sincerity, her high principles, her generous trust of others, and her patience under trials that would be great for much stronger heads. It is no wonder that the accomplished Henry Tilney falls in love with her when he finds that she is already a little in love with him; and when his father brutally sends her home from the Abbey where he has pressed her to visit his daughter on the belief that she is rich and will be a good match for his son, it is no wonder that Tilney follows her and offers himself to her. She prevails by her innocence and sweetness, and in spite of her romantic folly she has so much good heart that it serves her in place of good sense.

The chapters of the story relating to Catharine's stay at the Abbey are rather perfunctorily devoted to burlesquing romantic fiction, in accordance with the author's original design, and they have not the easy charm of the scenes at Bath, where Catharine, as the guest of Mrs. Allen, meets Henry Tilney at a public ball.

Mrs. Allen was one of that numerous class of females whose society can raise no other emotion than surprise at there being any men in the world who could like them well enough to marry them. . . . The air of a gentlewoman, a great deal of quiet, inactive good temper, and a trifling turn of mind were all that could account for her being the choice of a sensible, intelligent man like Mr. Allen. In one respect she was admirably fitted to introduce a young lady into public, being as fond of going everywhere, and seeing everything herself, as any young lady could.

But at the first ball she knows nobody, and she can only say to Catharine from time to time, 'I wish we had a large acquaintance here,' but at their next appearance in the Lower Rooms (how much the words say to the reader of old-fashioned fiction!) the master of ceremonies introduces a partner to Catharine.

His name was Tilney. He seemed to be about four or five and twenty, was rather tall, had a pleasing countenance, a very lively and intelligent eye, and, if not quite handsome, was very near it. . . . When they were seated at tea she found him as agreeable as she had already given him credit for being. . . . After chatting for some time on such matters as naturally arose from the objects around them, he suddenly addressed her with – 'I have hitherto been very remiss, madam, in the proper attentions of a partner here; I have not yet asked you how long you have been in Bath, whether you were ever here before, whether you have been at the Upper Rooms, the theatre, and the concert, and how you like the place altogether. I have been very negligent; but are you now at leisure to satisfy me in these particulars? If you are, I will begin directly.' 'You need not give yourself that trouble, sir.' 'No trouble, I assure you, madam.' Then, forming his features in a set smile, and affectedly softening his voice, he added with a simpering air, 'Have you been long in Bath, madam?' 'About a week, sir,' replied Catharine, trying not to laugh. 'Really!' with affected astonishment. 'Why should you be surprised, sir?' 'Why, indeed?' said he in his natural tone. 'But some emotion must appear to be raised by your reply, and surprise is more easily assumed, and not less reasonable, than any other. Now let us go on. Were you ever here before, madam?' 'Never, sir.' 'Indeed! Have you yet honored the Upper Rooms?' 'Yes, sir; I was there last Monday.' 'Have you been to the theatre?' 'Yes, sir; I was at the play on Tuesday.' 'To the concert?' 'Yes, sir; on Wednesday.' 'And you are altogether pleased with Bath?' 'Yes, I like it very well.' 'Now, I must give one more smirk, and then we may be rational again.' Catharine turned away her head, not knowing whether she ought venture to laugh. 'I see what you think of me,' said he gravely. 'I shall make but a poor figure in your journal to-morrow. . . . I know exactly what you will say. Friday went to the Lower Rooms; wore my sprigged muslin robe with blue trimmings, plain black shoes; appeared to much advantage, but was strangely harassed by a queer, half-witted man who would make me dance with him, and distressed me by his nonsense.' 'Indeed I shall say no such thing.' 'Shall I tell you what you ought to say?' 'If you please.' 'I danced with a very agreeable young man, had a good deal of conversation with him, seems a most extraordinary genius; hope I may know more of him. *That*, madam, is what I *wish* you to say.' 'But perhaps I keep no journal.' 'Perhaps you are not sitting in this room, and I am not sitting beside you.'

It is plain from the beginning what must be Catharine's fate with a young man who can laugh at her so caressingly, and what must be his with a girl so helplessly transparent to his eyes. Henry Tilney is as good as he is subtle, and he knows how to value her wholesome honesty aright; but all her friends are not witty young clergymen, and one of them is as little like him in appreciation of Catharine's rare nature as she is like Catharine in the qualities which take him. This is putting it rather too severely if it conveys the reproach of wilful bad faith in the case of Isabella Thorp, who becomes the bosom friend of Catharine at a moment's notice, and the betrothed of Catharine's brother with very little more delay. She is simply what she was born, a self-centred jilt in every motion of her being, and not to be blamed for fulfilling the jilt's function in a world where she is divined in almost her modern importance. In this character, the author forecasts the supremacy of a type which had scarcely been recognized before, but which has since played so dominant a part in fiction, and as with the several types of snobs, proves herself not only artist but prophet. Isabella is not of the lineage of the high and mighty flirts, the dark and deadly flirts, who deal destruction round among the hearts of men. She is what was known in her time as a 'rattle'; her tongue runs while her eyes fly, and her charms are perpetually alert for admiration. She is involved in an incessant drama of fictitious occurrences; she is as romantic in her own way as Catharine is in hers; she peoples an unreal world with conquests, while Catharine dwells in the devotion of one true, if quite imaginary lover. As Catharine cannot make anything of such a character, she decides to love and believe in her utterly, and she cannot well do more after Isabella becomes engaged to her brother James, and declares that she is going to withdraw from the world in his absence, and vows that though she may go to the assembly she will do it merely because Catharine asks it. '"But do not insist upon my being very agreeable, for my heart you know will be forty miles off; and as for dancing, do not mention it, I beg; *that* is quite out of the question."'

Catharine takes her friend so literally that when Tilney asks her in behalf of his handsome brother the question whether Miss Thorp would have any objection to dancing,

'Your brother will not mind it, I know,' said she, 'because I heard him say before that he hated dancing; but it was very good-natured of him to think of it. I suppose he saw Isabella sitting down, and fancied she might wish for a partner, but . . . she would not dance on any account in the world.' Henry smiled and said, 'How very little trouble it can give you to understand the motive of other people's actions.' 'Why, what do you mean?' . . . 'I only meant that your attributing my brother's wish of dancing with Miss Thorp to good-nature, convinced me of your being superior in good-nature yourself to all the rest of the world.' Catharine blushed and disclaimed. . . . She drew back for some time, forgetting to speak or to listen . . . till roused by the voice of Isabella, she looked up and saw her with Captain Tilney preparing to give their hands across. Isabella shrugged her shoulders and smiled, the only explanation of this extraordinary change which could at that time be given. Catharine . . . spoke her astonishment in very plain terms to her partner. 'I cannot think how it could happen. Isabella was so determined not to dance.' 'And did Isabella never change her mind before?' 'Oh! but because – and your brother! After what you told him from me, how could he think of going to ask her?' . . . 'The fairness of your friend was an open attraction; her firmness, you know, could only be understood by yourself.' 'You are laughing; but

I assure you Isabella is very firm in general.' . . . The friends were not able to get together . . . till after the dancing was over; but then as they walked about the room arm in arm, Isabella thus explained herself: 'I do not wonder at your surprise, and I am really fatigued to death. . . . I would have given the world to sit still.' 'Then why did not you?' . . . 'Oh, my dear, it would have looked so particular, and you know how I abhor doing that. . . . You have no idea how he pressed me. . . . I found there would be no peace if I did not stand up. Besides, I thought Mrs. Hughes, who introduced him, might take it ill if I did; and your dear brother, I am sure, would have been miserable if I had sat down the whole evening. My spirits are quite jaded, listening to his nonsense; and then being such a smart young fellow, I saw every eye was upon us.' 'He is very handsome indeed.' 'Handsome? Yes, I suppose he may . . . But he is not at all in my style of beauty. I hate a florid complexion and dark eyes in a man. However, he is very well. Amazingly conceited, I am sure. I took him down, several times, you know, in my way.'

The born jilt, the jilt so natured that the part she perpetually plays is as unconscious with her as the circulation of the blood, has never been more perfectly presented than in Isabella Thorp, in whom she was first presented; and her whole family, so thoroughly false that they live in an atmosphere of lies, are miracles of art. The soft, kindly, really well-meaning mother, is as great a liar as her hollow-hearted, hollow-headed daughter, or her braggart son who babbles blasphemous falsehoods because they are his native speech, with only the purpose of a momentary effect, and hardly the hope or wish of deceit. His pursuit of the trusting Catharine, who desires to believe in him as the friend of her brother, is the farcical element of the pretty comedy. The farce darkens into as much tragedy as the scheme will suffer when General Tilney, a liar in his own way, is taken in by John Thorp's talk, and believes her very rich; but it all brightens into the sweetest and loveliest comedy again, when Henry Tilney follows her home from his father's house, and the cheerful scene is not again eclipsed till the curtain goes down upon her radiant happiness.

SOURCE: extract from *Heroines of Fiction* (1901) pp. 58–64.

Reginald Farrer

A BIG STRIDE FORWARD (1917)

... In *Northanger Abbey* Jane Austen takes a big stride forward. Developing her taste for technical problems, she here tackles a very difficult one – in an artist's consciousness of the problem, indeed, but with youth's indomitable unconsciousness of its full difficulty. A lesser writer, or a maturer, would have either jibbed at such a task as that of interweaving two motives, of parody and serious drama, or would have crashed heavily through their thin ice. In buoyancy of youth and certainty of power, Jane Austen skims straight across the peril, and achieves a triumph so complete that easy readers run the risk of missing both triumph and problem, in mere joy of the book. She even allows herself to dally here with her own delight, and personally steps forward in the tale with her three great personal outbreaks, – on Novels, on Folly in Females, and on the Vanity of Feminine Motives in Dress. As for the reader, the closer his study of the dovetailing of the two motives, the profounder his pleasure. Parody rules, up to the arrival of Catherine at Northanger, which is the pivot of the composition; after which the drama, long-brewing out of the comic motive, runs current with it, and soon predominates. The requisite hyphen is provided by John and Isabella Thorpe, as differently important in one aspect of the tale as in the other. Each moment of the drama artfully echoes some note of the parody that had prevailed before; and the General's final outburst is just what had been foreshadowed long before, in burlesque, of Mrs Allen. Catherine herself suffers by this very nicety of poise and adjustment; she is really our most delightful of all *ingénues*, but her story is kept so constantly comic that one has no time to concentrate on its chief figure.

Fun, too, tends to overshadow the emotional skill with which the movement is developed. Even the processes by which Catherine so plausibly hardens herself into her grotesque belief that General Tilney killed his wife, even her stupefaction before the commonplaceness of the murdered martyr's room, pale beside the sudden comic tragedy of her awakening,[1] so convincing as it is, so completely blending the two motives of the book, and, in itself, so vibrant with an emotion as genuine as its generating causes are ridiculous. 'She raised her eyes to him more fully than she had ever done before,' is an early, but very notable, instance of Jane Austen's peculiar power of conveying intense feeling with a touch. In fact, *Northanger Abbey* marks the point of transition between the author's first period and her second. Already character is a serious rival to the story; henceforth it becomes more and more the main motive, till finally we reach *Persuasion*, than which no known novel of anything like equal calibre is so entirely devoid of any 'story' at all. . . .

SOURCE: extract from 'Jane Austen', in *Quarterly Review*, CCXXVIII (July 1917) 18–19.

NOTE

1. Jane Austen loves to have her heroine taken in, either by herself or some one else; so that author and reader can enjoy a private smile together.

Mary Lascelles

THE PATTERN OF BURLESQUE (1939)

. . . *Northanger Abbey* is a good point of departure, because of the boldness with which it flaunts its burlesque intention. The pattern of its burlesque element, however, is by no means simple. Though it is not subtly interwoven with the rest of the fabric, it is elaborately and ingeniously contrived.

It presents itself with a deceptive air of simplicity and broad, bold humour. The author herself seems to be explaining, in a clear, youthful, high-spirited voice, how her opening situation should develop according to the laws of the 'land of fiction'.[1] Since Catherine Morland is the heroine, it is her business to fit herself for this office, to emulate the heroines of Mrs. Radcliffe, Mrs. Roche, and countless others – to bring herself up after the pattern of Charlotte Smith's Emmeline (for example),[2] who, besides forming correct literary tastes in a ruined library, had 'of every useful and ornamental feminine employment . . . long since made herself mistress without any instruction'.[3] But Catherine, alas, 'never could learn or understand any thing before she was taught; and sometimes not even then, for she was often inattentive, and occasionally stupid'.[4] And whereas Emmeline 'had learned to play on the harp, by being present when Mrs. Ashwood received lessons on that instrument',[5] *she*, at the height of her career as heroine, had advanced no farther than to be able to 'listen to other people's performance with very little fatigue'.[6] This was not all – 'her greatest deficiency was in the pencil';[7] here she fell miserably short of Emmeline, who 'endeavoured to cultivate a genius for drawing, which she inherited from her father'. It is true that, 'for want of knowing a few general rules, what she produced had more of elegance and neatness than correctness and knowledge',[8] but when this small defect had been remedied by a friend's communication of these few general rules, she was able to execute a faultless portrait of her Delamere (and leave it, wrapped in silver paper, on the pianoforte, for him to discover there),[9] while poor Catherine, her looking-glass image and opposite, 'had no notion of drawing – not enough even to attempt a sketch of her lover's profile, that she might be detected in the design'.[10]

It is to be hoped, however (the author suggests), that the other characters will have a stricter notion of their responsibilities: Mrs. Morland will surely fill her daughter's mind with 'cautions against the violence of such noblemen and baronets as delight in forcing young ladies away to some remote farmhouse'[11] – but she does not promise well. '. . . Mrs. Morland knew so little of lords and baronets, that she entertained no notion of their general mischievousness, and was wholly unsuspicious of danger to her daughter from their machinations.'[12] Indeed, being fully occupied in rearing younger children, she had failed to put any ideas into her daughter's head at all, and so fitted her admirably for the part she was to play. Mrs. Allen may understand better what is expected of her – but she proves so unhelpful that it must be left to the reader 'to judge, in what manner her actions will hereafter tend to promote the general distress of the work, and how she will, probably, contribute to reduce poor Catherine to all the desperate wretchedness of which a last volume is capable . . .'.[13] As for the hero, he does not even know how to make a proper entrance: Catherine

had reached the age of seventeen, without having seen one amiable youth who could call forth her sensibility; without having inspired one real passion, and without having excited even any admiration but what was very moderate and very transient. This was strange indeed! But strange things may be generally accounted for if their cause be fairly searched out. There was not one lord in the neighbourhood; no – not even a baronet. There was not one family among their acquaintance who had reared and supported a boy accidentally found at their door – not one young man whose origin was unknown.[14]

And so the best that Henry Tilney can do is to get himself introduced to Catherine by the master of the ceremonies in the

Lower Rooms; and the small hope of mystery that this leaves is dissipated by Mr. Allen's inconsiderate inquiries.

And now, by a delightful piece of ingenuity, the authoress hands over to the newly arrived hero her own office of interpreter: it is he, from now on, who will remind Catherine of her duties as heroine, and point the difference between her situation as it should develop under the laws of fiction, and as it is actually developing. When the friendship between Catherine and Isabella breaks, he catechizes her:

'You feel, I suppose, that, in losing Isabella, you lose half yourself: you feel a void in your heart which nothing else can occupy. Society is becoming irksome; and as for the amusements in which you were wont to share at Bath, the very idea of them without her is abhorrent. You would not, for instance, now go to a ball for the world. You feel that you have no longer any friend to whom you can speak with unreserve; on whose regard you can place dependence; or whose counsel, in any difficulty, you could rely on. You feel all this?'

'No,' said Catherine, after a few moments' reflection, 'I do not – ought I?'[15]

This is not all: it now begins to appear that Jane Austen has something in reserve – that she is going to use more than one of the possible burlesque patterns. (The pleasure of surprise is rare in burlesque.) Catherine, hitherto ignorant of the world of illusion, is instructed in its laws by Isabella, 'four years older than Miss Morland, and at least four years better informed',[16] and surrenders to its enchantment. It is characteristic of Jane Austen's delicate moderation that once this enchantment has mastered Catherine's imagination, Henry Tilney relinquishes for a while his office of interpreter; we do not need them both to point – he consciously, she with her author's help – the difference between Udolpho and Bath. Catherine now goes forward on her journey burdened with delusions which events must challenge. Daylight gives place to limelight – Beechen Cliff 'puts her in mind of the country that Emily and her father travelled through, in the "Mysteries of Udolpho"'.[17] People begin to cast grotesque shadows: when General Tilney chooses another path than that which had been his wife's favourite, Catherine knows what to think about Mrs. Tilney.

Of her unhappiness in marriage, she felt persuaded. The General certainly had been an unkind husband. He did not love her walk: – could he therefore have loved her? And besides, handsome as he was, there was a something in the turn of his features which spoke his not having behaved well to her.[18]

She does not stop here; before long she is dallying with

the probability that Mrs. Tilney yet lived, shut up for causes unknown, and receiving from the pitiless hands of her husband a nightly supply of coarse food . . .[19] In support of the plausibility of this conjecture, it further occurred to her, that the forbidden gallery, in which lay the apartments of the unfortunate Mrs. Tilney, must be, as certainly as her memory could guide her, exactly over this suspected range of cells, and the stair-case by the side of those apartments of which she had caught a transient glimpse, communicating by some secret means with those cells, might well have favoured the barbarous proceedings of her husband. Down that stair-case she had perhaps been conveyed in a state of well-prepared insensibility!

Catherine sometimes started at the boldness of her own surmises, and sometimes hoped or feared that she had gone too far; but they were supported by such appearances as made their dismissal impossible.[20]

Indeed, they are as moderate as they are logical – judged by the canons of that world in which Madeline Clermont learns of her father's guilt by observing him look pointedly at a picture of Cain killing Abel.[21]

For all this, there is within Catherine herself an instinct, as of a wise child, that prevents her from abandoning her mind altogether to the world of illusion, and acquiring a taste for its poisonous magic fruit. Unlike Arabella, Cherubina, and the dreary company of heroines whom they ridicule, she is never deceived about those people in her little world who are true to themselves – she has a juster and more sensitive understanding of Eleanor Tilney than of Isabella Thorpe; nor is she deceived about herself: she never comes nearer to fancying herself a heroine than in the modest hope that 'since James's engagement had taught her what *could* be done'[22] Henry Tilney might in time return her affection. I believe Mr. Ralli to be at fault in finding Catherine and her folly incongruous: '. . . so delicate a mind' as hers, he says, 'requires less strong contrasts than the suggestions of Mrs. Radcliffe, the rough manners and want of sensitiveness of the Thorpes, and the rudeness of General Tilney . . .'.[23] This (if I have understood it) means that a more obtuse heroine would have served as well for the burlesque element in *Northanger Abbey*. But it is essential to Jane Austen's purpose that Catherine's perceptions should be naturally just, merely clouded for a while by the perplexities of the passage from child to woman, so that she may take leave of her folly unregretfully:

Charming as were all Mrs. Radcliffe's works, and charming even as were the works of all her imitators, it was not in them perhaps that human nature, at least in the midland counties of England, was to be looked for. Of the Alps and Pyrenees, with their pine forests and their vices, they might give a faithful delineation; and Italy, Switzerland, and the South of France, might be as fruitful in horrors as they were there represented. Catherine dared not doubt beyond her own country, and even of that, if hard pressed, would have yielded the northern and western extremities.[24]

And so she enters the real world with a good heart – all the better because it is, appropriately, no doctor of divinity but Henry Tilney himself who leads her over the threshold.

Thus, the burlesque element in *Northanger Abbey* has a pretty intricacy and variety. Its strands are ingeniously interwoven with one another – but not so well woven into the rest of the fabric. There is weakness in the slight connexion between Catherine's fancied and her actual adventures at the climax of the story. The General's interference with her fortunes is neither a consequence of her foolish misconception of him (as it would be in any of the stock burlesques of the age), nor an amusing looking-glass version of it. And not all the light, gay references to her heroineship at the end[25] can draw these two together. . . .

S o u r c e : extract from *Jane Austen and Her Art* (1939) pp. 59–64.

NOTES

1. Scott's phrase in his review of *Emma* (*Quarterly Review*, XIV, March 1816). The width of the satire in *Northanger Abbey*, its application to the novel of sentiment in Fanny Burney's tradition equally with the novel of romantic mystery in Mrs. Radcliffe's, has not been sufficiently recognised.

2. Charlotte Smith, *Emmeline, The Orphan of the Castle* (1788). I choose her as a good representative of the type, and because, taking into account the fact that J. A. already knew the book, I think it likely that she had this particular heroine present in her mind when she wrote *N.A.* But there is a great similarity among the heroines of that age.

3. *Emmeline*, vol. I, ch. 7.

4. *N.A.*, ch. 1, p. 14.

5. *Emmeline*, I, ch. 14.

6. *N.A.*, ch. 1, p. 16.

7. *N.A.*, ch. 1, p. 16.

8. *Emmeline*, I, ch. 7.

9. *Emmeline*, I, ch. 16.

10. *N.A.*, ch. 1, p. 16.

11. *N.A.*, ch. 2, p. 18. J. A. may possibly have been thinking of Cowper's disapproval of heroines:

Caught in a delicate soft silken net
By some lewd Earl, or rake-hell Baronet –

Progress of Error, ll. 313–14.

12. *N.A.*, p. 18.

13. *N.A.*, ch. 2, pp. 19, 20.

14. *N.A.*, ch. 1, p. 16.

15. *N.A.*, ch. 25, p. 207.

16. *N.A.*, ch. 4, p. 33.

17. *N.A.*, ch. 14, p. 106.

18. *N.A.*, ch. 22, p. 180.

19. *N.A.*, ch. 23, pp. 187–8.

20. *N.A.*, ch. 23, p. 188.

21. Regina Maria Roche, *Clermont* (1798), vol. IV, ch. 1.

22. *N.A.*, ch. 17, p. 138.

23. A. Ralli, *Critiques* (1927) p. 81.

24. *N.A.*, ch. 25, p. 200. I think that one of the threads of sympathy between J. A. and Scott shows itself in the similarity (both

as to thought and expression) between this passage and a passage
in Scott's life of Mrs Radcliffe: '. . . she has uniformly selected the
south of Europe for her place of action, whose passions, like the
weeds of the climate, are supposed to attain to portentous growth . . .':
Scott's *Miscellaneous Prose Works* (1827) III p. 439 – *Memoir of Mrs.
Radcliffe* (first published in *Lives of the Novelists*, 1820–4).

  25. E.g. *N.A.*, ch. 30 ,p. 243.

D. W. Harding

A NEIGHBOURHOOD OF VOLUNTARY SPIES (1940)

The impression of Jane Austen which has filtered through to the reading public down from the first-hand critics, through histories of literature, university courses, literary journalism and polite allusion, deters many who might be her best readers from bothering with her at all. How can this popular impression be described? In my experience the first idea to be absorbed from the atmosphere surroundering her work was that she offered exceptionally favourable openings to the exponents of urbanity. Gentlemen of an older generation than mine spoke of their intention of re-reading her on their deathbeds; Eric Linklater's cultured Prime Minister in *The Impregnable Women* passes from surreptitious to abandoned reading of her novels as a national crisis deepens. With this there also came the impression that she provided a refuge for the sensitive when the contemporary world grew too much for them. So Beatrice Kean Seymour writes (*Jane Austen*): 'In a society which has enthroned the machine-gun and carried it aloft even into the quiet heavens, there will always be men and women – Escapist or not, as you please – who will turn to her novels with an unending sense of relief and thankfulness.'

I was given to understand that her scope was of course extremely restricted, but that within her limits she succeeded admirably in expressing the gentler virtues of a civilised social order. She could do this because she lived at a time when, as a sensitive person of culture, she could still feel that she had a place in society and could address the reading public as sympathetic equals; she might introduce unpleasant people into her stories but she could confidently expose them to a public opinion that condemned them. Chiefly, so I gathered, she was a delicate satirist, revealing with inimitable lightness of touch the comic foibles and amiable weaknesses of the people whom she lived amongst and liked.

All this was enough to make me quite certain I didn't want to read her. And it is, I believe, a seriously misleading impression. Fragments of the truth have been incorporated in it but they are fitted into a pattern whose total effect is false. And yet the wide currency of this false impression is an indication of Jane Austen's success in an essential part of her complex intention as a writer: her books are, as she meant them to be, read and enjoyed by precisely the sort of people whom she disliked; she is a literary classic of the society which attitudes like hers, held widely enough, would undermine.

In order to enjoy her books without disturbance those who retain the conventional notion of her work always have had slightly to misread what she wrote at a number of scattered points, points where she took good care (not wittingly perhaps) that the misreading should be the easiest thing in the world. Unexpected astringencies occur which the comfortable reader probably overlooks, or else passes by as slight imperfections, trifling errors of tone brought about by a faulty choice of words. Look at the passage in *Northanger Abbey* where Henry Tilney offers a solemn reprimand of Catherine's fantastic suspicions about his father:

Dear Miss Morland, consider the dreadful nature of the suspicions you have entertained. What have you been judging from? Remember the country and the age in which we live. Remember that we are English, that we are Christians. Consult your own understanding, your own sense of the probable, your own observation of what is passing around you. Does our education prepare us for such atrocities? Do our laws connive at them? Could they be perpetrated without being known, in a country like this, where social and literary intercourse is on such a footing, and where roads and newspapers lay every thing open?

Had the passage really been as I quote it nothing would have been out of tone. But I omitted a clause. The last sentence actually runs: 'Could they be perpetrated without being known, in a country like this, where social and literary intercourse is

on such a footing, where every man is surrounded by a neighbourhood of voluntary spies, and where roads and newspapers
lay everything open?' 'Where every man is surrounded by a
neighbourhood of voluntary spies' – with its touch of paranoia
that surprising remark is badly out of tune both with 'Henry's
astonishing generosity and nobleness of conduct' and with the
accepted idea of Jane Austen.

Yet it comes quite understandably from someone of Jane
Austen's sensitive intelligence, living in her world of news and
gossip interchanged amongst and around a large family. She
writes to Cassandra (14 September 1804),

My mother is at this moment reading a letter from my aunt
Yours to Miss Irvine of which she had had the perusal (which by
the bye in your place I should not like) has thrown them into a
quandary about Charles and his prospects. The case is that my
mother had previously told my aunt, without restriction, that . . .
whereas you had replied to Miss Irvine's inquiries on the subject
with less explicitness and more caution. Never mind, let them
puzzle on together.

And when Fanny Knight (her niece) writes confidentially
about her love affair, Jane Austen describes ruses she adopted
to avoid having to read the letter to the family, and later
implores Fanny to 'write *something* that may do to be read or
told' (30 November 1814).

Why is it that, holding the view she did of people's spying,
Jane Austen should slip it in amongst Henry Tilney's eulogies
of the age? By doing so she achieves two ends, ends which she
may not have consciously aimed at. In such a speech from such
a character the remark is unexpected and unbelievable, with
the result that it is quite unlikely to be taken in at all by many
readers; it slips through their minds without creating a disturbance. It gets said, but with the minimum risk of setting
people's backs up. The second end achieved by giving the
remark such a context is that of off-setting it at once by more
appreciative views of society and so refraining from indulging
an exaggerated bitterness. The eulogy of the age is not nullified

by the bitter clause, but neither can it wipe out the impression the clause makes on those who attend to it.

One cannot say that here the two attitudes modify one another. The technique is too weak. Jane Austen can bring both attitudes into the picture but she has not at this point made one picture of them. In *Persuasion* she does something of the same kind more delicately. Miss Elliot's chagrin at having failed to marry her cousin is being descirbed in the terms of ordinary satire which invites the reading public to feel superior to Miss Elliot:

There was not a baronet from A to Z whom her feelings could have so willingly acknowledged as an equal. Yet so miserably had he conducted himself, that though she was at this present time (the summer of 1814) wearing black ribbons for his wife, she could not admit him to be worth thinking of again. The disgrace of his first marriage might, perhaps, as there was no reason to suppose it perpetuated by offspring, have been got over, had he not done worse;

– and then at this point the satire suddenly directs itself against the public instead of Miss Elliot: 'but he had, as by the accustomary intervention of kind friends they had been informed, spoken most disrespectfully of them all . . .' . . .

Source: extract from 'Regulated Hatred: An Aspect of the Work of Jane Austen', *Scrutiny*, viii (March 1940) 346–9.

Marvin Mudrick

'IRONY *VERSUS* GOTHICISM' (1952)

Irony, Jane Austen's characteristic response to that curious alien world beyond Steventon, may have turned her toward the eighteenth-century novel as toward a particularly favorable climate for incongruity. Yet it will not account for the fact that she found herself altogether and immediately at home in the novel. Irony is an attitude and an instrument, it brings into view and analyzes; but it does not create or predetermine a medium.

Every medium – even, perhaps above all, the novel, in its often fatally deceptive resemblance to casual, at any rate personal and unfocused, intelligent observation – requires its own special talents; and, for the novel, Jane Austen had these precociously also. Her special talent for thematic narrative is obvious in 'Love and Freindship', however limited by the demands of parody; still more, and more variously, in 'The Three Sisters'. Her talent for recasting and organizing personality in potential depth and development is just as obvious in the barely sketched figures of 'Lesley Castle' and 'The Three Sisters', and in the remarkable vignette (LF pp. 109 ff.) that introduces Lady Greville, first of Jane Austen's predatory female aristocrats. Her irony, as early as in her *juvenilia*, is already operating not only upon the novel, but within the special conditions of the novel.

By 1794, when *The Mysteries of Udolpho* captured the reading public for Mrs. Radcliffe and the Gothic novel, Jane Austen had at least four years of authorship behind her. Having cleared away the lachrymose debris, and in the process grown aware and confident of her literary powers,[1] she may have felt that simple parody, even of so promising and fresh a target as the Gothic novel, was too restrictive for her now; that striking out in novels of her own, which would treat the familiar, verifiable, renewable world, was a more stimulating prospect, for the time being at least. In the next three years, at any rate, she turned from her close preoccupation with parody and wrote two full-length domestic novels.[2]

Meanwhile, however, the Gothic enthusiasm had mounted to a fury,[3] the temptation to dismantle became too strong for the ironist; and *Northanger Abbey* was the result. Yet her talents could no longer be channeled into simple parody. This last formidable assault of hers on the illusionary world could not be as direct and single-minded as that of 'Love and Freindship' because the actual world could no longer be implicit or fragmentary as in her burlesques: she had already explored it and staked it out, not just socially as in her letters but artistically also, and she could not or would not exclude it from the focus of attention. *Northanger Abbey* – unlike 'Love and Freindship' – is as much domestic novel as parody. Irony overtly juxtaposes the Gothic and the bourgeois worlds, and allows them to comment on each other. The ironic contrast, the juxtaposition of these two sets of values is, in fact, so overt and extensive that the formal unity of the novel depends on the author's success in maintaining each one as a distinct, continuous, and self-consistent commentary on the other.

In 'Love and Freindship', Jane Austen parodied the lachrymose novel by reproducing its characters and situations and then allowing them both to overreach themselves into absurdity: the action of the parody was single and internal, with no reference but an implicit and general one to the actual world. In *Northanger Abbey*, for the maturing and more conscious artist, the problem of parody has become far more complex.[4] The parody of a novel must itself be a novel: the novelist who shows what is artistically irrelevant and improbable must at the same time show what is relevant and probable. To meet this new standard in *Northanger Abbey*, Jane Austen discards the central technique of 'Love and Freindship'. Instead of reproducing the Gothic types of character and situation, she presents their anti-types in the actual world, and organizes these into a domestic narrative that parallels or intersects, and at all points is intended to invalidate, the Gothic narrative to which it diligently corresponds. The problem is to write simultaneously a Gothic novel and a realistic novel, and to gain and keep the reader's acceptance of the latter while proving that the former is false and absurd.[5]

It is important to note, at this point, the particular quality and direction of the Gothic world that Jane Austen has under scrutiny in *Northanger Abbey*. Her 'Gothicism' derives, not from the stagey sensuality and diabolism of M. G. Lewis's *The Monk*,[6] but from that obvious offshoot of the lachrymose novel – the hybrid form which Mrs. Radcliffe developed to its height of effectiveness and popularity, and which had been earlier cultivated in such works as Sophia Lee's *The Recess* (1785) and Charlotte Smith's *Celestine* (1791). In these novels, sensibility is still the index of virtue and the motive of action. The difference is that mere extravagances of pathos, poverty, suffering, and parental misunderstanding are replaced by strangeness and terror – a change of atmosphere rather than of character or motive. For the reader, the only difference is that the gasp replaces the tear as the measurable unit of response. So it is not surprising to meet old friends from the lachrymose novel: the tyrannical father, the importunate and unscrupulous suitor, the hero and heroine of sensibility and of mysterious but noble birth, the confidante (that relic of the epistolary novel), the chaperone – all of them, however, having taken on the dismal coloration of their new surroundings.

Against this world, Jane Austen sets up her own domestic anti-types. As in the Radcliffean novel, the heroine's consciousness, or sensibility, is the center of action; but in *Northanger Abbey* the heroine's function is doubled with the doubling of the action. There is irony even in its internal point of view: in the fact that its two worlds must originate, converge, and be finally discriminated in the limited consciousness of that most ingenuous and domestic heroine, Catherine Morland. The double burden seems almost too much for so lightweight a mind.

Of course, the author helps. At the outset, nobody but the author knows that Catherine is a potential Gothic heroine:

No one who had ever seen Catherine Morland in her infancy, would have supposed her born to be a heroine. Her situation in life, the character of her father and mother, her own person and disposition, were all equally against her. Her father was a clergyman, without being neglected, or poor, and a very respectable man, though his name was Richard[7] – and he had never been handsome. He had a considerable independence, besides two good livings – and he was not in the least addicted to locking up his daughters. (*N.A.*, p. 13)

Moreover, Catherine 'had a thin awkward figure, a sallow skin without colour, dark lank hair, and strong features'. (*N.A.*, p. 13) Nor are her abilities those of a heroine:

She never could learn or understand anything before she was taught; and sometimes not even then, for she was often inattentive, and occasionally stupid. (*N.A.*, p. 14)

The day which dismissed the music-master was one of the happiest of Catherine's life. Her taste for drawing was not superior; though whenever she could obtain the outside of a letter from her mother, or seize upon any other odd piece of paper, she did what she could in that way, by drawing houses and trees, hens and chickens, all very much like one another.[8] (*N.A.*, p. 14)

As she grows up and becomes 'almost pretty', she begins to occupy, without yet being aware of, her role: '. . . from fifteen to seventeen she was in training for a heroine; she read all such works as heroines must read to supply their memories with those quotations which are so serviceable and so soothing in the vicissitudes of their eventful lives.'[9] (*N.A.*, p. 15) Unfortunately

She had reached the age of seventeen, without having seen one amiable youth who could call forth her sensibility; without having inspired one real passion, and without having excited even any admiration but what was very moderate and very transient. This was strange indeed! But strange things may be generally accounted for if their cause be fairly searched out. There was not one lord in the neighbourhood; no – not even a baronet. There was not one family among their acquaintance who had reared and supported a boy accidentally found at their door – not one young man whose origin was unknown. Her father had no ward, and the squire of the parish no children. (*N.A.*, p. 16)

Catherine's luck changes when Mr. and Mrs. Allen, a childless couple in the village, invite her to accompany them to Bath. Even now, Mrs. Morland fails to act as a heroine's mother should:

Cautions against the violence of such noblemen and baronets as delight in forcing young ladies away to some remote farmhouse, must, at such a moment, relieve the fulness of her heart. Who would not think so? But Mrs. Morland knew so little of lords and baronets, that she entertained no notion of their general mischievousness, and was wholly unsuspicious of danger to her daughter from their machinations. (*N.A.*, p. 18)

So the party leaves: and Catherine, entrusted to the care of Mrs. Allen, happily anticipates the excitements of a resort.

Jane Austen never lets us doubt her dual intention in the narrative. She places before us both what a character should be if he were to conform to the Gothic mode, and what he really is. As long as Catherine, still uninstructed by Isabella, remains incapable of manufacturing her own illusionary world to offset the real one, the author will manufacture it for her. Here, for example, is what Mrs. Allen should be:

It is now expedient to give some description of Mrs. Allen, that the reader may be able to judge, in what manner her actions will hereafter tend to promote the general distress of the work, and how she will, probably, contribute to reduce poor Catherine to all the desperate wretchedness of which a last volume is capable – whether by her imprudence, vulgarity, or jealousy – whether by interrupting her letters, ruining her character, or turning her out of doors.[10] (*N.A.*, p. 19 f.)

And here is what she is:

. . . one of that numerous class of females, whose society can raise no other emotion than surprise at there being any men in the world who could like them well enough to marry them. She had neither beauty, genius, accomplishment, nor manner. The air of a gentle-woman, a great deal of quiet, inactive good temper, and a trifling turn of mind, were all that could account for her being the choice of a sensible, intelligent man, like Mr. Allen. (*N.A.*, p. 20)

Unlike the Gothic chaperone, she is neither wicked nor vigilant. She is content to let Catherine walk and visit where she pleases, to bring her to balls, and always to sit placidly by, whether later with a gossipy friend, or at first serenely deploring the fact that Catherine has not been asked to dance and so helping the author (for Catherine is still unaware of her role in the parallel story) to define the Gothic convention that the hero and heroine, drawn toward each other by a natural affinity, scorn so artificial a method as the formal introduction.

Nevertheless, this is the method by which Catherine meets Henry Tilney: they are introduced by the master of ceremonies at the ballroom. Henry is not even of mysterious birth or voca-tion. Mr. Allen finds out before the evening is ended that he is a clergyman, and 'of a very respectable family in Gloucester-shire'. (*N.A.*, p. 30) And it soon becomes apparent not only that Henry fancies himself as an anti-hero, but that he will take over a large part of what has been up till now the author's function: to provide a non-committal running ironic commen-tary on the hypocrisy of social conventions and the incredibility of the literary conventions that parallel them. Not only is Henry within the two actions of the story, but he becomes our chief observer and interpreter of both.

Henry prides himself on his worldliness and his lack of sentimentality; and – like his author – he expresses either only through irony. Anything falsely emotional, like social conver-sation, inspires him to burlesque:

. . . forming his features into a set smile, and affectedly softening his voice, he added, with a simpering air, 'Have you been long in Bath, madam?'
'About a week, sir,' replied Catherine, trying not to laugh.
'Really!' with affected astonishment.
'Why should you be surprized, sir?'

'Why, indeed!' said he, in his natural tone – 'but some emotion must appear to be raised by your reply, and surprize is more easily assumed, and not less reasonable than any other. . . .' (*N.A.*, p. 26)

Later on, after Catherine has been thoroughly indoctrinated by Isabella and her own reading into the Gothic world, he will tease her with a minutely detailed burlesque on its improbabilities. In the meantime, he is cocksurely articulate about the wearing qualities of women's clothes and of their letters, about imprecision of language, about dancing and marriage, about the beauties of landscape. He is always informed and confident, and almost always flippant to the verge of, but saved by a lively irony from, cynicism. His role in Catherine's unsentimental education is clear. To become her chief mentor, all he needs beyond his personality is to be attracted by her; and Jane Austen herself, having made Catherine impeccably ignorant, guarantees that much: '. . . in justice to men . . . though to the larger and more trifling part of the sex, imbecility in females is a great enhancement of their personal charms, there is a portion of them too reasonable and too well informed themselves to desire any thing more in woman than ignorance.' (*N.A.*, p. 111)

It is Isabella Thorpe, however, who first explicitly introduces the Gothic theme. Isabella parades herself as a heroine; and Catherine, dazzled, is quite willing to play the confidante to this paragon of beauty and sensibility:

The progress of the friendship between Catherine and Isabella was quick as its beginning had been warm, and they passed so rapidly through every gradation of increasing tenderness, that there was shortly no fresh proof of it to be given to their friends or themselves. They called each other by their Christian name, were always arm in arm when they walked, pinned up each other's train for the dance, and were not to be divided in the set; and if a rainy morning deprived them of other enjoyments, they were still resolute in meeting in defiance of wet and dirt, and shut themselves up, to read novels together. (*N.A.*, p. 36 f.)

The Mysteries of Udolpho, appropriately, is the first novel that

Isabella brings Catherine to read; and she promises her also *The Italian* and seven other Gothic romances that she names.[11] Plunged into all this self-conscious heroism, Catherine has no difficulty in accepting Isabella's protestations of affection, altruism, and constancy:

'. . . I wish you knew Miss Andrews, you would be delighted with her. She is netting herself the sweetest cloak you can conceive. I think her as beautiful as an angel, and I am so vexed with the men for not admiring her! I scold them all amazingly about it.'
    'Scold them! Do you scold them for not admiring her?'
    'Yes, that I do. There is nothing I would not do for those who are really my friends. I have no notion of loving people by halves, it is not my nature. My attachments are always excessively strong. I told Capt. Hunt at one of our assemblies this winter, that if he was to tease me all night, I would not dance with him, unless he would allow Miss Andrews to be as beautiful as an angel. . . .' (*N.A.*, p. 40)

Catherine is moving steadily toward the Gothic world. Not only has she read the right books, but she has met her own particular hero (who, having left Bath 'mysteriously', can be mooned over) and an authentic heroine. She has many occasions to match her sensibility with Isabella's, and to find it adequate: '. . . they followed their chaperons, arm in arm, into the ball-room, whispering to each other whenever a thought occurred and supplying the place of many ideas by a squeeze of the hand or a smile of affection.' (*N.A.*, p. 52)

Her ingenuousness and ignorance have prevented her from suspecting Isabella's indefatigable coquetry, her malice toward women, her large foolish generalizations about men. Of course, Catherine does not yet imagine that she – not Isabella – has been destined for the role of heroine; even now that the atmosphere of literary sensibility is strongly established, she needs at least a villain or two, and a recognizable Gothic setting, to precipitate her into self-delusion.

It is typical of the explicitly realistic ground of Jane Austen's parody in *Northanger Abbey* that Catherine seems, not an hallucinated puppet,[12] but a credibly impressionable and ingenuous young girl, with enough common sense to require at least a show of evidence before she draws the Gothic conclusions. Catherine finds her villains, not simply because she is looking for them, but because the author finds villains in actual life and allows her a few. For all the malice, hypocrisy, treachery, and general wickedness at Udolpho, Jane Austen finds very satisfactory counterparts at Bath. What her irony does here, as elsewhere, is to diminish scale, to puncture the grandiose pretensions of the Gothic villains, to demonstrate what villainy is like when transferred to the everyday, middle-class, social world. In this juxtaposition of Gothic type and actual anti-type, the latter is undeniably villainous also: only, like the rest of the actual world, on a much smaller and more disposable scale. The ironist finds no iniquity at Bath, but there is enough contemptibleness and to spare.

Consider John Thorpe, Jane Austen's anti-type for the unwelcome suitor. Certainly, he is importunate and unscrupulous enough to carry the Gothic role; but there is nothing sinister about him. He is simply exasperating, vulgar, rude, and foolish. The author is quick to put her own social tag on him: 'He . . . seemed fearful of being too handsome unless he wore the dress of a groom, and too much like a gentleman unless he were easy when he ought to be civil, and impudent when he might be allowed to be easy.' (*N.A.*, p. 45) He cannot let off boasting of the quality of his possessions: the speed of his horse, the durability of his gig, his skill at billiards. One of his favorite epithets, which he applies to whomever he suspects of having money, is 'rich as a Jew'. (*N.A.*, pp. 63, 96) He has a relish for profanity and financial transactions:[13] 'My horse! oh, d— it! I would not sell my horse for a hundred. . . .' (*N.A.*, p. 47) '. . . He asked fifty guineas; I closed with him directly, threw down the money, and the carriage was mine.' (*N.A.*, p. 46)

All these traits prepare the reader, if not Catherine (she is, naturally, prejudiced in favor of Isabella's brother), for Thorpe's villainy. Not that he abducts or tortures Catherine when she declines his attentions; he does not even connive with her father at marrying her against her will. His world and his talent are too limited for spectacular achievements; but he does as much mischief as he can.

He keeps forcing his presence and his garrulity on Catherine, in spite of her at first passive and later even obstinately active preference for other company. He has no scruple against lying to get her – or anyone else – to do or think as he wishes, and no feeling of guilt when caught in a lie. While Catherine is waiting to be visited by Henry and his sister, Thorpe tells her that he has seen them driving off elsewhere; later, when Catherine, driving with him, catches sight of them on their way to meet her, he is, in fact, only pleased with the success of his maneuver. His general offensiveness is so marked that Catherine herself, overawed at first by his continual, loud brashness and by his sister's authority, finds him tiring, and his hints at a proposal – her ingenuousness being reinforced by her reluctance to listen to him – comprehensible only as more rattling palaver. And finally – in accord with his function as anti-type to the villainous suitor – his boasting, his lying, his treachery, and his lack of scruple are all involved in his confidences to General Tilney, upon which the whole culminating Gothic adventure and its realistic aftermath depend.

The most interesting novelistic fact about all these characters is that – whatever else they may be – they are consistently, even rigidly, functional. They perform the special tasks of parody within a domestic setting, of action beside action: they behave as the author knows that bourgeois types behave, and in their behavior they suggest the corresponding Gothic types by being so different, by displaying the Gothic qualities reversed or contracted. Mrs. Allen, for example, is the Gothic chaperone reversed: Mrs. Allen all placid, submerged inertia and unconcern (a less well married Lady Bertram); the Gothic chaperone always deeply concerned, motivated – depending on whether the author needs her for a 'good' or a 'bad' character – either by an anxious propriety or by a busy malevolence. Isabella is the heroine's confidante reversed: sensibility into vulgarity, sympathy into egocentrism, chastity into man-chasing, thoughtfulness into frivolity. Thorpe, on the other hand, is the unwelcome suitor *contracted*: he too plagues the heroine and threatens her future happiness with his importunities, but his methods are ludicrously petty by comparison.

They are, then, consistently functional characters, and their function is to illustrate Jane Austen's double irony: that the Gothic world does not correspond to human nature as it may be seen at Bath; and that human nature as it may be seen at Bath is not necessarily more agreeable or more trustworthy than the Udolpho variety, though it *is* necessarily more limited. It remains to be considered whether these characters, or the rest, are more than functional, whether they go beyond merely illustrating the ironic intent of the novel.

One figure that seems more than merely functional is Henry Tilney. He is, of course, the Gothic hero reversed: he does not treat the heroine with solemn respect, he fails to fall in love with her at first sight, he does not even rescue her at any critical moment from a villain's clutches. Positively, however, he is witty, lively, talkative, didactic, and his common sense does rescue Catherine finally from delusion. He seems, in fact, the only perceptive person in the book; and he closely resembles, except for a few details of dress and appearance, the author herself.

This resemblance is more than superficial: his irritation with the use of words like 'nice' and 'amazing' to signify general approval of everything from looks to people, his defense of novel-reading, his delight in spinning out a worldly judgment or a circumstantial burlesque. Behind these characteristics, and uniting them all, is the impetus of irony, the unrelaxing wariness against a personal involvement.

Henry is constitutionally incapable of making a statement unqualified by irony. He can judiciously mock Catherine's opinion that history is a torment to little children:

'That little boys and girls should be tormented . . . is what no one at all acquainted with human nature in a civilized state can deny; but in behalf of our most distinguished historians, I must observe, that they might well be offended at being supposed to have no higher aim; and that by their method and style, they are perfectly well qualified to torment readers of the most advanced reason and mature time of life. I use the verb "to torment," as I observed to be your own method, instead of "to instruct," supposing them to be now admitted as synonimous.' (*N.A.*, p. 109)

In his eagerness to turn everything to ironic profit, he can even be unkind when his sister misunderstands Catherine's solemn announcement that 'something very shocking indeed, will soon come out in London'. (*N.A.*, p. 112)

'. . . my stupid sister has mistaken all your clearest expressions. You talked of expected horrors in London – and instead of instantly conceiving, as any rational creature would have done, that such words could relate only to a circulating library, she immediately pictured to herself a mob of three thousand men assembling in St. George's Fields; the Bank attacked, the Tower threatened, the streets of London flowing with blood, a detachment of the 12th Light Dragoons, (the hopes of the nation,) called up from Northampton to quell the insurgents, and the gallant Capt. Frederick Tilney, in the moment of charging at the head of his troop, knocked off his horse by a brickbat from an upper window. Forgive her stupidity. The fears of the sister have added to the weakness of the woman; but she is by no means a simpleton in general.' (*N.A.*, p. 113)

When his sister asks him to apologize, he replies:

'Miss Morland, I think very highly of the understanding of all the women in the world – especially of those – whoever they may be – with whom I happen to be in company.'
'That is not enough. Be more serious.'
'Miss Morland, no one can think more highly of the understanding of women than I do. In my opinion, nature has given them so much, that they never find it necessary to use more than half.' (*N.A.*, p. 113 f.)

Henry Tilney is the willfully ironic and detached spectator as no one except the author herself is in any other of Jane Austen's novels. Whenever he speaks, he speaks from the outside, to amuse, to parry, to lead on, to instruct, to humble; never plainly and straightforwardly, or unwarily, to reveal or engage himself. Even when Catherine, obviously anxious, questions him about his brother's attentions to Isabella (who is now betrothed to her brother James), he can only put her off, reinforcing his irony with evasiveness, and relenting briefly into a final, false assurance that nothing is wrong. (*N.A.*, pp. 150 ff.) As for the few times in the novel when, according to the exigencies of the plot, we must be made aware of his increasing affection for Catherine, he cannot speak except in irony (*N.A.*, pp. 132 f., 206); and on the occasion of his visiting the Morlands' home to propose to Catherine – when irony seems inappropriate, besides, because of Catherine's recent indignities at the hands of his father – the author, wisely enough, keeps him silent, wrapped in a cloud of indirect expression and conventional novelistic explanations. The living Henry never made the trip at all.

To introduce this sort of spectator-character, especially into a novel like *Northanger Abbey*, is an obvious convenience for the novelist. In any novel, such a character may unify the action, and with the advantage over the author of being within it, by examining it totally. In an overtly double action like that of *Northanger Abbey*, since the novel's unity depends upon our sharp discrimination, simultaneously with our awareness of correspondence and symmetry, between two self-consistent worlds, a character like Henry Tilney – familiar with both worlds, and aware of all their correspondences and differences – helps to unify the novel from within, to fortify the author's own observations and implications, which are likely in themselves to have an air of imposition. In personal terms, moreover, Henry makes an ideal foil for Catherine: irony and straightforwardness, sophistication and naïveté, confidence and timidity, information and ignorance.

One disadvantage is that such a character, by his very superiority of awareness and insight, may in contrast make the other characters look too confined and predictable. He may damage or destroy the illusion of their personal freedom, may come to seem himself no more than an arbitrary self-projection by the author. The other characters may seem, not personal, but functional only, without will. In a combination of Gothic novel and domestic novel like *Northanger Abbey*, where the gallery of characters is obliged at the same time to illustrate one rigorously defined set of values and to suggest the other, such a failure of will becomes more probable yet.

It is not merely what Henry says and thinks about the other characters that makes us suspect him, but his position of relative immunity in an atmosphere contagious with irony. Jane Austen does make fun of his youthful pedantry from time to time, she lets him fall in love with Catherine out of gratitude for Catherine's attachment to him (*N.A.*, p. 243), and out of a didactic delight in her ignorance; but that is the sum of the charges. Otherwise, he is allowed to know about as much as the author does, to pass similar judgments, to respond with a similarly persistent and inviolable irony toward all characters and events that come within his range. The effect of Henry's resemblance to the author is, finally, to make us wonder just how present the author is; or, rather, to strengthen our impression that she is present intrusively, in the need to assert her own non-commitment, and at the expense of the personal depth and independence of her characters.

There is, of course, besides this compulsion, the fact of her inexperience: among her large-scale works in the forms in which they survive,[14] *Northanger Abbey* is probably the earliest.[15] At any rate, *Northanger Abbey* has its share of the common literary property upon which even a novelist of genius is likely to draw in early work: characters like James Morland, who exists only to be deceived by Isabella; Eleanor Tilney, a wraith of female gentility hardly more substantial than Catherine's Gothic imaginings; Mr. Allen, who might as well have stayed home in Fullerton for all that we see or learn of him at Bath. This is the kind of failure to which the author is liable simply by being a novice, however precocious and brilliant, and more especially by undertaking so complex a scheme.

The other kind of failure in *Northanger Abbey* is peculiar to the author: a product of inexperience and compulsion at once. Jane Austen's compulsion toward irony persists throughout the novels until *Persuasion*, but she learns to accommodate it more and more skillfully to the requirements of her story. After *Northanger Abbey*, there are no all-knowing Henry Tilneys: the only privileged spectator is the author, and character and situation tend to establish and contain their own level of irony. In *Northanger Abbey*, however, the irony – always somewhat excessive for its material – is besides repeatedly expressed and spotlighted by the author from the outside. Jane Austen has yet neither the mature skill to direct wholly within the action of her novel, nor the social qualms to replace by bourgeois morality, her characteristic response of irony to all the phenomena she is willing to recognize. In *Northanger Abbey*, she cannot help intruding to assert her own detachment, not simply from society as in her letters, or from the illusionary world as in her youthful burlesques, but from the events and the people that she herself has created.

This enforced detachment justifies itself, with her pleasant characters, by denying them any depth or complexity of feeling; and with her unpleasant ones, by denying them not only feeling but any favorable qualities at all. There is, of course, the thematic need of invalidating the Gothic world by a detached observation and exposure; but Jane Austen goes further and in her flippancy tends now and then to suspend our belief or interest in her domestic world as well. In *Northanger Abbey*, her irony is too often in excess of the immediate need.

We can never believe, for example, that Catherine or her troubles are of much moment because the author so deliberately makes light of them. This depreciation begins mildly enough, as part of the specific parody of romantic love. Catherine, having fallen in love, perversely fails to lose either appetite or sleep; on the contrary, her reaction takes the form of an

... extraordinary hunger, and when that was appeased, changed into an earnest longing to be in bed; such was the extreme point of her distress; for when there she immediately fell into a sound sleep which lasted nine hours, and from which she awoke perfectly revived, in excellent spirits, with fresh hopes and fresh schemes. (*N.A.*, p. 60)

After a while, however, Jane Austen's early remark that Catherine is quite ignorant and unworldly seems as much an excuse for the author's condescension as a foreshadowing of the character's behavior. Parody tends here to become an affirmation of superiority. Catherine is never allowed to display a sensitivity that might engage our sympathy or transcend her author's ironic vigilance. She fails to measure up, not only to the idea of a Gothic heroine, but even to our idea of an interesting person. Unrelieved as it is, her naïveté begins to resemble dullness. She is too easily hoodwinked by Isabella. Even the impossible Mr. Thorpe she finds tolerable for a time. Her wide-eyed infatuation with Henry becomes tedious because we are not allowed to believe that it is anything more. Whenever we suspect that she deserves our concern – as when Thorpe tricks her into giving up an afternoon with Henry – the author takes pains to undeceive us: 'And now I may dismiss my heroine to the sleepless couch, which is the true heroine's portion; to a pillow strewed with thorns and wet with tears. And lucky may she think herself, if she get another good night's rest in the course of the next three months.' (*N.A.*, p. 90)

Catherine is the center of the action: yet she is neither the borrowed heroine of a pure burlesque, like Laura in 'Love and Freindship', nor as interesting and complex a person as she would have to be – intellectually or emotionally – to sustain the necessary tensions at the center of a realistic novel. We can neither treat her as a joke, nor take her at the value her position in the novel requires. She is credible enough; she functions amusingly in her dual role; but she is too simple and too slight, too narrowly a symbol of the author's rejection of romantic nonsense, to assert the claim of personal feeling and value beyond mere function. Jane Austen's rejection of romance develops into a rejection – at least, the spectator's implicit rejection – of personality: whatever value or autonomous feeling the action even begins to suggest for Catherine is immediately drowned in the author's irony.

To the other characters, Jane Austen denies even a suspicion of depth. They are ironically defined at the beginning in terms of their function, and allowed thereafter to act only on the basis of this definition. Mrs. Allen sits gossiping forever; Isabella pursues and jilts men and women equally; Thorpe swears to his improbable achievements and extends his lying as a matter of course; only General Tilney is permitted for a time to evade definition, for the sake of the plot: but none of them ever gives a hint of compunction or self-knowledge, of penetrability past or latent. They have no history; they are flatly in the present, beneath the author's irony.

Still, the most striking evidence of Jane Austen's compelled detachment lies, not in the behavior of her characters, but in her own explicit intrusions into the story, as in her treatment of Catherine sleepless with tears (*N.A.*, p. 90): in her own imposed direction, tone, and commentary. She cannot yet adjust her ironic attack nicely to the strength of its object, the flimsy and false-fronted Gothic world; she overreaches into her own realistic world and shakes that also, dangerously. She can never, for example, quite moderate her attack on the literary platitudes about affection. We have seen how she disposes of Catherine in love and in the disappointments of love. In her friendship with Isabella, Catherine is just as severely treated: the two girls supply 'the place of many ideas by a squeeze of the hand or a smile of affection' (*N.A.*, p. 52); and Catherine, having found so good a friend at the Pump-room, considers 'that building . . . so favourable for the discovery of female excellence, and the completion of female intimacy, so admirably adapted for secret discourses and unlimited confidence, that she was most reasonably encouraged to expect another friend from within its walls'. (*N.A.*, p. 60) The irony here is especially loaded and supererogatory because at Isabella's earliest appearance we are put to no trouble at all to discover her motives from her words alone: the fact that Catherine is ingenuous to be deceived by her requires no underlining. As for friendship between those two inoffensive, aging vegetables, Mrs. Allen and Mrs. Thorpe, the author cannot restrain her contempt. At an unexpected meeting in Bath, 'Their joy . . . was very great, as well it might, since they had been contented to know nothing of each other for the last fifteen years.' (*N.A.*, pp. 31 f.) And Mrs. Allen is later '. . . never satisfied with the day unless she spent the chief of it by the side of Mrs. Thorpe, in what they called conversation, but in which there was scarcely any exchange of opinion, and not often any resemblance of subject, for Mrs. Thorpe talked chiefly of her children, and Mrs. Allen of her gowns'. (*N.A.*, p. 36)

It is not that Jane Austen fails to illustrate her characters by incident for the most part, but that she cannot resist establishing her distance from them in her own voice as well, as if she does not trust – or is not yet aware of – the power of her art alone, without the arbitrary expression of her will, to cut down and isolate the middle-class world for detached examination and so to safeguard her against involvement.

Function and commentary are the two dimensions of *Northanger Abbey*; and though we may be on the verge of a third now and then – as when Catherine apologizes in the eager rush of explanation to Henry:

'Oh! Mr. Tilney, I have been quite wild to speak to you, and make my apologies. You must have thought me so rude; but indeed it was not my own fault, – was it, Mrs. Allen? Did not they tell me that Mr. Tilney and his sister were gone out in a phaeton together? and then what could I do? But I had ten thousand times rather have been with you; now had not I, Mrs. Allen?' (*N.A.*, p. 93 f.)

or when we share the Tilneys' sense of strain in their father's presence and in his unctuousness toward Catherine – the author always pulls herself up in time.

It is true that General Tilney arouses enough interest in his nature and his motives to show promise of a personal dimension. Functionally, of course, he is not only effective but crucial. Without him, there would be no suspense and no climax, Gothic or otherwise. We wonder from his first appearance about this impressive-looking father of whom his otherwise lively and irreverent son never speaks. We wonder even more at his sudden courtliness toward Catherine in the midst of hints about his irascibility and in the face of information from Henry and Eleanor that he would never allow his son Frederick to marry a girl like Isabella, without 'consequence and fortune'. (*N.A.*, p. 208) And, conveniently, he lives in an abbey – made over but still with traces of antiquity – in a room of which Catherine, her head turned by too much Gothic reading and by growing evidence of the General's willful bad temper, conjures up her night-terrors of a mysterious manuscript and a murdered or imprisoned wife. Without the suspense aroused by our uncertainty about him, the Gothic episode in *Northanger Abbey* would in fact have no realistic scaffolding at all.

Yet, having borrowed[16] and fitted in so useful a character, Jane Austen seems concerned, ultimately, much less to make him consistent than to keep him at his function. It is not that she might not have done both at once; but, in his case at least, her desire to do the latter inhibits her ability to do the former. General Tilney keeps escaping into his own life; but he must be cut down to size, he must be converted into a small piece of amusement for the author-spectator. So, in the end, we are not even allowed to observe his climactic – and, perhaps, impressive – rage at being deceived about the Morlands' affluence. We are merely expected to believe that man of great, almost monomaniacal pride and ambition of place, of unbending severity, who considers 'consequence' as well as 'fortune' indispensable to any prospective member of his family, who by the harshness of his authority has driven his otherwise inde-pendent-spirited children into frightened submission, whom we never see humble himself to anyone else, would treat with the most fatuous, pliant, immoderate deference a very young girl 'without consequence' solely in the belief that she will bring his son a large dowry. There may be somewhere such a com-mingling of traits; but Jane Austen does nothing to make it seem probable, to ease and vindicate the transition between the General with Catherine and the General without her. The final explanation of the General's conduct amounts to a be-trayal, for it involves dropping out of sight most of what we have learned about him. The two lines of his conduct remain as disparate as they ever were, and the one element that kept them simultaneously acceptable – the author's skillful implication that they would be resolved in the end – has been sunk in her desire to leave him contemptible only, to cram him back into the limits of his function: the tyrannical parent contracted.

Catherine, too, shows signs of by-passing her function: into a plain matter-of-factness, without the intervention of the Gothic climax called for in the formal design of *Northanger Abbey*. Catherine, like the General, has got away somewhat from her author and threatens to become unmanageable. It is not strange, therefore, that the Gothic episode, in which she is returned and rigidly fitted to her function, is the most inflexible and uncreative episode in the book. It is pat and single-textured; atmospherically unprepared and discontinuous with the rest of the novel; too literally a carrying-out of the Radcliffean terror episode, and of Henry's amusing prophecy. Most injuriously, however, it sacrifices Catherine's consistency to her function. It demands too abrupt a transition from Catherine the matter-of-fact ingénue to Catherine the self-appointed Gothic heroine: we can see, in retrospect, the accumulation of evidence – the directed reading, the abbey, the mysterious and forbidding widower, the bedroom with its Gothic paraphernalia – by which the author has attempted to rationalize the change; but we can hardly believe that Catherine's present imaginative credulity is a natural development out of her previous unimaginative credulity. The key to Catherine's nature is, not credulity, but matter-of-factness, whether she is quite lost in Isabella's innuendoes about a vanished clergyman-lover of her own (*N.A.*, p. 36) or bewildered by Henry's evasiveness about the relations between Isabella and his brother. (*N.A.*, pp. 150 ff.) Catherine is incapable of discovering implications: she is credulous only because she believes exactly what people say, not because she draws false and sentimental inferences from what they say or do.

In *Northanger Abbey*, function is the only field for Jane Austen's irony. When her characters begin to slip away from her into attitudes unforeseen by function, to solicit sympathy or understanding, her only recourse is to force them back, by inconsistency of conduct or her own authoritative commentary, into the limits of their function. Her skill and tact in directing realistic characters – so different from the easily disparaged puppets of 'Love and Freindship' – have not yet developed to the point of tempering and assimilating the disparagement, the often arbitrary reduction of scale, the assumption that nothing need be taken seriously, upon all of which her irony in *Northanger Abbey* blandly insists. The denouement of the novel represents also the climax of this insistence. If Henry and Catherine are separated by General Tilney's unyielding will (which function has not accounted for and cannot deal with), our story, dear reader, is after all only a story and we can pull a viscount out of the hat:

The anxiety, which in this state of their attachment must be the portion of Henry and Catherine, and of all who loved either, as to its final event, can hardly extend, I fear, to the bosom of my readers, who will see in the tell-tale compression of the pages before them, that we are all hastening together to perfect felicity. The means by which their early marriage was effected can be the only doubt; what probable circumstance could work upon a temper like the General's? The circumstance which chiefly availed was the marriage of his daughter with a man of fortune and consequence. . . . (*N.A.*, p. 250)

So, carried back to the belatedly introduced hero of 'Jack and Alice', and conveniently ignoring the realistic ground of *Northanger Abbey*, the author dismisses her absurd finishing-off as a joke. It seems that Eleanor's husband, the viscount,

. . . was really deserving of her; independent of his peerage, his wealth, and his attachment, being to a precision the most charming young man in the world. Any further definition of his merits must be unnecessary; the most charming young man in the world is instantly before the imagination of us all. Concerning the one in question therefore I have only to add – (aware that the rules of composition forbid the introduction of a character not connected with my fable) – that this was the very gentleman whose negligent servant left behind him that collection of washing-bills, resulting from a long visit at Northanger, by which my heroine was involved in one of her most alarming adventures. (*N.A.*, p. 251)

And, in a final flourish of unconcern, she leaves the reader with a choice of morals: '. . . I leave it to be settled by whomsoever it may concern, whether the tendency of this work be altogether to recommend parental tyranny, or reward filial disobedience'. (*N.A.*, p. 252)

This is rejection outright, and from without. Jane Austen's irony is no longer able even to make a pretense of coping internally with its materials: she shrugs off altogether the artist's responsibility toward them. They are disposed of, and we must ask no questions. She might have found the key to the plausible development and resolution of the story elsewhere, she might perhaps have elaborated the double action out of this more consistent and more characteristically youthful aspect of Catherine:

. . . the inexplicability of the General's conduct dwelt much in her thoughts . . . why he should say one thing so positively, and mean another all the while, was most unaccountable! How were people, at that rate, to be understood? Who but Henry could have been aware of what his father was at? (*N.A.*, p. 211)

But irony comes too close to relinquishing its office here, too close in fact to defining its threat to human relationships, as in a mirror in which hypocrisy and irony come to much the same thing, weapons against commitment; and the author shies away, back to parody, to the predictable anti-types who, having demolished the Gothic delusion by their own inadequacy to its demands, must now be reduced to faceless inconsequence and dismissed in turn. The novelist gives way to the parodist; and irony, here as in 'Love and Freindship', as in all the *juvenilia*, hardens perceptibly into rejection: in *Northanger Abbey*, into a rejection not only of the illusionary world, but of the realistic characters who disprove it – indeed, of the whole realistic basis of the novel. Irony overrides the artist, and becomes rejection unlimited.

SOURCE: 'The Literary Pretext Continued: Irony *versus* Gothicism', ch. 2 in *Jane Austen: Irony as Defense and Discovery* (1952) pp. 37–59.

NOTES

1. The independent experimentation of the later *juvenilia*, and their evolution toward serious novelistic relationships, seem to reflect Jane Austen's growing confidence in her ability to handle the medium whose extravagances she is burlesquing. Besides, her family audience must always have been appreciative and encouraging: as early as 1797, her father tried to get published, at his own expense if necessary, 'a manuscript novel, comprising 3 vols., about the length of Miss Burney's *Evelina*' (W. and R. A. Austen-Leigh, *Jane Austen: Her Life and Letters*, London, 1913, p. 97): probably 'First Impressions' (see following note).

2. About these we know, besides that they were written in letters, that their names were 'Elinor and Marianne' (which, at least in its final incarnation and probably more markedly in its first, still took off from parody and retained notable parodic elements) and 'First Impressions', that the latter was offered for publication (see preceding note), and that they were later very thoroughly revised into, respectively, *Sense and Sensibility* and *Pride and Prejudice*. 'Elinor and Marianne' was written about 1795; 'First Impressions' was begun in October 1796 and finished in August 1797. (Ibid. p. 96.)

3. Michael Sadleir, having examined the file of catalogues of the Minerva Library, presents statistics which demonstrate that Gothic novels, fairly popular before *The Mysteries of Udolpho* was published but still far outnumbered by novels of sentiment and sensibility, flooded the market in the latter half of the 1790s. (M. Sadleir in J. Austen, *Northanger Abbey*, London, 1930, p. xiv.)

4. As it was for Fielding in *Joseph Andrews*; though through a large part of his novel he solved the problem by ignoring it – that is, by dropping parody altogether in favor of his own story.

5. The implication that *Northanger Abbey* is a work of transition between Jane Austen's youthful parody and her first domestic novels, *Sense and Sensibility* and *Pride and Prejudice* – though these were in first draft earlier (W. and R. A. Austen-Leigh, op. cit., p. 96) – must be considered. We have evidence that the latter two were thoroughly revised shortly before publication (in 1811 and 1812, respectively). According to Jane Austen's own note, *Northanger Abbey* was probably revised as late as 1803 (*N.A.*, p. 12): but there is no evidence of any later revision. It is worth pointing

out that the latest Gothic novel mention in Isabella's list
(*N.A.*, p. 40) was published in 1798. In any case, parody : especially of so minutely regulated a form as the Radcliffean
novel – imposes so many rigid requirements that the artist's
tendency to revise must be much impeded. As they stand, *Northanger
Abbey* seems clearly the earliest of the full-length novels: by
internal evidence as well, I hope to demonstrate.

6. Published in 1796, and followed by a library of blood-and-
sin novels culminating in C. R. Maturin's *Melmoth the Wanderer*
(1820) and – with no appreciable change of medium – in Byron's
dramas. Jane Austen was quite aware of this form: see the list of
novels which Isabella urges Catherine to read (*N.A.*, p. 40), and
which Michael Sadleir summarizes and comments upon in his
excellent essay on eighteenth-century Gothicism: *The Northanger
Novels* (The English Association, Pamphlet No. 68, Oxford, 1927);
but she never handled it, ironically or otherwise. It was not nearly
so easy to handle with ironic detachment as the more ladylike
variety of Gothic novel.

7. Another indication that *Northanger Abbey* is in detail, as well
as in spirit, the earliest of the novels, the closest to the family-
diversion atmosphere of the *juvenilia*. The name 'Richard' was a
private family joke: 'Mr. Richard Harvey's match is put off till he
has got a Better Christian name, of which he has great Hopes.
Mr. Children's two Sons are both going to be married, John &
George—. They are to have one wife between them; a Miss Holwell,
who belongs to the Black Hole at Calcutta.' (*Letters of Jane Austen*,
ed. R. W. Chapman, Oxford, 1932, I 15, 15 Sep 1796).

8. Miss Lascelles has pointed out that this whole introduction
of Catherine Morland is a close parody of Charlotte Smith's
Emmeline, The Orphan of the Castle (1788), that midway marker
between the lachrymose and the Gothic novels. (M. Lascelles, *Jane
Austen and Her Art*, Oxford, 1939, p. 60.) [See herein, page 62 – Ed.]

9. One of the most conspicuous symptoms of the lachrymose and
Gothic novels is their rash of portentous quotations: invariably on
the title-page, and abundantly scattered through the text.

10. In this description of a wicked chaperone, which could apply
pretty closely to, say, Mrs. Jewkes in *Pamela*, the continuity of
sentimental impetus in the eighteenth-century novel – from Richard-
son through the lachrymose novelists to Mrs. Radcliffe – is clear
enough. The sentimental types remain strikingly constant, though
their milieu becomes progressively remote and improbable.

11. M. Sadleir (op. cit.) demonstrates how representative these romances are of the leading Gothic trends.

12. Like the heroines of other burlesque novels of the late eighteenth century. See Miss Lascelles' summary, op. cit., p. 16 f.

13. Jane Austen's only character who does. John Thorpe is, in fact, her only quite unmannerly character (unmannerly, that is, to a society becoming middle-class, reconciled to money but not to trade or to marketplace language). When she illustrates vulgarity later, she works it more subtly into the framework of manners, which are used as a defense, rather than violated, by the character.

14. Except for the revised chapters of *Persuasion* (J. Austen, *Two Chapters of Persuasion*, ed. R. W. Chapman, Oxford, 1926), no manuscript of the novels survives.

15. For such evidence as there is, see above Note 5.

16. The General derives, of course, from the tyrannical father or guardian; Catherine specifically compares him to Mrs. Radcliffe's Montoni. (*N.A.*, p. 187)

Elizabeth Hardwick

AN ENGAGING STORY OF HUMAN BEINGS (1965)

... Her difficulties with the publication of her work may have had a good deal to do with some of the secondary aspects of *Northanger Abbey*. By secondary I mean the part of the novel designed to be a satire on the extremely popular Gothic mysteries of the time, particularly *The Mysteries of Udolpho*, by Mrs. Radcliffe. It is a relief, reading *Northanger Abbey* once more after a span of years, to find that the business about the *Mysteries* is actually the merest side issue, not even a true subplot, and that it is the weakest part of a strong novel. The Gothic satire is one of those matters of contemporary interest authors seize upon to give their books a hold upon the reader's attention. The romantic architecture of Northanger Abbey, Catherine's suspicious fantasies about old passageways and the like, are spots of fictional landscaping.

The popularity of Mrs. Radcliffe must have been a threat to a serious artist like Jane Austen, and I, at least, have no doubt that she felt it strongly. It was quite clear that her work could not flourish in the Gothic atmosphere. And elsewhere in *Northanger Abbey* there are brief excusions into literary comment that appear to indicate a natural desire on the part of this fabulous fictional genius to make her way as a writer. Her pride in her work and in the profession of novelist is shown in this interesting outburst: 'Yes, novels; for I will not adopt that ungenerous and impolitic custom, so common with novelwriters, of degrading, by their contemptuous censure, the very performances to the number of which they are themselves adding. . . . Let us not desert one another; we are an injured body.' It does not please Jane Austen that a young lady might be ashamed to be seen reading a novel but would proudly show herself with a copy of the *Spectator*.

Still, *Northanger Abbey* is not a work of literary criticism and not primarily taken up with the fancies of young girls who have been too freely feeding upon *The Mysteries of Udolpho*. It is, instead, an engaging story of human beings in pursuit of love, money, and pleasure. And it should be said at once that this pursuit is not always lighthearted and innocently romantic. A good deal of cynicism accompanies the chase and we feel throughout the intense competition of the selfish, the heat of ambition in the plans of gay young girls, and a piercing sadness when trusting people are brutally overrun. The plot, on the surface, seems amusing enough, but there is genuine cruelty in the working out of it.

Northanger Abbey begins with Catherine Morland's visit to Bath. The visit to the celebrated resort is more than a diversion of a few weeks, a mere vacation and interlude. It is undertaken as a sort of primitive rite, a momentous initiation. Bath represents the very opening of independent life for Catherine. It is truly everything and occurs at that moment when a young person is poised between the past and the future. The very atmosphere at Bath is charged with promise and also with the fear of failure; romantic hope and intermittent despair define the days. Of course, this postpuberty rite is a comedy, and its ritual is singularly prosaic: joy is a partner for the dance and despair is having left the pump-room at just the moment the loved one entered.

Catherine is, at the opening of the story, maliciously patronized by Jane Austen. The author obviously feels superior to her creation and, in any case, it is not exactly Catherine's role to be impressive; the fictional scheme does not want her to dazzle. She is openly made fun of: 'Not that Catherine was always stupid – by no means; she learnt the fable of "The Hare and Many Friends" as quickly as any girl in England.' In addition to this, poor Catherine is far from beautiful; the best that can be said for her is that she is better looking than she used to be: '. . . had the company only seen her three years before, they would now have thought her exceedingly handsome.'

Bath itself is almost the central character of the first part of the book, just as Northanger Abbey, and all it means, is at the center of the second half of the novel. At Bath 'crowds of people were every moment passing in and out, up the steps and down . . .'; teatime in the pump-room is agony and ecstasy; and there are dances at which it is difficult for a young girl to meet a suitable young man, and yet it is always by some miracle possible. Jane Austen had made a good many visits to Bath, and her family spent the years from 1801 to 1805 in residence there after her father died. She has a special feeling for the rites, disappointments, and rules of the place. Innocent and frantic flirtations set the pace: social pressures are fearful to contemplate. In the midst of strolls and chatter about the shop windows there is much shame-making eagerness and social suffering.

At every point it is relevant that Catherine is the daughter of a well-to-do, if not rich, clergyman. She is surrounded by a respectable, somewhat ordinary world. Her chaperon in Bath, Mrs. Allen, is a conventional comic character, identified by an outstanding trait, a ruling passion. Her trait is a relentless occupation with matters of dress, her own and that of other women. Mrs. Allen is likely to cry out: '. . . There goes a strange-looking woman! What an odd gown she has got on! How old-fashioned it is! Look at the back.'

While it is, to repeat, hard to meet suitable escorts at Bath, we do find that once couples have met, commitments follow with astonishing rapidity. The voracious intentions of all these respectably bred young persons is part of the comedy – and we of a later time can make of them what we will. For instance, we are struck by the immediate intensity of Catherine's wish to become engaged to Henry Tilney. And even more breathlessly reckless is the engagement of Isabella Thorpe and Catherine's brother, James Morland. Jane Austen, unmarried herself, knew the inglorious fervor of these girls in pursuit of a husband. It is funny and yet there is a suggestive edge of degradation in the miserable impatience. Isabella Thorpe is a characterization of considerable interest. She has an ongoing vigor and sustaining ambition and a pure purposefulness that daze the sensible, villagy Catherine. Isabella's heartless self-interest does not really make a villain of her. She is hardened by her lack of money and the necessity to find a husband to make up for the lack.

General Tilney's invitation to Catherine to visit Northanger Abbey has been thought by some critics to be mechanical and unconvincing. Catherine's middling charms and prospects, of which we have been quite fully informed by the author, make her an unlikely candidate for the general's dreams for his son. The invitation, however, is the useful vehicle in which the action moves forward. The results are not a weekend of Gothic titillation but the discovery of coldheartedness, snobbery, and downright meanness.

Revelations of human perfidy are particularly startling in Jane Austen's later novels. When you read, in *Persuasion*, of Sir Walter Elliot's grotesque sense of his social importance and of the insignificance, in his view, of everyone else, you are not simply being introduced to a comic exaggeration. Elliot is a man of true meanness and serious dishonesty. His daughter, Elizabeth, shares his selfishness and claims for herself the right to every indulgence. The family is in deep debt and must retrench; Elizabeth cannot think of anything she could consent to give up except a 'few unnecessary charities'.

The plot of *Northanger Abbey* finally rests upon love of money, or perhaps we should use the stronger word, greed. Money precedes even the reverence for social position. It is the very essence of love in many instances and plays its part in the most natural and pure affections. Isabella Thorpe's engagement to Catherine's brother provides a vivid instance of the power of money to create or destroy love. When the financial arrangements and expectations are announced by the young man's father – and they mean genuine sacrifices on the part of the Morlands – the disappointment of Isabella and her mother is immediately clear. The air is filled with chagrin and anger in this masterly scene. They make the usual empty protestations of gratitude, but the very words reveal them as ungrateful,

greedy, and completely contemptible in their lack of appreciation for the kindness of the father. 'Everybody has a right to
do what they like with their own money,' Isabella says crypti-
cally, implying that the Reverend Morland might have
endowed more generously if he had wished. It is not long after,
of course, that further proof of Isabella's lack of feeling is
provided by the news that she has taken up an excited flirtation
with Captain Tilney, the brother of Henry. She sees this, we
guess, as a social and financial improvement, but she does not
realize that Captain Tilney is also unable to love, or at least to
marry, without money and would never take seriously a penniless girl like herself. We are left to feel in all this that calculations
rather than love went astray.

The discovery of an even greater cynicism is to be the lot of
Catherine, although Catherine can hardly be said to have the
nature of a 'discoverer'. She is given over to her feelings and
tries to bring them under the control of common sense, and
when that cannot be done, she simply endures the wounds.
Northanger Abbey is much more grand – both as a great house
and as a style of life – than anything Catherine has been used
to. It is the grandeur of reality, of privilege, rather than of the
ineffable, the romantic. The mysterious delights she had been
expecting are dissolved by common sense. But there are moral
horrors at Northanger Abbey, and common sense is not quite
prepared for them. We never for a moment doubt that Catherine and Henry will be all right in the end; still, General
Tilney's deceitful enthusiasm for Catherine passes beyond the
puzzling and has about it an element of the pathological. He
has courted and flattered the young girl in a most unlikely
degree, and then suddenly, in the midst of her happiness,
she is brutally turned out of the house. It is the final
degradation that Catherine should be sent away *immediately*,
unattended, unregarded, without even the time to notify her
family.

When we learn that General Tilney had mistakenly thought
Catherine to be an important heiress and that his hospitality
had been based upon an error, we are still not satisfied. His

malevolence exceeds the circumstances. And indeed, Catherine is not penniless at all, but moderately and comfortably endowed. The general is a monster. This sort of character, extreme, fantastic, will appear later in Dickens.

Social cruelty is common in the novels of Jane Austen. Selfishness is naturally one of the common human failings that will be seized upon by the satirist. But the selfishness is not always amusing; in these novels, as in Dickens, it inflicts pain upon helpless persons. There is suffering to be endured. And this is one of the contradictions in Jane Austen. She herself can inflict pain by her cleverness, mowing down clumsy or ill-bred people with a turn of phrase. And yet she remains alive to the suffering, to the wounds of indifference and cruelty. And we feel she had known these firsthand. Can one think of General Tilney and Sir Walter Elliot as caricatures? Greed and family pride were more readily displayed in Jane Austen's day than in our own. We expect hypocrisy or courtesy to blur these harsh feelings, and we are shocked by the sharpness of the assault upon a heroine like Catherine.

The characters in *Northanger Abbey* are more sketchily drawn than in the later novels, but they are steadily interesting and lifelike. Henry Tilney is a very successful creation – masculine, witty, generously sane, and attractive. He is in some sense a preview of Mr. Knightly in *Emma*. Henry is spared the acquisitive meanness of his father, but he is sufficiently worldly to hold his own in the society around him. In Jane Austen we hardly expect the characters to escape their social destiny by mere temperament, but she does allow them to modify the acceptance of their environment by moral strength and by ironic understanding. We are relieved when the charming, unpretentious Eleanor Tilney makes a splendid marriage to a rich viscount. We do not feel Eleanor would be improved by necessitous circumstances or that any valuable moral law would be served by a less brilliant marriage. And yet few would go so far in delight as the malicious General Tilney, who had never 'loved his daughter so well in all her hours of companionship, utility, and patient endurance as when he first hailed her "Your Ladyship!" '.

The chaos beneath an orderly world is clearly brought home to Catherine in the impulsive infidelity of Isabella and the fraudulent friendship of General Tilney. These are hard lessons from a hard world. And there is John Thorpe, Isabella's brother, who is a liar and a loud, coarse-grained, thoroughly disturbing young man. Or think of the cold indictment in *Persuasion*: 'The real circumstances of this pathetic piece of family history were that the Musgroves had the ill fortune of a very troublesome, hopeless son and the good fortune to lose him before he reached his twentieth year; that he had been sent to sea because he was stupid and unmanageable on shore; that he had been very little cared for at any time by his family, though quite as much as he deserved; seldom heard of, and scarcely at all regretted, when the intelligence of his death abroad had worked its way to Uppercross, two years before.' English literature does not offer a harsher bit of character description and social indifference than this.

Jane Austen was not a placid spinster, taking up her manuscripts between bouts of sewing and chattering. And she was not a 'natural' writer, writing simply for pleasure, without ambition. Her seriousness about her work, her important revisions, have been studied by Mrs. Leavis and others. As Walter Allen says, 'to blunder into perfection in six consecutive novels would be inconceivable'. And the evidence of the books themselves indicates great concern for craft.

True, we know little about Jane Austen. Her biography isn't busy with incident, and it is still hard to get a picture, from contemporary evidence, of the sort of person she might have been. Many of her most important letters were destroyed. Virginia Woolf sums it up well: 'It is probable that if Miss Cassandra Austen had had her way, we should have had nothing of Jane Austen's except her novels. To her elder sister alone did she write freely; to her alone she confided her hopes and, if rumour is true, the one great disappointment of her life; but when Miss Cassandra Austen grew old, and the growth of her sister's fame made her suspect that a time might come when strangers would pry and scholars speculate, she burnt, at great cost to herself, every letter that could gratify their curiosity, and spared only what she judged too trivial to be of interest.'

In the novels there is wit and balance and proportion, but there is something else between the lines that speaks of moral rebellion against the ways of the world. Professor Marvin Mudrick thinks that Jane Austen's irony is a way of keeping her distance, that this irony stands between her and moral engagement. We can hardly deny the claims for Mudrick's view because they are too strong. And yet, at the same time, there is simply too much knowledge of wickedness, too much skill in the portrayal of contemptible characters, for us to feel unengaged. In the novels the final happiness is simply a mechanical resolution of the plot. The plot itself, amusing and brilliantly witty as it may be, often rests upon heartlessness and sorrow. The ability to nail down unpleasant bits of character, to stab pretension, must inevitably be the fruit of intense introspection and involvement. For myself, I believe the records that say Jane Austen was taciturn and stiff. I don't think her superb intelligence brought her happiness in the world she had been given. And she had sympathy for the weak. In the beginning of *Northanger Abbey* the scorn for Catherine is a bit chilling. But we are gradually led to admire Catherine; her honesty and her simplicity are appealing. We and Jane Austen think she deserves happiness. We decide that Henry Tilney, one of the author's most attractive characters, might well have married her.

Source: extract from the Afterword in the New English Library edition of *Northanger Abbey* (1965) pp. 214–21.

Marilyn Butler

THE ANTI-JACOBIN POSITION (1975)

We are often told that Jane Austen's original satirical inspiration was fed by dislike for a literary manner, rather than for a
moral idea. The juvenilia are, according to this view, 'burlesques': though definition and re-definition tends to surround
the word, since it is by no means easy to see what, precisely, is
being burlesqued. Goldsmith's history-writing, in 'The History
of England . . . by a partial, prejudiced and ignorant Histo-
rian'? Surely not. The conventions of the sentimental novel,
variously in 'Volume the First'? The great majority of these
short fragments seem meant for nothing more ambitious than
to raise a laugh in a fireside circle by that favourite eighteenth-
century comic recourse, extreme verbal incongruity. The
heroine Alice 'has many rare and charming qualities, but
sobriety is not one of them'.[1]

'Love and Friendship' is another matter. Here there is an
unequivocal relationship with the sentimental novel, a tilt at
both form and content. Mackenzie [in *Julia de Roubigné* – Ed.]
had used the letter-novel not as a means of contrasting different
characters, but in order to indulge his heroine's propensity for
narcissistic self-examination. 'Love and Friendship' presents an
uninterrupted stream of letters from the heroine, Laura, who
dismisses the occasional criticisms of others in favour of a com-
placent view of her own character. 'A sensibility too tremblingly
alive to every affliction of my Friends, my Acquaintance, and
particularly to every affliction of my own was my only fault, if
a fault it could be called.'[2] But though this may be parody, it
is directed not at manner but at substance: Laura (and
Mackenzie's Julia) pretend to a virtue which Jane Austen
wishes to deny them. The capacity to feel was presented as the
transcendent merit of every sentimental heroine from Julie to

Delphine, enough in itself to lift them above the common run of mortals. Laura is placed in a numerous company when she is made to applaud her own refinement and dismiss the more utilitarian or extrovert qualities of others:

She [Bridget] could not be supposed to possess either exalted Ideas, Delicate Feelings or refined Sensibilities –. She was nothing more than a mere good-tempered, civil and obliging Young Woman; as such we could scarcely dislike her – she was only an Object of Contempt.[3]

The intention in satirizing Laura is above all to expose the selfishness of the sentimental system. Here is a heroine governed by self-admiration, and aware only of those others so similar in tastes and temperament that she can think of them as extensions of herself. Her rejection of the claims of the rest of humanity arises either from hostility to those who try to thwart her, or from unawareness of the claims of anyone outside the charmed circle of sentimental friendship. The co-heroine, Sophia, cannot even visit her beloved, Augustus, in Newgate – ' "my feelings are sufficiently shocked by the *recital*, of his Distress, but to behold it will overpower my Sensibility" '.[4] Laura remembers to mention the death of her parents only because it is a factor in making her destitute.[5] Rather more subtle, perhaps, is Jane Austen's mocking observation of the solipsism which may lie behind the sentimentalist's paraded sensitivity to nature:

'What a beautiful sky! (said I) How charmingly is the azure varied by those delicate streaks of white!' 'Oh! my Laura (replied she hastily withdrawing her Eyes from a momentary glance at the sky) do not thus distress me by calling my Attention to an object which so cruelly reminds me of my Augustus's blue satin waistcoat striped with white!'[6]

Although Jane Austen's sentimentalists act in a way that is at the very least equivocal, for in practice they appear ruthlessly self-interested, it is no part of her intention to suggest that they are insincere. In her view the contradiction is inherent in the

creed: she wants to show that the realization of self, an apparently idealistic goal, is in fact necessarily destructive and
delusory. As a formal burlesque rather than a novel, 'Love and
Friendship' is quite apart from Jane Austen's later career.
Thematically, however, it makes the first chapter of a consistent
story.

Of the early work, 'Catharine, or the Bower' is the nearest
attempt at true fiction: in fact it is the first recognizable effort
at the classic Jane Austen form of novel. As in so many works
of the period, an inexperienced young girl is on the threshold
of life. One source of interest for the reader was clearly to have
been Catharine's assessment of 'the world': her eventual discriminations about Camilla Stanley, the girl who offers her
false sentimental friendship, and Camilla's brother Edward,
who, as a lover, threatens her peace more substantially. In
dramatizing this process of growing discernment Jane Austen
achieves a technique which already belongs to the era of Maria
Edgeworth rather than of Fanny Burney. The dialogue offers
the reader direct evidence about the character of the two girls:

'You have read Mrs. Smith's Novels, I suppose?' said she to her
Companion –. 'Oh! Yes,' replied the other, 'and I am quite delighted
with them – They are the sweetest things in the world –' 'And
which do you prefer of them?' 'Oh! dear, I think there is no comparison between them – Emmeline is *so much* better than any of the
others –' 'Many people think so, I know; but there does not appear
so great a disproportion in their Merits to *me*; do you think it is
better written?' 'Oh! I do not know anything about *that* – but it is
better in *everything* – Besides, Ethelinde is so long –' 'That is a very
common Objection, I believe,' said Kitty, 'but for my own part, if
a book is well written, I always find it too short.' 'So do I, only I get
tired of it before it is finished.'⁷

The characteristic of Camilla's mind as revealed here is carelessness, a habit of exaggeration and inaccuracy. She is not
interested in the books they are talking about, though Catharine
is. The striking feature of the conversation is its implicit moral

frame of reference. Catharine is right to take the issue seriously, because it is a test case, a trial attempt at defining the good, which is the process upon which the moral life depends.

Dialogue of this kind is developed in *Northanger Abbey*, and in far subtler forms in the later novels, beginning with *Pride and Prejudice*. It is always associated with a narrative prose which so closely tracks the heroine's consciousness that it often approximates to 'free indirect speech'. Jane Austen never gives up her option of insinuating comments into her heroine's thought-process that in fact could have emanated only from the author, but in 'Catharine' she is still clumsy about such interventions. Catharine's introduction to Camilla is spoilt by the superfluous observation that Camilla 'professed a love of Books without Reading, was lively without Wit, and generally goodhumoured without Merit'. But in the passage that follows, the author's comment, though officious, shows a kindly insight into the heroine's dangerous intellectual isolation:

> . . . and Catharine, who was prejudiced by her appearance, and who from her solitary Situation was ready to like anyone, tho' her Understanding and Judgement would not otherwise have been easily satisfied, felt almost convinced when she saw her, that Miss Stanley would be the very companion she wanted. . . .[8]

Here is the first example of Jane Austen's technique of comparing the evidence given to the mind with the mind's insidious habit of perverting evidence: two planes of reality, the objective and the subjective, respectively presented in dialogue and in a form which approaches internal monologue. Catherine Morland's thoughts about Isabella, Elizabeth's about Mr. Wickham, and Emma's about Frank Churchill, are anticipated in Catharine's self-deceiving trains of thought about Camilla and afterwards about Edward:

> The Evening passed off as agreably as the one that had preceded it; they continued talking to each other, during the chief part of it, and such was the power of his Address, & the Brilliancy of his Eyes, that when they parted for the Night, tho' Catherine had but a few hours before totally given up the idea, yet she felt almost

convinced again that he was really in love with her. . . . The more
she had seen of him, the more inclined was she to like him, & the
more desirous that he should like *her*. She was convinced of his
being naturally very clever and very well disposed, and that his
thoughtlessness & negligence, which tho' they appeared to *her* as
very becoming in *him*, she was aware would by many people be
considered as defects in his Character, merely proceeded from a
vivacity always pleasing in Young Men, & were far from testifying
a weak or vacant Understanding.[9]

If Jane Austen was no more than sixteen when she wrote this,
it is something of a *tour de force*; and what makes it more
remarkable is that the resourceful use of language supports
other appropriate narrative techniques. Catharine's situation is
well prepared in the opening pages of exposition. We are
shown that she is especially vulnerable because she is solitary:
her childhood friends, the Wynnes, have gone away, and she is
left in the company of her aunt, Mrs. Percival, who is fussy and
prosaic. Catharine likes to indulge her sentimental regret for
the Wynnes alone in her 'Bower', a romantic spot which, as the
sub-title indicates, was to have been given special symbolic
significance. Mrs. Percival, a prototype perhaps for Mrs.
Jennings or Miss Bates, objects to her habit of going there, but
for valetudinarian reasons which at the moment Catharine
finds it easy to dismiss. The real threat offered by the Bower
was clearly to have been to her moral health, for it encourages
her in a dangerously solipsistic reverie; and it is there, appropriately, that Edward Stanley appeals to her emotions by
seizing her hand. It is clear even from these short beginnings
that the story was to have encompassed both the natural
evolution of Catharine's error, and its moral implications, so
that in conception and, primitively, in technique, it belongs to
the series that culminates with *Emma*.

The first of Jane Austen's novels to be completed for publication, *Northanger Abbey*,[10] makes use of all the same important
features. A naïve, inexperienced heroine stands at the threshold

of life and needs to discriminate between true friends and false. The evidence she is given are words and the system of value they express; so that the reader, cleverer or at least more cleverly directed than Catherine, is able to make the correct discriminations for himself as the action unfolds. In one important respect the second Catherine is a coarser conception than the first, for she has been crossed with the burlesque heroine of the 'female quixote' variety, so that many of her intellectual errors are grosser and far more improbable. Yet although *Northanger Abbey* is often remembered for its sequence at the abbey, when Catherine is led by her reading of (presumably) Mrs. Radcliffe's *Romance of the Forest*[11] into fantastic imaginings, the central impulse of *Northanger Abbey*, and its serious achievement, has nothing to do with burlesque. Like 'Catharine', it uses the literary conversation not for the sake of the subject, but in order to give an appropriate morally objective ground against which character can be judged.

Catherine Morland has five important conversations about the Gothic novel: with Isabella Thorpe (vol. 1, ch. 6); with John Thorpe (1 7); with Eleanor and Henry Tilney (1 14); with Henry Tilney, in his phaeton on the way to Northanger Abbey (11 5); and with Henry Tilney again, when he uncovers her suspicions of his father, the General (11 9). In all of these conversations, as in 'Catharine', the reader is not asked to criticize certain novels, nor the habit of novel-reading,[12] but rather to consider the habits of mind which the different speakers reveal. For example, when Isabella and Catherine first discuss horrid novels together, in chapter 6 of the first volume, Isabella's knowledge proves superficial: she is dependent on her friend Miss Andrews for all her information, and Miss Andrews knows what is current, but not *Sir Charles Grandison*. From this conversation it emerges that Isabella's mind is not held by novels, for it continually runs after young men, whereas Catherine's comments are characterized by extreme, if naïve, interest. 'I do not pretend to say that I was not very much pleased with him [Henry Tilney]; but while I have *Udolpho* to read, I feel as if nobody could make me

miserable.'[13] Again, when Catherine raises the subject 'which
had long been uppermost in her thoughts' with John Thorpe,
it is to discover that despite his assurance he does not know
Udolpho is by Mrs. Radcliffe, and that he has got less than half-
way in the first volume of the five-volume *Camilla*. On the other
hand, the characteristic of the Tilneys which emerges when
Catherine raises the subject with them is informed interest. 'I
have read all Mrs. Radcliffe's works,' says Henry, 'and most of
them with great pleasure.'[14] The mild qualification is important,
for the proper attitude of the person who reads is a discriminating exactness – the quality Henry shows when he challenges
Catherine's word 'nice', and Eleanor when she emends it to
'interesting'.[15]

After discussing novels the Tilneys move on to the subject of
history, just as the earlier Catharine of the juvenilia did. Both
topics, together with the Tilneys' choice of landscape, enable
Jane Austen to illustrate character at a light and amusing level
without imputing triviality. Choice of these as subjects for
conversation already implies a certain degree of thoughtfulness
and rationality – unlike John Thorpe's topics of horses, curricles,
drink, and money, and Isabella's of 'dress, balls, flirtations and
quizzes'.[16] Thus far at least the conversations about Gothic
novels in *Northanger Abbey* belong to the over-all strategy of the
novel, which is concerned first to reveal the character of the
heroine, second to contrast the minds of her two sets of friends,
the Thorpes and the Tilneys.

The clarity of Jane Austen's conception appears to waver in
the second volume. Henry's teasing conversation with Catherine
during their drive to the abbey is, as earlier dialogues were not,
a series of observations directed *at* the Gothic mode. What
Henry invents is a burlesque Gothic story, compounded of
various clichés – ancient housekeeper, isolated chamber, secret
passage, instruments of torture, hidden manuscripts, and extin-
guished candle – though it should also be noticed, since it is
typical of the discriminating reader in the period, that he puts
as much stress upon verbal blunders as upon extravagances of
plot. He imagines Catherine surmounting an *'unconquerable'*

horror of the bed, and discovering a secret door through 'a division in the tapestry so artfully constructed as to defy the minutest inspection'.[17] Henry's lively and critical approach to his Gothic material is thus contrasted with Catherine's selection of precisely the wrong aspect to comment on. 'Oh! Mr. Tilney, how frightful! – This is just like a book! – But it cannot really happen to me. I am sure your housekeeper is not really Dorothy.'[18]

The memory of Henry's intelligent detachment in this conversation lingers as an unspoken commentary on Catherine's series of interior monologues at Northanger – while she searches her room, or lies terror-stricken in bed, or concocts wild fantasies concerning the General and the death of Mrs. Tilney. Typically, it is in the 'objective' form of dialogue, where we are equally detached from both parties, and not in subjective thought-processes, that we hear, reliably, the note of rationality. And it is through another speech from Henry that Catherine is brought at last to an understanding of the 'real' world of long-lasting social and religious institutions:

'What have you been judging from? Remember the country and the age in which we live. Remember that we are English, that we are Christians. Consult your own understanding, your own sense of the probable, your own observation of what is passing around you – Does our education prepare us for such atrocities? Do our laws connive at them? Could they be perpetrated without being known, in a country like this, where social and literary intercourse is on such a footing; where every man is surrounded by a neighbourhood of voluntary spies, and where roads and newspapers lay everything open? Dearest Miss Morland, what ideas have you been admitting?'[19]

There is clearly a difference in Jane Austen's use of dialogue in the first volume and in the second. In the first, it is the reader alone who is enlightened, by comparable dialogues between Catherine and the Thorpes, and Catherine and the Tilneys. During the same period the heroine neither learns to discriminate between her two groups of friends, nor to be discriminating about them. Although Henry Tilney has been setting her a good example for virtually a full volume, Catherine returns from her walk with him and Eleanor nearly as unenlightened as when she set out:

> It was no effort to Catherine to believe that Henry Tilney could never be wrong. His manner might sometimes surprize, but his meaning must always be just: – and what she did not understand, she was almost as ready to admire, as what she did.[20]

In the second volume the impact on Catherine of Henry's remarks and, negatively, of Isabella's letters, is far greater. Aided no doubt by prosaic external evidence at the Abbey, she is brought sharply to a sense of reality:

> The visions of romance were over. Catherine was completely awakened. Henry's address, short as it had been, had more thoroughly opened her eyes to the extravagance of her late fancies than all their several disappointments had done. Most grievously was she humbled. Most bitterly did she cry.[21]

When she becomes more tranquil, Catherine continues soberly to recognize that 'it had been all a voluntary, self-created delusion, each trifling circumstance receiving importance from an imagination resolved on alarm, and everything forced to bend to one purpose by a mind which, before she entered the Abbey, had been craving to be frightened'.[22] This, then, is the typical moment of *éclaircissement* towards which all the Austen actions tend, the moment when a key character abandons her error and humbly submits to objective reality.

During the period of *Northanger Abbey*'s evolution, before its near-appearance as 'Susan' in 1803, Maria Edgeworth was experimenting with similar devices. *Belinda* has precisely the same stylized arrangement of characters, according to their contrasting philosophies of life, and perhaps an even more fully developed sense of the relationship between verbal style and quality of mind. What is very different in *Northanger Abbey*, however, different even from Maria Edgeworth's rather undistinguished execution in *Angelina*, is Jane Austen's reluctance to commit herself to her heroine's consciousness. It is not merely Catherine's emotional distress after she discovers her errors that receives hurried treatment; her actual mental processes are also summarily dealt with. From the consistent *naïveté* of her earlier thinking to her final state of enlightenment is a long step, but Jane Austen is not really concerned to examine it. Ultimately this is because, unlike Maria Edgeworth, she does not value the personal process of learning to reason as an end in itself. What is required of Catherine is rather a suspension of a particular kind of mental activity, her habit of romantic invention; at the moment Jane Austen is not concerned to define positively what kind of regular mental process it is that will keep Catherine sensible. For the naturalistic treatment of an individual's inner history which was promised in the first 'Catharine', here we have to make do with facetious stylization, and allusion to a ready-made inner world acquired from reading other people's books. We are shown that Catherine has learnt a significant general rule, that human nature is worse than she first thought: for, apart from her aberration over the General, she has successively overrated the Thorpes, Frederick Tilney, and perhaps even Henry, with all the sentimentalist's optimism about human nature. The reader is asked to take on trust that henceforth she will apply more caution, more scepticism, more concern for the objective evidence. Of the actual change in her habits of mind that would make such a revolution possible he sees little or nothing.

Jane Austen was slower to handle the inner life confidently than to deploy dialogue: her next novel with a similar format, *Pride and Prejudice*, also fails to give Elizabeth's train of thought with the same clarity and brilliance with which it presents the dialogue. Yet *Northanger Abbey* is consistent and ingenious in dramatizing the author's point of view, like all Jane Austen's novels to employ a fallible heroine. It establishes the antiphonal role of dialogue and free indirect speech which is to be so important in Jane Austen's career. It deploys characters around the heroine with the kind of antithetical precision that is typical of Mrs. West, but much more amusingly and naturally. Even if Catherine's mind is a somewhat implausible blank, the arrangement of the two pairs of brothers and sisters, the Tilneys and the Thorpes, virtually forces the reader into a series of ethical comparisons between them on the author's terms. However strong his training and his inclination to involve himself uncritically in the heroine's emotions, he is manipulated into undertaking an unfamiliar kind of intellectual activity. Stylistically the novel induces him to value sincerity and accuracy, rather than those emotions which are harder to account for or specify. Formally it requires him to use his judgement and not his feeling.

At the same time *Northanger Abbey* is very much a novel, which is to say that it succeeds in creating and maintaining an autonomous fictional world. The story is not a parody of a novel story, but actually, like *Pride and Prejudice*, employs the common novelist's fantasy of the poor girl who meets, and after a series of vicissitudes marries, the rich young man. Catherine may not be a 'heroine' in the idealized mode of sentimental fiction, but she is a very good heroine at the level which matters. She invites and keeps our sympathy, and she makes us feel that what happens to her matters to us. No wonder, indeed, that in the famous passage in chapter five Jane Austen ironically refuses to condemn the novel: for *Northanger Abbey* is quite as much a novel as *Udolpho* is.

It is perhaps because Catherine is so pleasing, even when she blunders, that some recent critics have felt that Jane Austen ends *Northanger Abbey* by reversing its whole moral tendency; that she turns her irony on the good sense advocated by Henry Tilney, and at least in part vindicates Catherine's intuition. The central piece of evidence cited is that the General, Montoni-like, turns Catherine out of Northanger Abbey, and thus proves to be a villain after all. But an act of rudeness is not villainy. It is not even, to use Andrew Wright's term, 'violence'.[23] It arises from the ill-tempered pique of a snobbish man who has just discovered that Catherine is a person of no social account. There is plenty of evidence throughout the novel that Henry and Eleanor are aware of their father's bad temper, as well as of his snobbery and formality: Eleanor's instant obedience on all occasions, for example, suggests that she has learnt to fear the General's anger. His treatment of Catherine comes nearer to confirming their view of him than hers, although it is perhaps not fully in keeping with either.[24]

Again, after Catherine returns home her romantic feelings are opposed to Mrs. Morland's worthy moralizing, and here at least Jane Austen appears to be on Catherine's side: 'There was a great deal of good sense in all this; but there are some situations of the human mind in which good sense has very little power; and Catherine's feelings contradicted almost every position her mother advanced.'[25]

But it is only by taking this observation out of context that we can read into it a serious meaning which relates to the whole book. The nice little vignette of Catherine's relations with her mother after her return home is surely yet another literary borrowing, this time from Fanny Burney's *Camilla*. Camilla's parents think that Camilla has been spoilt by high life, when really she is pining for the loss of her lover, Edgar Mandlebert; and Mrs. Morland is mistaken in just the same way. Had she really tried to cure a case of true love by fetching down a volume of *The Mirror* (containing 'a very clever Essay ... about young girls that have been spoilt for home by great acquaintance'),[26] the incident might indeed suggest that Jane Austen was after all merely balancing the merits of feeling and sense. In fact Mrs. Morland's error is no more than a joke designed to reintroduce the hero in the lightest and least emotional manner possible.

Northanger Abbey is a novel, and it works as a novel, while at the same time it subjects the conventional matter of the merely subjective novel to consistently critical handling. Ideologically it is a very clear statement of the anti-jacobin position; though, compared with other anti-jacobin novels, it is distinctive for the virtuosity with which it handles familiar clichés of the type. Very pleasing, for example, is the cleverly oblique presentation of the subject under attack.

Most anti-jacobin novels include characters who profess the new ideology, and are never tired of canvassing it in conversation. In *Northanger Abbey* there is no overtly partisan talk at all. ('By an easy transition [Henry] . . . shortly found himself arrived at politics; and from politics, it was an easy step to silence.')[27] But in *Northanger Abbey* Jane Austen develops, perhaps from the prototypes the Stanleys in 'Catharine', her version of the revolutionary character, the man or woman who by acting on a system of selfishness, threatens friends of more orthodox principles; and ultimately, through cold-blooded cynicism in relation to the key social institution of marriage, threatens human happiness at a very fundamental level. Isabella Thorpe, worldly, opportunist, bent on self-gratification, is one of a series of dangerous women created by Jane Austen. Lucy Steele, Lady Susan, Mary Crawford, all like Isabella pursue the modern creed of self, and as such are Jane Austen's reinterpretation of a standard figure of the period, the desirable, amoral woman whose activities threaten manners and morals. Moreover, already in *Northanger Abbey* the opportunists find allies where they should properly be most vigorously opposed – among those who uphold only the forms, and not the essence, of orthodoxy. The pompous but mercenary General is as much implicated as John Thorpe in the pursuit of Catherine's mythical fortune. In the same vein, Henry and Mary Crawford meet no resistance, but encouragement, when they threaten to introduce anarchy into Mr. Rushworth's ancestral estate. And William Walter Elliot finds an easy dupe, even an ally, in the empty figure-head he despises, Sir Walter.

That Jane Austen is perfectly clear what she is doing can be demonstrated by identifying the same cluster of themes and characters in *Sense and Sensibility*. Inheriting a set of conservative dogmas, and some impossibly theatrical characters – notably the revolutionary villain – already in her first two full-length novels she produces a more natural equivalent, on a scale appropriate to comedy. Her villains are not only better art than her rivals'; they are also better propaganda. The tendency among the routine anti-jacobins was to create Satanic demon-villains who were dangerously close in the temper of the times to being heroes. Jane Austen's intelligence, like Burke's, is more subtle. Her selfish characters are consistently smaller and meaner than their orthodox opponents, the heroines; they are restricted within the bounds of their own being, and their hearts and minds are impoverished. Jane Austen's achievement, the feat of the subtlest technician among the English novelists, is to rethink the material of the conservative novel in terms that are at once naturalistic and intellectually consistent.

SOURCE: 'The Juvenilia and *Northanger Abbey*', ch. 7 in *Jane Austen and the War of Ideas* (1975) pp. 168–81.

NOTES

1. *Minor Works*, ed. R. W. Chapman, rev. ed. (Oxford, 1963) p. 23. But for the argument that literary burlesque is pervasive in the juvenilia, cf. B. C. Southam, *Jane Austen's Literary Manuscripts* (Oxford, 1964) p. 9 and *passim*.
2. *Minor Works*, p. 78.
3. Ibid. pp. 100–1.
4. Ibid. p. 89.
5. Ibid. pp. 89–90.
6. Ibid. p. 98.
7. Ibid. p. 199.
8. Ibid. p. 198.
9. Ibid. pp. 235–6.
10. To discuss *Northanger Abbey* before *Sense and Sensibility* is a somewhat arbitrary decision. In conception *S. & S.* is the earlier: the letter-version, 'Elinor and Marianne', dates from 1795, while the novel as we know it was begun in Nov 1797. In structure and theme *S. & S.* is a typical novel of 1795–6, while *N.A.*, which in part reacts to the rage for Gothic of 1796–8, belongs historically a little later. And yet *N.A.*, which was accepted for publication by Cadell under its title of 'Susan' in 1803, was probably ready by then in substantially its present form. Cf. Alan D. McKillop, 'Critical Realism in *Northanger Abbey*', *From Jane Austen to Joseph Conrad*, ed. R. C. Rathburn and M. Steinmann, Jr (Minneapolis, 1958); and Southam, *Literary Manuscripts*, p. 62.

11. It was Adeline, heroine of that novel, who stayed at a ruined abbey and found a secret chamber behind the arras, containing a rusty dagger and a roll of paper which told the story of the man kept prisoner there.

12. One of the commonest misconceptions about *Northanger Abbey* is that Isabella leads Catherine astray by introducing her to a world of horror and make-believe. But Catherine's worst error, to be taken in by Isabella, occurs before she has begun to read popular novels. Cf. Kenneth L. Moler, *Jane Austen's Art of Allusion* (Nebraska, 1969) pp. 19–20.

13. *Northanger Abbey*, ed. R. W. Chapman, 3rd ed. (Oxford, 1933) p. 41.

14. *N.A.*, p. 106.

15. *N.A.*, p. 108.

16. *N.A.*, p. 33.

17. *N.A.*, p. 159.

18. *N.A.*, p. 159.

19. *N.A.*, pp. 197–8.

20. *N.A.*, p. 114.

21. *N.A.*, p. 199.

22. *N.A.*, pp. 199–200.

23. Professor Wright is one of the most influential critics to hold that Catherine's view of the General is not altogether illusory (*Jane Austen's Novels: A Study of Structure*, London, 1954, pp. 106–7). Among others who have taken the same line, with incidental variations, are John K. Mathison, '*Northanger Abbey* and JA's Conception of the Value of Fiction', *English Literary History*, xxiv (1957) 138–52; Lionel Trilling, *The Opposing Self* (1955) p. 217; Frank J. Kearful, 'Satire and the Form of the Novel: the Problem of Aesthetic Unity in *Northanger Abbey*', *English Literary History*, xxxii (1965) 511–27; Henrietta Ten Harmsel, *Jane Austen: a Study in Fictional Conventions* (The Hague, 1964) pp. 25–6; and A. Walton Litz, *Jane Austen: A Study of her Artistic Development* (London, 1965) p. 63. But cf. Kenneth L. Moler, *Jane Austen's Art of Allusion*, pp. 38–40.

24. The General's behaviour was so out of line with gentlemanly standards in the period that early readers found it incredible. Maria Edgeworth called it 'out of drawing and out of nature' (letter to Mrs. Ruxton, 21 Feb 1818: Mrs. Edgeworth, *Memoir of Maria Edgeworth*, privately published, 1867, ii, 6). Hitherto we have

thought of him as over-formal, and there is no room to modify his character sufficiently.

25. *N.A.*, p. 241.
26. *N.A.*, p. 239.
27. *N.A.*, p. 111.

B. C. Southam

'"REGULATED HATRED" REVISITED' (1976)

D. W. Harding's famous essay, 'Regulated Hatred: An Aspect of the Work of Jane Austen', is a landmark in the criticism of Jane Austen. Published in *Scrutiny*, VIII (March 1940), it appeared at a time when the prevailing image of the writer was still 'Gentle Jane'. Harding's Jane Austen was quite ungentle, a powerful and astringent satirist. His account was daring and unconventional, an essay in 'iconoclasm', according to the great Jane Austen editor–bibliographer R. W. Chapman. It cut right across the cosy drawing-room image. Harding's offence was not just to attack the cult. Far worse. He also suggested that the Janeite reading of the novels was a misreading that Jane Austen makes possible as part of her ironic strategy. He argued that there are devices of style which conceal from the unwary, the unobservant or the otherwise unworthy, the hard fact that her satire is edged against them, that her books 'are, as she meant them to be, read and enjoyed by precisely the sort of people whom she disliked'. Harding explains how these readers are taken in: 'at a number of scattered points, points where she took good care (not wittingly perhaps) that the misreading should be the easiest thing in the world. Unexpected astringencies occur which the comfortable reader probably overlooks, or else passes by as slight imperfections, trifling errors of tone brought about by a faulty choice of words'. For his first example, Harding quoted the paragraph in chapter 24 of *Northanger Abbey* when Henry Tilney reprimands Catherine Morland for her Gothic fantasies about his father and his dead mother, the shadowy idea that the General might have murdered her:

'If I understand you rightly, you had formed a surmise of such horror as I have hardly words to – Dear Miss Morland, consider the dreadful nature of the suspicions you have entertained. What have you been judging from? Remember the country and the age in which we live. Remember that we are English, that we are Christians. Consult your own understanding, your own sense of the probable, your own observation of what is passing around you – Does our education prepare us for such atrocities? Do our laws connive at them? Could they be perpetrated without being known, in a country like this, where social and literary intercourse is on such a footing, where every man is surrounded by a neighbourhood of voluntary spies, and where roads and newspapers lay every thing open? Dearest Miss Morland, what ideas have you been admitting?'

The words in question are 'where every man is surrounded by a neighbourhood of voluntary spies'. Professor Harding comments, 'with its touch of paranoia that surprising remark is badly out of tune both with "Henry's astonishing generosity and nobleness of conduct" and with the accepted idea of Jane Austen'. He explains this seeming anomaly with the suggestion, firstly, that in the context it is a remark so 'unexpected and unbelievable' that it is 'unlikely to be taken in at all by many readers' and 'slips through their minds without creating a disturbance'. Secondly, that Henry's appreciative remarks, with their eulogy of the age, take away the edge of bitterness that the words might otherwise have. This, then, is a notable instance where the 'hatred', Jane Austen's violence of feeling, is 'regulated' by a literary device.

But the reference to 'a neighbourhood of voluntary spies', while memorable as a figurative turn-of-phrase, also possesses a literal historical meaning. In the period following the end of the Napoleonic wars in 1814 an extensive 'Spy-System' (as it was known) was maintained by the government to infiltrate the associations that working men had set up to protect their interests, their particular object to get the vote, which was then largely restricted to property-owners and left the working population voteless. In Regency England, the idea of parliamentary democracy awakened fears of bloody revolution, the French terror re-enacted on English soil. The official establishment view is summed up in the words of Castlereagh, the

Prime Minister, when he addressed Parliament in the summer of 1817, arguing that 'morality, religion, and social order, are best defended at home by spies and informers'. Working-class agitation was making the authorities as jittery as they had been twenty-five years earlier, in the 1790s, when the spy-system was being used against the earliest radical groups, in an attempt to stifle the spread of democratic and revolutionary thinking. The property-owning middle classes were strongly behind the government in this policy; nevertheless, the spy-system, and the argument that informing was a patriotic act, part of a citizen's duty (hence, perhaps, the force of Jane Austen's 'voluntary spies'), came under attack as an encroachment on liberty and an instrument of repression. In 1812, one critic described the police as 'a system of tyranny; an organised army of spies and informers, for the destruction of all public liberty and the disturbance of all private happiness'. There is no melodrama in this protest. It emerges from the most repressive period in English history since the Civil War.

So Henry Tilney's declaration that 'every man is surrounded by a neighbourhood of voluntary spies', delivered so reassuringly, puts him in very curious light. So indeed does the entire speech when we relate it to the historical situation. In 1818, a contemporary reader of *Northanger Abbey* who responded to Tilney's appeal – and 'remembered' 'the country and the age' in which he lived, 'consulted' his 'own sense of the probable', his 'own observation of what' was 'passing around' him – would come up with an answer wholly disconcerting, wholly at variance with the effect that Tilney is trying for in this little burst of mock-rhetoric. With Catherine, Tilney succeeds: she runs off 'with tears of shame'. Her Gothic ghosts are laid. But for the Regency reader, the joke has a hollow ring, and Tilney, at this point, at least, an equivocal voice.

A similar example occurs earlier in the novel, in chapter 14, where Tilney makes fun of his sister for jumping to the conclusion that Catherine's mysterious, unexplained remarks about having just heard from London of 'something very shocking indeed' – 'uncommonly dreadful! I shall expect murder and every thing of the kind' – are about a dreadful 'riot' that has really taken place. Tilney indulges himself, conjuring up a comic-macabre fantasy from Eleanor's fearful imaginings: 'she immediately pictured to herself a mob of three thousand men assembling in St George's Fields; the Bank attacked, the Tower threatened, the streets of London flowing with blood . . .'. This is delivered in tones of the purest ridicule – how could anyone be so silly and hysterical! It takes a man to set them right! But in fact his sister's train of thought is completely credible; and the fantasy he elaborates, all too possible. In 1795, there was a meeting of the radical London Correspondence Society in St George's Fields. There was an enormous crowd, reportedly as large as 100,000. The speeches were inflammatory, with wild talk of 'the holy blood of Patriotism, streaming from the severing axe'. A few months later, in October, George III was jeered on his way to the state opening of Parliament; his carriage was pelted and a window cracked by flying stones. The following day, horse-guards and troops had to clear the mobs out of his way to the theatre. So Eleanor's misunderstanding and Tilney's joke touch upon circumstances bizarrely close to the truth, even his comic conclusion, with 'a detachment of the 12th Light Dragoons (the hopes of the nation,) called up from Northampton to quell the insurgents, and the gallant Capt. Frederick Tilney, in the moment of charging at the head of his troop, knocked off his horse by a brickbat from an upper window'. The literary device here is anticlimax, achieved through bathos, a descent from the blood-curdling sublime to the trivial ridiculous. But a brickbatted Captain would be precisely the kind of detail that contemporary newspapers could include, just as we would expect the jingoistic press to throw in a patriotic cheer – 'the hopes of the nation' – for the 12th Light Dragoons. Tilney's repertoire of adroit mockery runs to a pastiche of popular journalism.

But beneath these layers of literary humour – Jane Austen's own and those she operates through Henry Tilney – the reflective readers of *Northanger Abbey* in 1818 would arrive at a stratum of unamusing fact, distant in time but not remote. The historical substance behind these images was not a single event in 1795, nor other isolated occasions when the London mob had to be brought to order by force, nor other instances of wild and threatening rhetoric, but the spectre of revolution that haunted the government and the middle classes from the 1790s onwards and found a terrible nemesis in the deaths of Peterloo.

In these two passages, Jane Austen allows into *Northanger Abbey* an oblique and fleeting glimpse of some of the shadows on the darker side of Regency England, an England of unrest, repression and violence, where there were events more horrifying than anything imagined in the wildest flights of Gothic fiction, where there could be a real Gothicism, real danger, real disorder, real reasons for being afraid, events far worse than the example of General Tilney's 'villainy' which is usually made so much of – his crude gesture of contempt in ordering Catherine off the premises and exposing her to the scandal and disgrace of travelling alone on a public coach on a Sunday, where she was liable to be regarded, perhaps even accosted, as an available young woman. Jane Austen handles this material perfectly. There is no break in the surface of comedy. The aesthetic mode of the novel never falters. Both passages are cast wholly within Tilney's normal style of ironic banter. Jane Austen had learnt her lessons from Swift and Pope – that the force of satire is a feat of literary devices and literary contrivance, that its power to sting is a function of its capacity to amuse, with its virtuosity, its poise and lightness of wit, a display of artistry which conceals a harder purpose. Tilney is condemned out of his own mouth. With his urbanity, his fluency and charm, his elaborate and witty *reasonableness*, he can convince a Catherine Morland. But the fertility of his rational, enlightened imagination betrays him into conjuring up the very Gothicism he supposes himself to be denying. At these points, Jane Austen's irony is profound. It strikes at the heart of the shallow, fragile complacency of the prosperous middle classes – that, for them, at least, the present period in history, despite all its threats and uncertainties, was triumphantly *the* moment to enjoy the blessings of English society at its Regency zenith. It is a complacency that sounds assertively, stridently, throughout the Tory literature of the period. It is caught in Southey's rejoicing, in 1818, to belong 'to the middle rank of life . . . which in this country and at this time is beyond doubt the most favourable situation wherein man has ever been placed for the cultivation of his moral and intellectual nature'. This note sounds again in the words of Henry Tilney. Jane Austen presents him for our inspection, quietly and blandly. Her portrait of the ultra-reasonable man is finely drawn and even-toned, a supreme instance of her 'hatred' artistically, disarmingly and insidiously 'regulated'.

NOTE

No editor or critic of *Northanger Abbey* has so far explored the possible historical references of these passages. Most editors are content to follow R. W. Chapman's lead (in the Oxford edition, 1923) in making no comment on 'the neighbourhood of voluntary spies' and relegating the St George's Fields meeting to long before (*vide* Chapman's note that Tilney's reference 'makes it certain that he is thinking of the Gordon Riots of 1780' (p. xiii)). One reason for this is that the novels have traditionally been read as if they somehow exist out of time in a kind of 'period'-present and that to understand them what we principally need is not information but intelligence, alertness to the levels of tone and irony, responsiveness to the characters and so on. The highly verbal and semantic qualities of Jane Austen's writing have encouraged highly verbal and analytical interpretations. The survival, popularity, and continuing fascination of the novels is the proof of their permanence and timelessness as works of art. But these essential truths should not blind us to Jane Austen's intention in writing contemporary novels addressed to a contemporary audience and taking up contemporary issues and themes.

SOURCE: essay first published in this Casebook; © B. C. Southam 1976.

PART TWO
Persuasion

1. CONTEMPORARY AND VICTORIAN OPINIONS

RICHARD WHATELY (1821): Superior to All

. . . *Persuasion*, which is more strictly to be considered as a posthumous work, possesses that superiority which might be expected from the more mature age at which it was written, and is second, we think, to none of the former ones, if not superior to all. In the humorous delineation of character it does not abound quite so much as some of the others, though it has great merit even on that score; but it has more of that tender and yet elevated kind of interest which is aimed at by the generality of novels, and in pursuit of which they seldom fail of running into romantic extravagance: on the whole, it is one of the most elegant fictions of common life we ever remember to have met with.

Sir Walter Elliot, a silly and conceited baronet, has three daughters, the eldest two, unmarried, and the third, Mary, the wife of a neighbouring gentleman, Mr. Charles Musgrove, heir to a considerable fortune, and living in a genteel cottage in the neighbourhood of the Great house which he is hereafter to inherit. The second daughter, Anne, who is the heroine, and the only one of the family possessed of good sense, (a quality which Miss Austin is as sparing of in her novels, as we fear her great mistress, Nature, has been in real life,) when on a visit to her sister, is, by that sort of instinct which generally points out to all parties the person on whose judgment and temper they may rely, appealed to in all the little family differences which arise, and which are described with infinite spirit and detail.

The following touch reminds us, in its minute fidelity to nature, of some of the happiest strokes in the subordinate parts of Hogarth's prints: Mr. C. Musgrove has an aunt whom he wishes to treat with becoming attention, but who, from being of a somewhat inferior class in point of family and fashion, is studiously shunned by his wife, who has all the family pride of her father and eldest sister: he takes the opportunity of a walk with a large party on a fine day, to visit this despised relation, but cannot persuade his wife to accompany him; she pleads fatigue, and remains with the rest to await his return, and he walks home with her, not much pleased at the incivility she has shown. [Quotes ch. 10 'She joined Charles' to 'along at all'.] But the principal interest arises from a combination of events which cannot be better explained than by a part of the prefatory narrative, which forms, in general, an Euripidean prologue to Miss Austin's novels. [Quotes ch. 4 'He was not' to 'unnatural beginning'.]

After an absence of eight years, he returns to her neighbourhood, and circumstances throw them frequently in contact. Nothing can be more exquisitely painted than her feelings on such occasions. First, dread of the meeting, – then, as that is removed by custom, renewed regret for the happiness she has thrown away, and the constantly recurring contrast, though known only to herself, between the distance of their intercourse and her involuntary sympathy with all his feelings, and instant comprehension of all his thoughts, of the meaning of every glance of his eye, and curl of his lip, and intonation of his voice. In him her mild good sense and elegance gradually re-awake long-forgotten attachment: but with it return the usual accompaniments of undeclared love, distrust of her sentiments towards him, and suspicions of their being favourable to another. In this state of regretful jealousy he overhears, while writing a letter, a conversation she is holding with his friend Captain Harville, respecting another naval friend, Captain Benwick, who had been engaged to the sister of the former, and very speedily after her death had formed a fresh engagement: we cannot refrain from inserting an extract from this conversation, which is exquisitely beautiful. [Quotes ch. 23 '"Your feelings"' to '"too much oppressed."']

While this conversation has been going on, he has been replying to it on paper, under the appearance of finishing his letter: he puts the paper into her hand, and hurries away. [Quotes ch. 23 the letter from Wentworth.]

We ventured in a former article, to remonstrate against the dethronement of the once powerful God of Love, in his own most especial domain, the novel; and to suggest that, in shunning the ordinary fault of recommending by examples a romantic and uncalculating extravagance of passion, Miss Austin had rather fallen into the opposite extreme of exclusively patronizing what are called prudent matches, and too much disparaging sentimental enthusiasm. We urged, that, mischievous as is the extreme on this side, it is not the one into which the young folks of the present day are the most likely to run: the prevailing fault is not now, whatever it may have been, to sacrifice all for love:

> Venit enim magnum donandi parca juventus,
> Nec. tantum Veneris quantum studiosa culinæ.[1]

We may now, without retracting our opinion, bestow unqualified approbation; for the distresses of the present heroine all arise from her prudent refusal to listen to the suggestions of her heart. The catastrophe however is happy, and we are left in doubt whether it would have been better for her or not, to accept the first proposal; and this we conceive is precisely the proper medium; for, though we would not have prudential calculations the sole principle to be regarded in marriage, we are far from advocating their exclusion. To disregard the advice of sober-minded friends on an important point of conduct, is an imprudence we would by no means recommend; indeed, it is a species of selfishness, if, in listening only to the dictates of passion, a man sacrifices to its gratification the happiness of those most dear to him as well as his own; though it is not now-a-days the most prevalent form of selfishness. But it is no condemnation of a sentiment to say, that it becomes blameable when it interferes with duty, and is uncontrouled by conscience: the desire of riches, power, or distinction, – the taste for ease and comfort, – are to be condemned when they transgress these bounds; and love, if it keep within them, even though it be somewhat tinged with enthusiasm, and a little at variance with what the worldly call prudence, i.e. regard for pecuniary advantage, may afford a better moral discipline to the mind than most other passions. It will not at least be denied, that it has often proved a powerful stimulus to exertion where others have failed, and has called forth talents unknown before even to the possessor. What, though the pursuit may be fruitless, and the hopes visionary? The result may be a real and substantial benefit, though of another kind; the vineyard may have been cultivated by digging in it for the treasure which is never to be found. What, though the perfections with which imagination has decorated the beloved object, may, in fact, exist but in a slender degree? still they are believed in and admired as real; if not, the love is such as does not merit the name; and it is proverbially true that men become assimilated to the character (i.e. what they *think* the character) of the being they fervently adore: thus, as in the noblest exhibitions of the stage, though that which is contemplated be but a fiction, it may be realized in the mind of the beholder; and, though grasping at a cloud, he may become worthy of possessing a real goddess. Many a generous sentiment, and many a virtuous resolution, have been called forth and matured by admiration of one, who may herself perhaps have been incapable of either. It matters not what the object is that a man aspires to be worthy of, and proposes as a model for imitation, if he does but *believe* it to be excellent. Moreover, all doubts of success (and they are seldom, if ever, entirely wanting) must either produce or exercise humility; and the endeavour to study another's interests and inclinations, and prefer them to one's own, may outlast the present occasion. Every thing, in short, which tends to abstract a man in any degree, or in any way, from self, – from self-admiration and self-interest, has, so far at least, a beneficial influence in forming the character.

On the whole, Miss Austin's works may safely be recommended, not only as among the most unexceptionable of their class, but as combining, in an eminent degree, instruction with amusement, though without the direct effort at the former, of which we have complained, as sometimes defeating its object.

For those who cannot, or will not, *learn* any thing from productions of this kind, she has provided entertainment which entitles her to thanks; for mere innocent amusement is in itself a good, when it interferes with no greater; especially as it may occupy the place of some other that may *not* be innocent. The Eastern monarch who proclaimed a reward to him who should discover a new pleasure, would have deserved well of mankind had he stipulated that it should be blameless. Those, again, who delight in the study of human nature, may improve in the knowledge of it, and in the profitable application of that knowledge, by the perusal of such fictions as those before us.

SOURCE: extract from unsigned article in *Quarterly Review*, XXIV (January 1821) 352–76.

NOTE

1. 'For she came unwilling to give much to young men, wanting food rather than love.'

JULIA KAVANAGH (1862): The Tender and the Sad

... Beyond any other of Miss Austen's tales, *Persuasion* shows us the phase of her literary character which she chose to keep most in the shade: the tender and the sad. In this work, as in *Sense and Sensibility*, and in *Mansfield Park*, but with more power than in either, she showed what can be the feelings of a woman compelled to see the love she most longs for, leaving her day by day. The judicious Elinor is, indeed, conscious that she is beloved; but her lover is not free, and she long thinks him lost. Fanny is her lover's *confidante*, and must be miserable when he is blest, or happy when he is wretched. The position of Anne Elliot has something more desolate still. The opposition of her relatives, and the advice of friends, induce her to break with a young naval officer, Captain Frederick Wentworth, to whom she is engaged, and the only man whom she can love. They part, he in anger, she in sorrow; he to rise in his profession, become a rich man, and outlive his grief; she to pine at home, and lose youth and beauty in unavailing regret. Years have passed when they meet again. Captain Wentworth is still young, still handsome and agreeable. He wishes to marry, and is looking for a wife. Anne Elliot, pale, faded, and sad, knows it, and sees it – she sees the looks, the smiles of fresher and younger beauties seeking him, and apparently not seeking him in vain.

Here we see the first genuine picture of that silent torture of an unloved woman, condemned to suffer thus because she is a woman and must not speak, and which, many years later, was wakened into such passionate eloquence by the author of *Jane Eyre*. Subdued though the picture is in Miss Austen's pages, it is not the less keen, not the less painful. The tale ends happily. Captain Wentworth's coldness yields to old love, Anne's beauty returns, they are married, yet the sorrowful tone of the tale is not effaced by that happy close. The shadow of a long disappointment, of secret grief, and ill-repressed jealousy will ever hang over Anne Elliot.

This melancholy cast, the result, perhaps, of some secret personal disappointment, distinguishes *Persuasion* from Miss Austen's other tales. They were never cheerful, for even the gentlest of satire precludes cheerfulness; but this is sad.

Of the popularity of Miss Austen's six novels, of the estimation in which they are held, we need not speak. It is honourable to the public that she should be so thoroughly appreciated, not merely by men like Sir Walter Scott and Lord Macaulay, but by all who take up her books for mere amusement. Wonderful, indeed, is the power that out of materials so slender, out of characters so imperfectly marked, could fashion a story. This is her great, her prevailing merit, and yet, it cannot be denied, it is one that injures her with many readers. It seems so natural that she should have told things and painted people as they are, so natural and so easy, that we are apt to forget the performance in the sense of its reality. The literary taste of the majority is always tinged with coarseness; it loves exaggeration, and slights the modesty of truth.

Another of Miss Austen's excellencies is also a disadvantage. She does not paint or analyze her characters; they speak for themselves. Her people have never those set sayings or phrases which we may refer to the author, and of which we may think, how clever! They talk as people talk in the world, and quietly betray their inner being in their folly, falsehood, or assumption. For instance, Sir Walter Elliot is handsome; we are merely told so; but we never forget it, for he does not. He considers men born to be handsome, and, deploring the fatal effect of a seafaring life on manly beauty, he candidly regrets that 'naval gentleman are not knocked on the head at once', so disgusted has he been with Admiral Baldwin's mahogany complexion and dilapidated appearance. And this worship of personal appearance is perfectly unaffected and sincere. Sir Walter Elliot's good looks have acted on him internally; his own daughter Anne rises in his opinion as her complexion grows clearer, and his first inquiry concerning his married daughter, Mary, is 'How is she looking? The last time he, Sir Walter, saw her, she had a red nose, and he hopes that may not happen every day.' He is assured that the red nose must have been accidental, upon which the affectionate father exclaims kindly: 'If I thought it would not tempt her to go out in sharp winds, and grow coarse, I would send her a new hat and pelisse.' . . .

SOURCE: extract from *English Women of Letters* (1862).

RICHARD SIMPSON (1870): The Most Charming of the Novels

. . . *Persuasion* [is] the last and altogether the most charming of the novels. In Anne Elliot we have a reproduction of the same character of 'sense' that was first displayed by Elinor in *Sense and Sensibility*. It cannot be denied that it is in some degree a retraction of former theories. It seems written to show that, whatever may have been the author's apparent meaning, she never intended really to separate the heart and the head, intellect and passion. In this novel, therefore, she traces the

course of a love founded equally upon esteem and passion,
interrupted by the interference of friends, and kept unsoldered
for eight years by the heat of the man's anger at his unmerited
rejection. Anne Elliot is Shakespeare's Viola translated into an
English girl of the nineteenth century. Like Viola, she never
tells her love, or rather never talks of it after its extinguishing,
but sits like patience on a monument smiling at grief; the
green and yellow melancholy feeds on her, and wastes her
beauty. Like Viola, too, she meekly ministers to the woman who
is unknowingly her rival. Miss Austen must surely have had
Shakespeare's *Twelfth Night* in her mind while she was writing
this novel; for not only is the general conception of the situation the same, but also the chapters which she wrote during the
last months of her life are directly founded upon Shakespeare.
They contain Anne's conversation with Captain Harville on the
different characteristics of men's and women's love, through
overhearing which Wentworth, the hero, is convinced of her
constancy, and comes forward again, after his long estrangement.

> There is no woman's sides
> Can bide the beating of so strong a passion
> As love doth give my heart; no woman's heart
> So big to hold so much; they lack retention.

So says the Duke; and Viola, disguised as Cæsario, replies,

> In faith they are as true in heart as we,

and gives the example of her supposed sister pining in thought.
'Was not this love indeed?' she asks.

> We men may say more, swear more; but indeed
> Our shows are more than will.

Similarly, Captain Harville believes that as men's bodies are
the strongest so are their feelings capable of bearing most

rough usage, and riding out the heaviest weather. 'Your feelings may be the strongest,' replies Anne, 'but the same spirit of analogy will authorize me to assert that ours are the most tender. Man is more robust than woman, but he is not longer lived, which exactly explains my view of the nature of their attachments. . . . All the privilege I claim for my sex (it is not a very enviable one; you need not covet it), is that of loving longest, when existence or when hope is gone.' This is the song of the dying swan, in which she makes ample recantation for all her heresies, more apparent than real, against the Majesty of Love; in it she displays a poetical vein which her previous writings hardly justified one in suspecting. It is exquisitely beautiful, in spite of the affected logical precision which gives too great a prosiness to the expression to allow it to take the poetical rank which its ideas deserve.

There is then a decided growth in the general intention of Miss Austen's novels; she goes over the same ground, trying other ways of producing the same effects, and attempting the same ends by means less artificial, and of more innate origin. . . .

. . . We may compare with Mr. Collins Sir Walter Elliot in *Persuasion*. He is at bottom a fool, with two fixed ideas to guide all his judgments. Vain of his own rank and good looks, these two points form his scale of comparison and rule of judgment for all men and all things: 'I have two strong grounds of objection to the navy. First, as being the means of bringing persons of obscure birth into undue distinction, and raising men to honours which their fathers and grandfathers never dreamed of; and, secondly, as it cuts up a man's youth and vigour most horribly; a sailor grows old sooner than any other man.' Sir Walter is a character constructed in the same way as Mr. Collins, with simpler means and less caricature. Altogether, he is a less factitious and artificial personage than Mr. Collins, who is rather built on the lines habitually adopted by Mr. Dickens. Miss Austen, in her earlier fools, seems scarcely as yet to have realized the Aristotelian maxim that all things, even stones, fishes, and fools, pursue their proper end. Now, Mr. Collins's fixed ideas have nothing to do with his objects in life. They govern his talk and his behaviour, but not his conduct. Sir Walter Elliot, however, is superior to Mr. Collins in making his ideas his rule of life; so his portrait becomes equal in absurdity, but superior in naturalness. . . .

SOURCE: extract from article in *North British Review*, LII (April 1870).

MARGARET OLIPHANT (1882): *Persuasion* Stands by Itself

. . . *Persuasion* stands by itself among the busy chapters of common existence in which so many of the humours of life are exhibited to us, as a story with one sustained and serious interest of a graver kind. To be sure there are abundance of amusing characters and sketches, but Anne Elliot herself, pensive and overcast with the shadow of disappointment and wistful uncertainty, fixes our regard from beginning to end with a sentimental interest which is not to be found in any other of Miss Austen's works. Nothing can be further from a love-lorn damsel than the serious and charming young woman whose vicissitudes of feeling we follow with so much sympathy: but this is the only exclusively love-story in the series, far more distinctive as such than the duel between Darcy and Elizabeth, and intellectual trial of strength which ends in the mutual subjugation of these two favourite figures. Anne is introduced to us in her dignified and sweet seriousness, always very courageous and cheerful, and in full command of herself, but paled out of her first bloom, and with a little tremor of anticipation and wistful wonder whether all is over, continually about her in the very air. And to us too is transferred that sense of suppressed anxiety and mute fear and hope. We follow her about always with our ears alive to every sound, amused in passing by the other people's eccentricities, but most occupied with her and with what is going to happen to her. Miss Austen is not a sentimentalist – love in her books takes no more than its proper place in life. Never from her lips would that artificial creed

' 'Tis woman's whole existence' have come. One can fancy the glow of lambent laughter with which she would have demonstrated the foolishness of any such melodramatic dogma. But her little cycle of clearest life-philosophy would not have been complete had she not once given its full importance to this most momentous of human sentiments. Nobody knew better that Anne Elliot would have lived and made herself a worthy life anyhow, even if Captain Wentworth had not been faithful; but there would have been a shadow upon that life – the sky would have been overcast, a cloud would have hung between her and the sun: and as step by step we get to see that her lover is faithful, the world cheers and lightens for us, and we recognise the divinity of happiness. It is the least amusing of Miss Austen's books, but perhaps the most interesting, with its one *motif* distinct and fine, the thread that runs through all. . . .

SOURCE: extract from *The Literary History of the Nineteenth Century* (1882) pp. 233–5.

2. TWENTIETH-CENTURY STUDIES

W. D. *Howells*

GREAT NOVELTY AND DARING (1901)

. . . People will prefer Anne Eliot to Elizabeth Bennet according as they enjoy a gentle sufferance in women more than a lively rebellion; and it would not be profitable to try converting the worshippers of the one to the cult of the other. But without offence to either following, it may be maintained that *Persuasion* is imagined with as great novelty and daring as *Pride and Prejudice*, and that Anne is as genuinely a heroine as Elizabeth.

In *Persuasion* Jane Austen made bold to take the case of a girl, neither weak nor ambitious, who lets the doubts and dislikes of her family and friends prevail with her, and gives up the man she loves because they think him beneath her in family and fortune. She yields because she is gentle and diffident of herself, and her indignant lover resents and despises her submission if he does not despise her. He is a young officer of the navy, rising to prominence in the service which was then giving England the supremacy of the seas, but he is not thought the equal of a daughter of such a baronet as Sir Walter Eliot. It is quite possible that in her portrayal of the odious situation Jane Austen avenges with personal satisfaction the new order against the old, for her brothers were of the navy, and the family hope and pride of the Austens were bound up with its glories. At any rate, when Sir Walter's debts oblige him to let Kellynch Hall, and live on a simple scale in Bath, it is a newly made admiral who becomes his tenant; and it is the brother of the admiral's wife who is Anne's rejected lover, and who now comes to visit his sister, full of victory and prize-money, with the avowed purpose of marrying and settling in life.

Seven years have passed since Frederick Wentworth angrily

parted with Anne Eliot. They have never really ceased to love each other; but the effect has been very different with the active, successful man, and the quiet, dispirited girl. No longer in her first youth, she devotes herself to a little round of duties, principally in the family of her foolish, peevish younger sister; and finds her chief consolation in the friendship of the woman who so conscientiously urged her to her great mistake. The lovers meet in the Musgrove family into which Anne's sister has married, and Wentworth's fancy seems taken with one of the pretty daughters. Divers transparent devices are then employed rather to pique the reader's interest than to persuade him that the end is going to be other than what it must be. Nothing can be quite said to determine it among the things that happen; Wentworth and Anne simply live back into the mutual recognition of their love. He learns to know better her lovely and unselfish nature, and so far from having formally to forgive her, he prizes her the more for the very qualities which made their unhappiness possible. For her part, she has merely to own again the affection which has been a dull ache in her heart for seven years. Her father's pride is reconciled to her marriage, which is now with a somebody instead of the nobody Captain Wentworth once was. Sir Walter 'was much struck with his personal claims, and felt that his superiority of appearance might not be unfairly balanced against her superiority of rank. ... He was now esteemed quite worthy to address the daughter of a foolish, spendthrift baronet who had not principle or sense enough to maintain himself in the situation in which Providence had placed him.' As for Anne's mischievous, well-meaning friend who had urged her to break with Wentworth before, 'there was nothing less for Lady Russell to do than to admit that she had been completely wrong, and to take up a new set of opinions and hopes'.

This outline of the story gives no just sense of its quality, which resides mainly in its constancy to nature; and it gives no sufficient notion of the variety or character involved in the uneventful, quiet action. Anne's arrogant and selfish father, her cold-hearted, selfish elder sister, and her mean, silly, empty-headed younger sister, with the simple, kindly Musgrove family, form rather the witnesses than the persons of the drama, which transacts itself with the connivance rather than the participation of Sir Walter's heir-at-law, the clever, depraved and unscrupulous cousin, William Walter Eliot; Lady Russell, the ill-advised adviser of the broken engagement; the low-born, manœuvring Mrs. Clay, who all but captures the unwary Sir Walter; the frank, warm-hearted Admiral Crofts and his wife, and the whole sympathetic naval contingent at Lyme Regis. They brighten the reality of the picture, and form its atmosphere; they could not be spared, and yet, with the exception of Louisa Musgrove, who jumps from the sea-wall at Regis, and by her happy accident brings about the final understanding of the lovers, none of them actively contributes to the event, which for the most part accomplishes itself subjectively through the nature of Anne and Wentworth.

Of the two Anne is by far the more interesting and important personage; her story is distinctly the story of a heroine; yet never was there a heroine so little self-assertive, so far from forth-putting. When the book opens we find her neglected and condemned by her father and elder sister, and sunken passively if not willingly into mere aunthood to her younger sister's children, with no friend who feels her value but that Lady Russell who has helped her to spoil her life. She goes to pay a long visit to her sister as soon as Kellynch Hall is taken by the Croftses, and it is in a characteristic moment of her usefulness there that Wentworth happens upon her, after their first cold and distant meeting before others.

The mother, as usual, had left a sick child to Anne's care, when

Captain Wentworth walked into the drawing-room at the Cottage; where were only herself and the little invalid Charles, who was lying on the sofa. . . . He started, and could only say, 'I thought the Miss Musgroves had been here; Mrs. Musgrove told me I should find them here,' before he walked to the window to recollect himself, and feel how he ought to behave. 'They are up-stairs with my sister; they will be down in a few minutes, I dare say,' had been Anne's reply in all the confusion that was natural; and if the child had not called to her to come and do something for him, she would have been out of the room the next moment, and released Captain Wentworth as well as herself. He continued at the window, and after calmly and politely saying, 'I hope the little boy is better,' was silent. She was obliged to kneel by the sofa, and remain there to satisfy her patient, and thus they continued a few minutes, when, to her very great satisfaction, she heard some other person crossing the vestibule. It proved to be Charles Hayter,

who supposes Wentworth to be his rival for one of the Miss Musgroves. He seats himself, and takes up a newspaper, ignoring Wentworth's willingness to talk.

Another minute brought another addition. The younger boy, a remarkably stout, forward child of two years old, having got the door opened, made his determined appearance among them, and went straight to the sofa to see what was going on, and put in his claim to anything good that might be given away. There being nothing to eat, he could only have some play, and as his aunt would not let him tease his sick brother, he began to fasten himself upon her, as she knelt, in a way that, busy as she was about Charles, she could not shake him off. She spoke to him, ordered, insisted, and entreated in vain. Once she did contrive to push him away, but the boy had the greater pleasure in getting upon her back again directly. 'Walter,' said she, 'get down this moment. You are extremely troublesome. I am very angry with you.' 'Walter,' cried Charles Hayter, 'why do you not do as you are bid? . . . Come to me, Walter.' But not a bit did Walter stir. In another moment she found herself in the state of being released from him; some one was taking him from her, though he had bent down her head so much that his sturdy little hands were unfastened from around her neck and he was resolutely borne away, before she knew that Captain Wentworth had done it. . . . She could not even thank him. She could only hang over little Charles with most disordered feelings . . . with the conviction soon forced upon her by the noise he was studiously making with the child, that he meant to avoid hearing her thanks . . . till enabled by the entrance of Mary and the Miss Musgroves to make over her patient to their care and leave the room. She could not

stay. . . . She was ashamed of herself, quite ashamed of being so
nervous, and of being over-come by such a trifle; but so it was, and
it required a long application of solitude and reflection to recover
her.

As any practised reader of fiction could easily demonstrate,
this is not the sort of rescue to bring about a reconciliation
between lovers in a *true* novel. There it must be something more
formidable than a naughty little boy that the heroine is saved
from: it must be a deadly miscreant, or a mad bull, or a frightened horse, or an express train, or a sinking ship. Still it cannot
be denied that this simple, this homely scene, is very pretty,
and is very like things that happen in life, where there is reason
to think love is oftener shown in quality than quantity, and
does its effect as perfectly in the little as in the great events.
Even the most tremendous incident of the book, the famous
passage which made Tennyson, when he visited Lyme Regis,
wish to see first of all the place where Louisa Musgrove fell
from the Cobb, has hardly heroic proportions, though it is of
greater intensity in its lifelikeness, and it reverses the relations
of Anne and Wentworth in the characters of helper and helped.

There was too much wind to make the high part of the new Cobb
pleasant for the ladies, and they agreed to get down the steps to the
lower, and all were contented to pass quietly and safely down the
steep steps excepting Louisa; she must be jumped down them by
Captain Wentworth. . . . She was safely down, and instantly to
shew her enjoyment, ran up the steps to be jumped down again.
He advised her against it, thought the jar too great; but no, he
reasoned and talked in vain, she smiled and said, 'I am determined
I will': he put out his hands; she was too precipitate by half a
second; she fell on the pavement on the Lower Cobb, and was taken
up lifeless! There was no wound, no visible bruise; but her eyes
were closed, she breathed not, her face was like death. . . . Captain
Wentworth, who had caught her up, knelt with her in his arms,
looking on her with a face as pallid as her own in an agony of
silence. 'She is dead!' screamed Mary, catching hold of her husband,
and contributing with her own horror to make him immovable;
and in the same moment, Henrietta, sinking under the conviction,
lost her senses, too, and would have fallen on the steps, but for

Captain Benwick and Anne, who supported her between them. 'Is there no one to help me?' were the first words that burst from Captain Wentworth. 'Go to him; go to him,' cried Anne; 'for Heaven's sake, go to him. Leave me and go to him. Rub her hands, rub her temples; here are salts; take them, take them.' Louisa was raised up and supported between them. Everything was done that Anne had prompted, but in vain; while Captain Wentworth, staggering against the wall for his support, exclaimed in the bitterest agony, 'Oh, God! Her father and mother!' 'A surgeon!' said Anne. He caught at the word; it seemed to rouse him at once; and saying only, 'True, true; a surgeon this instant.' . . . Anne, attending with all the strength and zeal and thought, which instinct supplied, to Henrietta, still tried, at intervals, to suggest comfort to the others, tried to quiet Mary, to animate Charles, to assuage the feelings of Captain Wentworth. Both seemed to look to her for direction. 'Anne, Anne,' cried Charles, 'what in Heaven's name is to be done next?' Captain Wentworth's eyes were also turned towards her. 'Had she not better be carried to the inn? Yes, I am sure; carry her to the inn.' 'Yes, yes, to the inn,' repeated Wentworth. . . . 'I will carry her myself.'

Anne has to show, with all this presence of mind, a greatness of mind superior to the misery of imagining that Wentworth is in love with Louisa, and that his impassioned remorse is an expression of his love. Only when they are going home together, to tell Louisa's parents of the accident, does she make one meek little tacit reflection in her own behalf.

'Don't talk of it, don't talk of it,' he cried. 'Oh, God! that I had not given way to her at that fatal moment! Had I done as I ought! But so eager and so resolute! Dear, sweet Louisa!' Anne wondered whether it ever occurred to him now to question the justness of his own previous opinion as to the universal felicity and advantage of firmness of character. . . . She thought it could scarcely escape him to feel that a persuadable temper might sometimes be as much in favor of happiness as a very resolute character.

SOURCE: extract from *Heroines of Fiction* (1901) pp. 50–7.

Reginald Farrer

ONE OF FICTION'S GREATEST
HEROINES (1917)

. . . Sentimentality has busied itself over the mellowing in-
fluences of approaching death, evident in *Persuasion*. The only
such evidences are to be found in its wearinesses and uneven-
nesses, and in the reappearance of that bed-rock hardness
which only in 'Lady Susan' stands out so naked. Jane Austen
herself felt its faults more strongly than subsequent generations
have done. She was depressed about the whole book. And
what she meant, however much one may disagree, is plain.
Persuasion has its uncertainties; the touch is sometimes vague,
too heavy here, too feeble there – Mrs Smith is introduced with
too much elaboration, Anne Elliot with too little; balance is
lost, and the even, assured sweep of *Emma* changes to a fitful
wayward beauty. This is at once the warmest and the coldest
of Jane Austen's works, the softest and the hardest. It is
inspired, on the one hand, by a quite new note of glacial
contempt for the characters she doesn't like, and, on the other,
by an intensified tenderness for those she does. The veil of her
impersonality wears thin; *Persuasion* is no Comedy, like *Emma*,
and contains no woven pattern of Austenian irony. The author
allows herself to tell her tale almost openly, and, in her strait
treatment of Lady Russell and the Dowager Viscountess, shows
very plainly her own characteristic attitude towards the artificial claims of rank – with such decision, indeed, that one
wonders why, with *Persuasion* to his hand, Mr Goldwin Smith
should have been at pains to note a mere flash of 'radical
sympathy' in 'poor Miss Taylor' (where, in point of fact, there
is no trace of it). As for Mrs Clay, she is introduced with so
much more emphasis than her ultimate place in the story
warrants, that it looks as if she had originally been meant to
play a much larger part in it. And worst of all is the violent and

ill-contrived exposure of William Elliot, which is also wholly unnecessary, since we are expressly told that not even for Kellynch could Anne have brought herself to marry the man associated with it. In fact, the whole Clay–Elliot imbroglio that cuts the non-existent knot at the end of the book is perhaps the clumsiest of Jane Austen's *coups de theatre*, though not deliberately false as that of *Mansfield Park*.

And yet, when everything is said and done in criticism, those who love *Persuasion* best of all Jane Austen's books have no poor case to put forward. For *Persuasion* is primarily Anne Elliot. And Anne Elliot is a puzzling figure in our literature. She is not a *jeune fille*, she is not gay or happy, brilliant or conspicuous; she is languidly, if not awkwardly brought on the stage, unemphasised, unemphatic. And yet Anne Elliot is one of fiction's greatest heroines. Gradually her greatness dawns. The more you know of her, the more you realise how perfectly she incarnates the absolute lady, the very counterpart, in her sex, of the καλοκἀγαθὸς among men. And yet there is so little that is obvious to show for all this. For the book is purely a cry of feeling; and, if you miss the feeling, you miss all. It sweeps through the whole story in a vibrating flood of loveliness; yet nothing very much is ever said. Jane Austen has here reached the culminating point in her art of conveying emotion without expression. Though *Persuasion* moves very quietly, without sobs or screams, in drawing-rooms and country lanes, it is yet among the most emotional novels in our literature.

Anne Elliot suffers tensely, hopelessly, hopefully; she never violates the decencies of silence, she is never expounded or exposed. And the result is that, for such as can feel at all, there is more intensity of emotion in Anne's calm (at the opposite pole to Marianne's 'sensibility') than in the wildest passion-tatterings of Maggie Tulliver or Lucy Snowe; and that culminating little heart-breaking scene between Harville and Anne (quite apart from the amazing technical skill of its contrivance) towers to such a poignancy of beauty that it takes rank with the last dialogue of mother and daughter in the *Iphigeneia*, as one of the very sacred things of literature that one dares not trust oneself to read aloud. And any other ending would be unbearable. So completely, in fact, do Anne and her feelings consume the book that the object of them becomes negligible. Wentworth, delightful jolly fellow that he is (with his jolly set of sailor-friends, whom Anne so wanted for hers), quite fades out of our interest, and almost out of our sight.

It is not so with the rest of the people, however. I have had curious testimony to their singular actuality. A great friend of mine, a man who never opens a book by any chance, if a newspaper be to hand, finding himself shut up for weeks in a tiny Chinese town on the borders of Tibet, was driven at last, in sheer desperation of dulness, to Jane Austen. I watched the experiment with awe and anguish. I might have spared myself. *Emma* baffled him indeed, but *Pride and Prejudice* took him by storm. And then, to my terror, he took up *Persuasion*; for surely of all her works, the appeal of *Persuasion* is the most delicate and elusive. But again I might have spared my fears. *Persuasion* had the greatest success of all; for days, if not weeks, my friend went mouthing its phrases, and chewing the cud of its felicities. 'That Sir Walter,' he would never weary of repeating, 'he's a *nib*!' And when I tried to find out what had so specially delighted him in *Persuasion*, he suddenly and finally summed up the whole of Jane Austen and her work: – 'Why, all those people, they're – they're *real*!'

SOURCE: extract from 'Jane Austen', in *Quarterly Review*, CCXXVIII (July 1917) 28–30.

Virginia Woolf

A PECULIAR BEAUTY AND A PECULIAR DULLNESS (1925)

. . . The balance of her gifts was singularly perfect. Among her finished novels there are no failures, and among her many chapters few that sink markedly below the level of the others. But, after all, she died at the age of forty-two. She died at the height of her powers. She was still subject to those changes which often make the final period of a writer's career the most interesting of all. Vivacious, irrepressible, gifted with an invention of great vitality, there can be no doubt that she would have written more, had she lived, and it is tempting to consider whether she would not have written differently. The boundaries were marked; moons, mountains, and castles lay on the other side. But was she not sometimes tempted to trespass for a minute? Was she not beginning, in her own gay and brilliant manner, to contemplate a little voyage of discovery?

Let us take *Persuasion*, the last completed novel, and look by its light at the books she might have written had she lived. There is a peculiar beauty and a peculiar dullness in *Persuasion*. The dullness is that which so often marks the transition stage between two different periods. The writer is a little bored. She has grown too familiar with the ways of her world; she no longer notes them freshly. There is an asperity in her comedy which suggests that she has almost ceased to be amused by the vanities of a Sir Walter or the snobbery of a Miss Elliott. The satire is harsh, and the comedy crude. She is no longer so freshly aware of the amusements of daily life. Her mind is not altogether on her object. But, while we feel that Jane Austen has done this before, and done it better, we also feel that she is trying to do something which she has never yet attempted. There is a new element in *Persuasion*, the quality, perhaps, that made Dr. Whewell fire up and insist that it was 'the most beautiful of her works.' She is beginning to discover that the world is larger, more mysterious, and more romantic than she had supposed. We feel it to be true of herself when she says of Anne: 'She had been forced into prudence in her youth, she learned romance as she grew older – the natural sequel of an unnatural beginning.' She dwells frequently upon the beauty and the melancholy of nature, upon the autumn where she had been wont to dwell upon the spring. She talks of the 'influence so sweet and so sad of autumnal months in the country'. She marks 'the tawny leaves and withered hedges'. 'One does not love a place the less because one has suffered in it,' she observes. But it is not only in a new sensibility to nature that we detect the change. Her attitude to life itself is altered. She is seeing it, for the greater part of the book, through the eyes of a woman who, unhappy herself, has a special sympathy for the happiness and unhappiness of others, which, until the very end, she is forced to comment upon in silence. Therefore the observation is less of facts and more of feelings than is usual. There is an expressed emotion in the scene at the concert and in the famous talk about woman's constancy which proves not merely the biographical fact that Jane Austen had loved, but the æsthetic fact that she was no longer afraid to say so. Experience, when it was of a serious kind, had to sink very deep, and to be thoroughly disinfected by the passage of time, before she allowed herself to deal with it in fiction. But now, in 1817, she was ready. Outwardly, too, in her circumstances, a change was imminent. Her fame had grown very slowly. 'I doubt', wrote Mr. Austen Leigh, 'whether it would be possible to mention any other author of note whose personal obscurity was so complete.' Had she lived a few more years only, all that would have been altered. She would have stayed in London, dined out, lunched out, met famous people, made new friends, read, travelled, and carried back to the quiet country cottage a hoard of observations to feast upon at leisure.

And what effect would all this have had upon the six novels that Jane Austen did not write? She would not have written of crime, of passion, or of adventure. She would not have been rushed by the importunity of publishers or the flattery of friends into slovenliness or insincerity. But she would have known more. Her sense of security would have been shaken. Her comedy would have suffered. She would have trusted less (this is already perceptible in *Persuasion*) to dialogue and more to reflection to give us a knowledge of her characters. Those marvellous little speeches which sum up, in a few minutes' chatter, all that we need in order to know an Admiral Croft or a Mrs. Musgrove for ever, that shorthand, hit-or-miss method which contains chapters of analysis and psychology, would have become too crude to hold all that she now perceived of the complexity of human nature. She would have devised a method, clear and composed as ever, but deeper and more suggestive, for conveying, not only what people say, but what they leave unsaid; not only what they are, but what life is. She would have stood farther away from her characters, and seen them more as a group, less as individuals. Her satire, while it played less incessantly, would have been more stringent and severe. She would have been the forerunner of Henry James and of Proust – but enough. Vain are these speculations; the most perfect artist among women, the writer whose books are immortal, died 'just as she was beginning to feel confidence in her own success'.

SOURCE: extract from *The Common Reader* (1925) pp. 142–4.

Mary Lascelles

ON *PERSUASION* (1939)

. . . In *Persuasion*, new possibilities are seen opening out. The mockery of false taste is more subtly conceived, and finds its expression in a more intricate pattern of self-deceptions than Emma's. The key to this mockery is hidden in the episode on the Cobb, which, to the casual eye, looks so disconcertingly like a perfunctory bringing about of the conventional catastrophe – a clumsy contrivance to increase the tension to breaking-point. The young Musgroves, with Anne Elliot and their friends at Lyme Regis, walk out along the Cobb, and Louisa, exhilarated by the attentions of Captain Wentworth, begins to play childish pranks and insists that he shall 'jump' her from one ledge to the other; '. . . she was too precipitate by half a second, she fell on the pavement of the Lower Cobb, and was taken up lifeless!'[1] The rest believe her to be dead, and they react characteristically to this shock: Mary falls into hysterics, Henrietta faints; Anne and Captain Wentworth take command and arrange for Louisa to be carried indoors. And then, in the close of the episode, a familiar voice penetrates the babble of the poor Musgroves, a voice which no one who has heard it before can fail to recognize for Jane Austen's own: 'By this time the report of the accident had spread among the workmen and boatmen about the Cobb, and many were collected near them, to be useful if wanted, at any rate, to enjoy the sight of a dead young lady, nay, two dead young ladies, for it proved twice as fine as the first report.'[2] The mockery sheathed in that phrase – 'nay, two dead young ladies' – pricks in an instant the bubble catastrophe; for its import is perfectly clear to any one who has observed Jane Austen's honourable dealings with her readers, her civil unwillingness to let them suffer (sympathetically) under a misapprehension. She will not allow them to misapprehend, here, the nature of the catastrophe: while it is not a mock climax to the action (like *Emma's*), nor an anticlimax (like the farce of disinheritance in *Sense and Sensibility*), it is yet not quite what it seems to be. It is a climax to the earlier part of the action in that it brings to a head, and solves, a problem which that had set – the knot tied by Wentworth's fancied preference for Louisa, her fanciful infatuation with him. But the catastrophe which the spectators think they are witnessing is an illusion. Louisa is not dead – nor even injured. True, she has fallen on her head; but it had never been a very good one, and the blow seems to have cleared it – for she acquires a taste for poetry and learns to attach herself to a man who can return her affection. And yet Mr. Read offers this scene as an example of Jane Austen's failure in serious emotional writing. Her style, he complains, 'becomes almost ludicrous . . . under the strain of dramatic action',[3] and he quotes a passage from this episode, and goes on to pick from it phrases 'which are not congruous with the tragedy of the situation'.[4] Moreover, he contrasts with its insignificance the urgency of the scene in which Heathcliffe is found dead – a real with a counterfeit catastrophe. His quotation, however, stops short of the *two dead young ladies*, and so misses the key to the ironical tone of the episode.

Here is not the irony of indifference – not that aloof tone of voice which suggests the gradual withdrawal of the authoress from the darkening landscape of *Mansfield Park*. Jane Austen can be careless in the contriving of violent action, but I do not think it is carelessness that makes Louisa's accident hardly plausible.[5] This irony is no mere symptom; it is the very tongue in which *Persuasion* is written. Before the episode, in the course of Anne's stay at Uppercross Cottage, a slender but tenacious thread of ironical suggestion has begun to weave itself into the pattern of this novel: the Musgroves of the 'Great House' are to visit the Musgroves of the Cottage, and Louisa, with laborious, youthful tact, explains that by bringing their harp she and Henrietta hope to lighten the visit, and raise their mother's spirits: '. . . she is thinking so much of poor Richard! And we agreed it would be best to have the harp, for it seems to amuse her more than the piano-forte.'[6] A chance allusion has recalled 'poor Richard' to her mind – 'So we must all be as merry as we can, that she may not be dwelling upon such gloomy things.'[7] Then follows directly a relentlessly matter-of-fact explanation:

> The real circumstances of this pathetic piece of family history were, that the Musgroves had had the ill fortune of a very troublesome, hopeless son; and the good fortune to lose him before he reached his twentieth year; that he had been sent to sea, because he was stupid and unmanageable on shore; that he had been very little cared for at any time by his family, though quite as much as he deserved; seldom heard of, and scarcely at all regretted, when the intelligence of his death abroad had worked its way to Uppercross, two years before

– and that 'his sisters were now doing all they could for him, by calling him "poor Richard"', while his mother, to whom chance only has recalled him, has been 'thrown . . . into greater grief for him than she had known on first hearing of his death'.[8] Mrs. Musgrove's creator, that is, has conceived of her creature's retrospective grief as half fanciful, and means to convey this conception of it to us: she shows what is unreal in it, to us – allows perception of it to cool even Anne's habitual warmth of sympathy – by the turn of Mrs. Musgrove's lamentation. So long as grief lived, she would surely be apt to forget the graceless boy in the child endearingly dependent on her forbearance. Now she dallies instead with the fiction of a brilliant future forestalled by death, and, seeing the Navy personified in Wentworth, laments to her ready sympathizer: 'Ah! Miss Anne, if it had pleased Heaven to spare my poor son, I dare say he would have been just such another by this time.'[9] And what is 'real and unabsurd' in her feelings – her author comments uncompromisingly – rarely wins the sympathy which is its right because it is awkwardly displayed: a comment which would seem so little relevant as to be merely captious, if it were not for the implied contrast which another character in the book presents. There is to be something of ironic reserve in the first mention of Captain Benwick: Wentworth's commendation of him 'had been followed by a little history of his private life, which rendered him perfectly interesting in the eyes of all the ladies. He had been engaged to Captain Harville's sister, and was now mourning her loss.'[10] And his introduction to the Musgrove party confirms this impression: 'He had a pleasing face and a melancholy air, just as he ought to have, and drew back from conversation.'[11] Anne's bent for sympathy impels her to 'begin an acquaintance with him', and they fall into talk about books. When Jane Austen tells of taste in reading we can be sure that she has something of character and mood to disclose; we are to learn a little of Captain Benwick's character through his enjoyment of the lavish sadness of Scott and Byron. (Had she conceived otherwise of his sorrow, she might have allowed him to sympathize with the disagreeable, the positively uncomfortable, melancholy of Johnson and Cowper.) And a faint tone of ironical detachment is perceptible when Anne tries to be of service to him by discussing 'whether *Marmion* or *The Lady of the Lake* were to be preferred, and how ranked the *Giaour* and *The Bride of Abydos*; and moreover, how the *Giaour* was to be pronounced', while he responds by repeating 'with . . . tremulous feeling, the various lines which imaged a broken heart . . .', and looking '. . . entirely as if he meant to be understood'.[12] In fact, Captain Benwick, who can express what is now only fanciful in his grief more gracefully than poor Mrs. Musgrove could express what was still real in hers, deceives not only himself but even those who should know him best, the simple, feeling Harvilles. Anne alone remains not wholly convinced;[13] the strong feelings which she may not express make her sensitive to the force of feeling in others; she penetrates to Captain Harville's undiminished silent grief. If it were not for these two, and all that is implied in the talk between them, one might almost take *Persuasion* for a satire on the frailty of human sorrow and the support it seeks from delusion; it is they who reveal it as a delicate study in shades of distinction between the true and the not quite true. And, as usual, Jane

Austen associates self-deception with wrong-headed reading. 'Yes, yes, if you please, no reference to examples in books.'[14]

What are we to make, however, of that crude farce – the mutual seduction of Mr. Elliot and Mrs. Clay – thrust into this delicate comedy? As an intrigue between rogues, diamond cut diamond, it has finer possibilities than it ever develops; so have the two characters themselves. Mrs. Clay begins admirably: her plausible, sly loquacity when she sets herself to win Sir Walter's favour surely promises well. Other men, she tells him, less fortunate than he as to rank and person, must expect to

'lose the look of youth . . . Sailors do grow old betimes . . . Soldiers, in active service, are not at all better off: and even in the quieter professions, there is a toil and a labour of the mind, if not of the body, which seldom leaves a man's looks to the natural effect of time. The lawyer plods, quite care-worn; the physician is up at all hours, and travelling in all weather; and even the clergyman –' she stopt a moment to consider what might do for the clergyman'[15]

– and there she is left, considering what may do for the clergyman, until that solemn, insinuating rogue, Mr. Elliot, is ready for her. What has become of the first comic inspiration? I think it is possible, with the catastrophes of the other novels in mind, to make a shrewd guess. The flaw lies here: these two could not receive full life unless they should be conceived of as comic in virtue of the part they had to play together. . . .

THE POINT OF VANTAGE

. . . Constancy of position suits a story in which there is a secret to be kept: such a plot as that of *Emma*, consisting in a series of happenings which, once their cause is revealed, appear in their true significance as intimations of what has not been seen; a story whose pattern is a secret kept until the end. *Persuasion* offers a less obvious, perhaps a more interesting, illustration. Its principal pattern is formed by the change in Wentworth's feelings towards Anne; and of the progress of this change we are allowed to judge only from a train of incidents which comes under her observation.

The point of vantage which we are to share with Anne is precisely indicated in the opening of the story; there we are made acquainted with the range of her field of vision. We realize that we are in possession of knowledge which is denied to the other characters in the book; few of them are aware that Wentworth's life has impinged upon hers, and of those few none knows her present feelings; but we know what their first strength was, and that it is not diminished. We can perceive, too, how poor is the visibility from her solitary observation-post, in the earlier weeks at least of the autumn in which the story opens; besides chance allusions, in talk which she may never encourage, must not even seem to understand, she has 'only navy lists and newspapers for her authority' as to his fortunes, and 'no reason to believe him married'.[16] They encounter, but his formal manner, outcome of resentment, withholds from Anne the means of estimating his feelings.

At this point comes the first, and more important, of the exceptions to Jane Austen's maintenance of the consistent point of view in this novel: not only does she tell us in her own voice something of those feelings, but she goes on to present Wentworth in intimate, if not quite candid, talk of them with his sister. This I can only suppose to be an oversight; for it is altogether different from the right to interpret manner which Jane Austen habitually reserves to herself. The episode is comparable only to those scenes in Mansfield parsonage which disclose to us, but not to Fanny, knowledge of Crawford's intentions towards her; and it jars more than they, because the opening of *Persuasion* has suggested no such composite impression as had that of *Mansfield Park*. I surmise that Jane Austen had always been liable to fall back upon various means of explanation in momentary failures of confidence,[17] and that here, in a novel which had not had time to become a 'gradual performance', she had not yet noticed the inappropriateness of this one. It may be convenient to point out here the other, and lesser, oversight of this kind, the gossip about Anne and Mr. Elliot to which Captain Wentworth has to listen when Anne has left him and his companions behind her in the shop.[18]

Except in these two passages, Anne's point of view is steadily maintained: we share her alternating moods of confidence and diffidence as to her power to read Wentworth's manner and actions; with her, we sometimes overhear words of his that seem to bear a meaning beyond that addressed to the immediate listener;[19] or hear his friends' account of his intentions, wondering how much it is worth. We share, too, her gift for drawing people out, and so learn from Captain Harville of a strain of tenderness in Frederick Wentworth of which the Musgroves know nothing. Then these two are separated again, and Anne must make what she can of such news as comes her way, often unable to interpret it for want of the clue for which she may not ask – her position defined for us by her encounter with the Admiral, the teasing incompleteness of his news of Louisa's engagement to Benwick, and her fruitless inquiries as to its effect on Wentworth:

'It did certainly seem, last autumn,' she says, 'as if there were an attachment between him and Louisa Musgrove; but I hope it may be understood to have worn out on each side equally, and without violence. I hope his letter does not breathe the spirit of an ill-used man.'

'Not at all, not at all; there is not an oath or a murmur from beginning to end. . . . He very handsomely hopes they will be happy together, and there is nothing very unforgiving in that, I think.'

Anne did not receive the perfect conviction which the Admiral meant to convey, but it would have been useless to press the enquiry further.[20]

Again she and Wentworth are together; but his manner has become ambiguous. Now it seems that she wants but opportunity to read it: 'If she could only have a few minutes conversation with him again, she fancied she should be satisfied.'[21] Now she is puzzled by its implications, deliberate but seemingly inconsistent. And so this subterraneous pattern is kept fairly out of sight until the climax when, by Wentworth's confession to Anne of that gradual change in his feelings towards her which he has but now fully realized himself, it is united with the visible train of events to make a single composition.

Why is it that the secondary pattern of subterraneous progress and visible incident, that formed by the intrigue of Mr. Elliot and Mrs. Clay, is so much less satisfactory? Early enough in the story we are let into the secret of Anne's suspicions: 'With a great deal of quiet observation, and a knowledge, which she often wished less, of her father's character, she was sensible that results the most serious to his family from the intimacy, were more than possible.'[22] But Lady Russell barely prevents us from forgetting the matter until Sir Walter and Mrs. Clay are within sight again and some languidly invented conversation can bring it once more to our notice; and with no more than this, and some instances of Mrs. Clay's intimacy with Elizabeth, to prepare us, we are plunged into Mrs. Smith's news of the 'general idea among Sir Walter's acquaintance, of her meaning to be Lady Elliot',[23] on which our understanding of Mr. Elliot's character is to depend. In support of this, Mrs. Clay has to perform a tedious little act of duplicity before Anne's eyes; and then she and her accomplice are left at a loose end until the author *tidies them up* by informing us, in her own voice – and in tones of that voice which remind me of the end of 'Lady Susan' – that Sir Walter would have been willing to buy, at the price of a socially disgraceful marriage, flattery which he had been getting for nothing, while Mr. Elliot was prepared to pay for the removal of this danger by the sacrifice of his carefully acquired respectability – and we realize that we have never, in effect, had anything but her word for the whole affair.

How has Jane Austen come to let us suppose that she has forgotten, or neglected, to invent enough of those incidents that should intimate it to us? It may fairly be argued that Anne was not interested in it – but that obstacle could have been circumvented either by heightening her concern, or by the use of another consciousness besides hers as a means of communication; either device being well within Jane Austen's power. Surely the real explanation must be that, for a reason I have already suggested,[24] she was not interested in the intrigue herself.

The stream of those incidents which illustrate the other

pattern in *Persuasion*, that in which her real interest lies, has
never failed. This, however, is not its only virtue. The plot of
Tom Jones (and of *Amelia*, too, although it is not so clear an
illustration) had been of this double make, part visible, part to
be guessed at: the revelation of the circumstances of Jones's
birth – or, indeed, of Amelia's situation among persecuting
suitors – had eventually allowed us to perceive the significance
and interrelations of happenings which we had hitherto been
able only to observe. There had been no dearth of inventive
activity. Fielding indeed delights in the exacting demands
which this kind of narration makes on him – demand for
invention of illustrative incident as well as of invisible train of
development. This is how he concludes a passage which has
revealed the hidden causes of those parts of the action we have
been allowed to see:

These were several Matters, of which we thought necessary our
Reader should be informed; for, besides that it conduces greatly to
a perfect Understanding of all History, there is no Exercise of the
Mind of a sensible Reader more pleasant than the tracing the
several small and almost imperceptible Links in every Chain of
Events by which all the great Actions of the World are produced.[25]

And again: 'We shall endeavour to satisfy an Enquiry which
may arise in our most favourite Readers, (for so are the most
curious) . . .'.[26] But even if he had set himself the task of con-
cealing this activity of his it is hard to see how, given his
method of narration, it could have been accomplished; how he
would have made us forget that he is, at his own will and
pleasure, alternately vouchsafing and withholding information.
For that is indeed how he separates his invisible and his visible
stories, bringing this and this fact to our view to serve as illustrative incident, keeping that and that fact from sight, as
though in a game, and – as in a game – pretending to complain
that we are slack adversaries: those readers who misinterpret
one of his characters 'make a very bad and ungrateful Use of
that Knowledge which we have communicated to them'.[27] Yet
the incidents which illustrate the principal train of development

in *Persuasion* never give the impression of having been arbitrarily selected by the narrator; rather the choice seems to have been imposed by a necessity which binds her equally with us, that very necessity which must result from the establishing of a fixed point of view; for by sharing Anne's position we are of course precluded from seeing more than those incomplete indications of the progress of events which are visible to her. . . .

SOURCE: extracts from *Jane Austen and Her Art* (1939) pp. 76–81, 203–8.

NOTES

1. *Persuasion* (Oxford, 1933), ch. 12, p. 109.
2. *P.*, ch. 12, p. 111.
3. Herbert Read, *English Prose Style* (1928), p. 119.
4. Ibid. p. 120.
5. [For a suggestion as to the cause of this, Mary Lascelles refers to p. 129 of her study, not reproduced here – Ed.]
6. *P.*, ch. 6, p. 50.
7. *P.*, ch. 6, p. 50.
8. *P.*, ch. 6, pp. 50, 51.
9. *P.*, ch. 8, p. 64.
10. *P.*, ch. 11, p. 96.
11. *P.*, ch. 11, p. 97.
12. *P.*, ch. 11, p. 100.
13. She remembers afterwards that she had not thought him inconsolable (*P.*, ch. 18, p. 167).
14. *P.*, ch. 23, p. 234.
15. *P.*, ch. 3, p. 20.
16. *P.*, ch. 4, p. 30.
17. She felt, it seems, some anxiety that Henry Crawford should be rightly understood by the reader. 'Henry is going on with "Mansfield Park",' she writes to Cassandra. 'He admires H. Crawford: I mean properly, as a clever, pleasant man' (*Letters*, ed. R. W. Chapman, Oxford, 1932, pp. 377, 378).
18. *P.*, ch. 19, p. 177.
19. *P.*, ch. 10, p. 88.
20. *P.*, ch. 18, pp. 172, 173.

21. *P.*, ch. 19, p. 180.
22. *P.*, ch. 5, p. 34.
23. *P.*, ch. 21, p. 206.
24. [See herein, p. 158 – Ed.]
25. Henry Fielding, *Amelia*, book XII, ch. 1.
26. Ibid., ch. 5.
27. Henry Fielding, *Tom Jones*, book III, ch. 5.

Elizabeth Bowen

A MASTERPIECE OF DELICATE
STRENGTH (1957)

Jane Austen is, in the main, delighted in as a smiling satirist –
a person most herself in the comic vein. Her art could seem
drawn to the sparkling shallows rather than to the greater
depths of emotion. Extreme grief, turbulence or despair are
banished from her pages, where not shown as the penalties of
excessive romanticism. All but one of her heroines are youthful,
capable of feeling, but still untouched by the more searching
experiences of life. We observe that, throughout most of her
writing years, Jane Austen deliberately chose restraint – she
had, it is true, a warning in the absurd contortions of sensibility
to which some of her fellow-novelists could go, but we may be
certain that for her choice there was also some compelling
personal reason. Not till she came to write *Persuasion* did she
break with her self-set limitations. Did something in her demand
release, expression, before it was too late? This was, whether
or not she knew it, the last book she was to live to complete.

Persuasion strikes a note unheard hitherto. It is a masterpiece
of delicate strength, suggesting far more than is put on paper.
For it was not that the author abandoned or turned against
restraint: on the contrary, she made it her study – its hard cost
and no less its painful causes are shown. *Persuasion*, whose
lonely heroine, young no longer, seems committed to all but
silence, is in fact a novel about restraint. It is, too, a novel
about maturity.

Somebody, discussing fiction, remarked that whereas men
write better about a first love, women write better about a
second. For our sex, do the original raptures tend to evaporate
from the later memory? One would hardly think so; it takes,
at least, remarkably little to recall them – an ancient dance
tune, a desiccated flower in a drawer, a scrap of all but for-

gotten handwriting can bring back the magic of a moment. Possibly women's first feelings are less articulate – for it *is* a fact that the heart's awakenings, young love, whether in boy or girl, have been more lyrically pictured by male novelists. For instance, does any young girl in fiction rival Tolstoi's enchanting, enchanted, unwise Natasha of *War and Peace*? In *Persuasion*, Jane Austen does not, admittedly, deal with a second love – but she is concerned with a young love which has grown up, which has steadied, lasted, felt the stress of reality, woven itself into the fabric of a life. Anne Elliot is not a girl but a woman – though a woman doomed, it would seem, to unfulfilment. Because of a mistake she cannot retrieve, the future is to be empty for her. In Jane Austen's day, a spinster of twenty-seven was to all intents and purposes a nobody – a seat in the background, an anxious place on the margin of other people's activities were the most such an unfortunate might aspire to. When we first meet Anne Elliot, this is her lot. And worse, it is her lot by her own fault.

Tormentedly yielding to persuasion on the part of a worldlier older friend, Anne, at nineteen, had broken off her engagement to Frederick Wentworth, the then young, penniless naval officer. Nor had the love affair ended only thus: Anne has the additional pain of knowing that her weakmindedness (as it seemed to him) aroused Frederick Wentworth's contempt and anger – utterly she had failed and disappointed him. Now, for eight years, intense self-reproach has mingled with her regret. For his sake, the best she feels she can hope is that Wentworth by now has forgotten her – she has spoiled her own life: is that not enough?

There is present, in that early history of Anne's, everything that could have made a warped creature. Do we not all know women with poisoned temperaments, in whom some grievance or disappointment seems to fester like an embedded thorn? Today, with a hundred careers open, it is or should be easier to forget – but Anne, condemned to the idleness of her time and class, has not an interest or an ambition to distract her. Endlessly, if she so willed, she could fret and brood. But no: she shows an unbroken though gentle spirit and, with that, a calm which does not fail. From what inner source does her courage spring? Love, although lost to her, still inspires her. Her undying feeling for Frederick Wentworth, the unshadowed nobility of his image, still lights up for her the entire world. For Anne Elliot to love, to have loved, is a tremendous thing. Somehow, therefore, she is set apart from those whose easier longings have been satisfied.

Hence, I think, this reticent woman's hold on the reader – one is drawn to her as to no other more outwardly striking Jane Austen heroine; one feels honoured by being in her confidence; she is sympathetic rather than coldly 'admirable'. Her slender beauty is thrown into more relief by the bumptious, apple-cheeked charms of the young Miss Musgroves. Playing the piano while her juniors dance, listening to the long and imagined woes of a series of discontented matrons, Anne Elliot remains in her quiet way the mistress of any situation. Unlike the blameless Fanny of *Mansfield Park*, she never is over-meek, subservient or mousey. She never pities herself: who dare pity her? The dull young squire Charles Musgrove, now her brother-in-law, had been, we learn, Anne's unsuccessful suitor; in the course of the story she is to attract the eye of a jaded, roving man-of-the-world. If life *is* 'over' for Anne, it is so by force of her own decision – she can contemplate no form of the second-best.

Persuasion's heroine, when we first meet her, owes her poise to a sort of sad inner peace, the peace which comes with the end of hope. She does not expect, and she cannot wish, ever again to see Frederick Wentworth.

Yet, she must. And we watch her through that ordeal.

Frederick, now Captain Wentworth, a naval war hero enriched by prize-money, reappears in the Elliots' West-country neighbourhood. Here, in these same places, these rooms and gardens charged with so many associations, the former lovers are forced to meet face to face. Forced? – yes, for Anne it amounts to that. She hears the news of his coming with apprehension. He, by all signs, does not any more feel anything; she must conceal the fact that she feels so much. Nor is this all –

she is to look on at Captain Wentworth's flirtation with and apparent courtship of her sprightly young neighbour Louisa Musgrove. For Frederick, Anne seems to be hardly there. Is it, for him, as though she had never been?

No. His formal good manners to her have a touch of ice: he has not forgotten, for he has not forgiven. Meet as they may as strangers, he and she cannot be strangers truly. Always, they are in the presence of crowds of people; there are walking-parties, dances, country house merry-makings, and there is the expedition to Lyme Regis which so nearly has a tragic end. One thing Anne *is* spared – prying or mocking eyes. For that eight-years-ago engagement had been kept secret: no outside person other than Lady Russell (whose advice had wrecked it) had ever known of it. Now, Lady Russell is elsewhere. Nobody, therefore, suspects either Anne's anguish or its cause.

All through *Persuasion*, the scenes in the country, at the sea-side, the later episodes in Bath, we react to the tension of speechless feeling. Yet somehow the novel is not a thing of stress; it has the harmony of its autumnal setting. The landscape, the changing season, are part of the texture of the story. Here, as nowhere else in Jane Austen's work, brims over the poetry of Nature – uplands, woods and sea. We are tuned in to a mood, to a sensibility which (being at once Anne's and her creator's) rings beautifully true. And, as the plot of *Persuasion* unfolds itself, we follow each development through Anne's eyes. Or sometimes, we keep watch on her behalf. Is Frederick Wentworth relenting? – or, had his coldness, from the first, been a matter of self-protection? Has his indifference to this older Anne been less than she had imagined, or he had thought? So we suspect, some time before Anne herself has dared to envisage the possibility. We begin to be impatient for the *dénouement* – of its kind, the suspense set up by *Persuasion* is as keen as any I know in fiction.

Then it comes – that extraordinary scene in the Bath parlour when, while Anne is talking to other people, Frederick sits absorbed in writing a letter. Then, rising, he leaves the room hurriedly, 'without so much as a look'. But next:

Footsteps were heard returning; the door opened; it was himself. He begged their pardon, but he had forgotten his gloves, and instantly crossing the room to the writing table, and standing with his back to Mrs Musgrove, he drew out a letter from under the scattered paper, placed it before Anne with eyes of glowing entreaty fixed on her for a moment, and hastily collecting his gloves, was again out of the room, almost before Mrs Musgrove was aware of his being in it – the work of an instant!

The revolution which one instant had made in Anne was almost beyond expression. . . . On the contents of that letter depended all which the world could do for her!

There are, I know, those who find in *Persuasion* one fundamental improbability. *Would* Anne, even when very young, have let herself be persuaded by Lady Russell into making a break with her true love? The weakness, the lack of faith – the cowardice, almost – seem out of accord with the heroine whom we later know. One must recollect that Lady Russell's argument had been a wily one – she had represented to Anne that a penniless youthful marriage would be a fatal drag on Frederick's career. Anne had given up Frederick for (as she thought) his sake – though mistaken, her decision had been selfless. Also, at nineteen, repressed and young for her age, she was unaccustomed to trusting her own judgement. Ignored by an arrogant father and elder sister, she had found in the worldly-wise Lady Russell her first friend – whose word, accordingly, carried undue weight. The time, moreover, was long ago: girls deferred, instinctively, to adult authority. But should we not, before either decrying Anne or declaring her weakness to be 'impossible', think again about this question of influence? Dare we say that a friend's opinion, forcefully put, never has affected our own decisions? And is it not in regard to what matter most – for instance, some vital question of love – that we are most at the mercy of what is told us? Caught in a tempest of feeling, we lose our bearings: it may not be easy to know what is right or wrong. The truth, we may only perceive later – not, it is to be hoped, too late.

Jane Austen's otherwise open life contains one mystery: her

love affair. Nobody but her sister Cassandra knew of it; and Cassandra, who outlived Jane, kept silence – it is known that, before Cassandra's death, she destroyed revealing letters written by Jane. The probable scene and time of the love affair have been pieced together; no more can be established with any certainty. It is understood that the love was mutual, wholly happy, tender and full of promise, and that there would have been marriage had not the young man died. Had Jane Austen married, it seems likely that the world would never have had her greater later novels – fate, by dealing that blow to her, has enriched us. Balanced, wise and adorable are her comedies, but her true depth was not to be felt till this final book. This, I think, is her testimony to the valour, the enduringness of the human spirit. She believed, and she was to show, that love for another can be the light of a life – can rise above egotism, accept hardship, outlive hope of reward. Out of a hard-won knowledge she wrote *Persuasion*.

SOURCE: '*Persuasion*', in *London Magazine*, IV (June 1957) 47–51.

R. S. Crane

A SERIOUS COMEDY (1957)

The one continuous story Jane Austen tells in *Persuasion* is of a broken engagement finally restored, and with even deeper happiness for the heroine and hero, Anne Elliot and Captain Frederick Wentworth, than they had felt when the engagement was entered into eight years and a half before. It had not lasted long. Wentworth was then a young naval officer with no certain prospects, and Anne, a girl of nineteen, was soon persuaded by her friend Lady Russell, who stood to her as her dead mother, that the engagement would be an imprudent one for him no less than for herself. She therefore broke it off, though at the cost of much suffering and continued regret; she realized very quickly, in fact, that she would renew it at once if Wentworth asked her to. He, however, had left immediately for sea, greatly angered by her treatment of him and fully convinced that it showed 'a feebleness of character . . . which his own decided, confident temper could not endure'. This was still his state of mind when the two happened to meet again eight years later; he thought Anne's power with him was gone forever, and he was prepared to fall in love with almost any girl but her – any girl, at least, who possessed 'a strong mind, with sweetness of manner'. He did in fact become involved, half seriously, with one of Anne's friends, Louisa Musgrove, thinking her just the kind of woman Anne was not. Before long, however, he began to discover, on observing Anne more closely, that he had seriously misjudged her character; and with this recognition of his error, his old affection for her, which had been latent throughout in spite of his 'angry pride', began more and more to revive; her character, as he told her later, 'was now fixed on his mind as perfection itself, maintaining the loveliest medium of fortitude and gentleness'. He was unable to speak at once because of his involvement with Louisa, and then, when this difficulty was fortunately removed, he was held back for a time by his uncertainty about Anne's present feelings for him. She finally became aware, however, of his returning love and contrived to let him know how deeply welcome this was to her. Whereupon the engagement was restored, with a completer consciousness on both sides of one another's merits.

For a novel depicting such a simple series of events, there is a fairly large cast of characters. Leaving aside those who appear only once or twice in the narrative, these fall into two originally distinct groups: the family and friends of Anne and the family and friends of Wentworth. Anne is the daughter of Sir Walter Elliot, baronet, of Kellynch-hall in Somersetshire; she has an older sister, Elizabeth, a younger sister, Mary, and a cousin, William Walter Elliot, who is heir to the title and estate. Her closest friend is an older woman, Lady Russell of Kellynch-lodge, to whom her dead mother had committed her upbringing. Her immediate circle at the time of Wentworth's return also includes Elizabeth's friend Mrs. Clay, the widowed daughter of the Elliots' estate agent, and, on a much more intimate footing, the Musgrove family of the neighboring village of Uppercross: Mr. and Mrs. Musgrove, their son Charles, who had married Mary Elliot after Anne had refused him, and their daughters Henrietta and Louisa; there is also Mrs. Musgrove's nephew Charles Hayter. And later on, Anne sees a good deal of an old schoolmate of hers, Miss Hamilton, now Mrs. Smith, whose late husband had been for a time a friend of William Elliot.

The other group is smaller and consists almost entirely of naval persons, without notable family connections, who have become prosperous or at least comfortable as a result of the recent war: Wentworth himself; his sister and her husband, Admiral Croft; and his close friends, Captain and Mrs. Harville, and Captain Benwick. Wentworth also has a clergyman brother, who had been a curate in the Kellynch neighborhood at the time of his first meeting with Anne.

It is in this world of country gentry and their connections and of naval officers just out of service that the action of *Persuasion* takes place. The narrative begins in the summer of 1814, eight years after Anne had broken her engagement, so that we learn of this earlier event only retrospectively. From that point until its climax in February of 1815, it passes through five stages, marked off chiefly until the last one by the doings and movements of the subordinate characters. The main happenings in the first stage are Sir Walter Elliot's discovery that he must live at a less extravagant rate than has been his habit, his decision that he can do this best by letting Kellynch-hall to a tenant and going to live in Bath, his finding of a satisfactory tenant in Admiral Croft, and his departure, with Elizabeth and Mrs. Clay; Anne is to rejoin the family after Christmas and in the meantime she is to stay first with Mary in Uppercross and then with Lady Russell.

The second stage presents what goes on in Uppercross and the neighborhood while Anne is there: the coming of Wentworth on a visit to his sister and brother-in-law; his meeting with the Musgroves and consequently with Anne; their other meetings at parties, on walks, and in Mary's cottage; his attempts to attach himself to Louisa, her apparent reciprocation of his interest, and Anne's awareness of all this; and finally an excursion of all the younger people to Lyme Regis, where the Harvilles and Captain Benwick are now living; Anne's meeting with them, her chance glimpse of her cousin Mr. Elliot, and the shocking culmination of the holiday in Louisa's fall and concussion while attempting to display to Wentworth her firmness of character; after which Anne, who has been the one resolute person in the group during the crisis, is obliged to return to Uppercross.

The third stage is a brief one: after a day or two at Uppercross (Wentworth and the Charles Musgroves remaining with Louisa in Lyme), Anne goes as she has promised to Lady Russell, visits the Crofts at Kellynch-hall, hears reassuring news of Louisa, becomes convinced that Louisa and Wentworth will now certainly marry, and then, at the beginning of the new year, accompanies Lady Russell to Bath.

The fourth stage is one of absorption on Anne's part in family and personal matters of an immediate sort quite removed from Wentworth and the happenings at Uppercross: the continued presence of Mrs. Clay; the constant visits of Mr. Elliot; the successful efforts of Sir Walter to become reconciled with some aristocratic relations of his; Anne's reunion with Mrs. Smith, who is now living as an invalid in Bath; and Lady Russell's unsuccessful attempt to persuade her that she ought to marry her cousin, who is apparently on the point of proposing to her.

This stage ends abruptly, and the final stage begins, with the news that Louisa has become engaged to Captain Benwick. Wentworth now comes to Bath; and except for one episode – Anne's discovery through Mrs. Smith of Mr. William Elliot's real character – all the happenings until the end are parts of the delayed resolution: a first embarrassed meeting with Wentworth by chance in a shop; a second meeting at a concert, where Anne becomes aware both of his returning love and of his jealousy of Mr. Elliot, to whom rumor in Bath has it that she is already engaged; and then the occasions provided by the surprise visit of Mrs. Musgrove, Charles and Mary, and Captain Harville, for undeceiving him on this point.

The essential story of *Persuasion*, thus, is to all appearances a very simple one; it is a story, as presented in the narrative, that really involves only the private thoughts and emotions of two persons. Given the constancy and the strength of Anne's feelings for Wentworth, the renewal of the engagement is inevitable once he comes to realize his mistake about her character and the inadequacy of the standard by which he has judged her; there are no external obstacles of any sort on either side. Why then so many incidental happenings, and especially why so many subordinate characters? One answer, true as far as it goes, is that they serve to give concrete body and life – surface life, at any rate – to a story that might otherwise seem too far abstracted from the ordinary daily circumstances in which private changes of opinion and feeling about other persons actually come about. And there is no doubt that in *Persuasion*, as in Jane Austen's other novels, an all-important cause of our pleasure in reading is her ability to invent and depict a great variety of persons who are alive and intrinsically interesting quite apart from any artistic functions they may have: consider Sir Walter Elliot and Mary Musgrove, for instance, or, at the opposite extreme, the Crofts. But neither this nor the other kind of value in happenings and characters is incompatible with the artist's use of them as necessary or desirable expedients in the working out of his governing conception. They may be good in themselves and at the same time be good for the plot and its effects. And so we need to ask, as one of our main critical questions about *Persuasion*, what all the minor characters and surface events I have listed are doing in the novel in relation to its central story. To what extent are their presence and treatment determined, in one way or another, by Jane Austen's conception of the novel as a whole and the problems to which this gave rise?

Now *Persuasion* is clearly conceived as a serious work – serious ethically no less than artistically. While it is pervaded with morality of what seems to me a very fine sort, however, it has no moral and argues no thesis. It is a novel of personal relations: the relations of two persons who had once been everything to one another, than apparently nothing, and finally everything again, but on a higher level of affection and understanding. It is a love story, in short, which moves us as all good love stories do, not because its hero and heroine are embodiments of abstract values, ideological or social, larger than themselves, but simply because they are particular human persons who have fallen in love and suffer and are happy in the end. That is the way, I am sure, that we all read *Persuasion* when we are not bemused by critical theory: not as a typical case of anything or an embodiment of a 'theme', but as an individual history the course of which is determined by circumstances peculiar to itself, and the moral of which, if it can be called a moral, is merely that such things can conceivably happen, and that when they happen in fiction they tend to hold our interest as fellow human beings.

It is a love story but assuredly not a mere love story: not a love story, that is, which depends for its emotional power solely or chiefly on our general human sympathy with young lovers, whoever they may be. For most love stories, undoubtedly, this basis of appeal is enough; but not for *Persuasion* as Jane Austen conceived it. I think there can be little doubt about the quality of the response she wanted her novel to evoke at its climax. To perceive this, one has only to read the passage, in the next to the last chapter, that begins just after Charles Musgrove has apologized for leaving Anne alone with Wentworth on the streets of Bath:

There could not be an objection. There could be only a most proper alacrity, a most obliging compliance for public view; and smiles reined in and spirits dancing in private rapture. In half a minute, Charles was at the bottom of Union-Street again, and the other two proceeding together; and soon words enough had passed between them to decide their direction toward the comparatively quiet and retired gravel-walk, where the power of conversation would make the present hour a blessing indeed; and prepare for it all the immortality which the happiest recollections of their own future lives could bestow. There they exchanged again those feelings and those promises which had once before seemed to secure every thing, but which had been followed by so many, many years of division and estrangement. There they returned again into the past, more exquisitely happy, perhaps, in their re-union, than when it had been first projected; more tender, more tried, more fixed in a knowledge of each other's character, truth and attachment; more equal to act, more justified in acting. And there, as they slowly paced the gradual ascent, heedless of every group around them, seeing neither sauntering politicians, bustling housekeepers, flirting girls, nor nursery-maids and children, they could indulge in those retrospections and acknowledgments, and especially in those explanations of what had directly preceded the present moment, which were so poignant and so ceaseless in interest.

How many other love stories are there in which the resolution is achieved in lovelier prose? But it would surely not be appropriate to write thus about the reunion of two persons whose only claim on our interest is that they are generally likeable people coming together again after a long separation. Or to write as Jane Austen did in her earlier version of the same episode, in which the scene was laid in the house of Admiral Croft: 'There was time for all this to pass, with such interruptions only as enhanced the charm of the communication, and Bath could hardly contain any other two beings at once so rationally and so rapturously happy as during that evening occupied the sofa of Mrs. Croft's drawing-room in Gay Street.' We are invited in both passages to share sympathetically in the lovers' new-found happiness. But the desired response is clearly more than one of sympathy merely. The happiness of Anne and Wentworth is 'rational' as well as 'rapturous', and it is 'rational' because its basis is the fuller knowledge they have acquired since their first meeting many years before 'of each other's character, truth, and attachment'. It is the happiness, in short, not simply of lovers but of moral individuals – a happiness which can be achieved only by persons of superior minds and characters, and to which, consequently, when we are convinced that this is indeed the case, we tend to respond in a more complex way than to the merely 'sentimental' resolutions of ordinary love tales. What we feel is an effect compounded of sympathy and moral approbation; it is not simply that a marriage is to take place, but a good marriage, of the kind we would wish all persons we particularly value to have.

Jane Austen, in short, conceived of *Persuasion* as a serious comedy: a comedy in the general sense that its plot moves from unhappiness to happiness; and a serious comedy in the sense that what makes its events interesting and moving for us is not so much their intrinsic painfulness and pleasurableness as the fact that they happen to persons for whom we have a special concern by reason of their merits as individuals. Consequently, her primary task in writing the novel was to do whatever was necessary with her materials to mold them effectively to this form, and more particularly to justify by all that she did before the climactic scene the peculiar kind and degree of emotion she clearly wished it to evoke.

But this was not all. For given her basic story as outlined above, there were obviously several ways in which she might have presented this to us. She might have begun with the original meeting of Anne and Wentworth and moved continuously from that point to the end (as she had done with the stories of *Pride and Prejudice* and *Mansfield Park*); and she might, again, have contrived a narrative that allowed us to enter as fully into Wentworth's thoughts and feelings, from the beginning on, as into Anne's. Actually, of course, she did neither of these things. We are introduced to the story only on the eve of Wentworth's return, eight years after the first engagement had been broken, so that we know of the earlier events only through the generalized narrative of chapter 4; and except in the opening exposition and in a relatively few scattered passages later on we are given no more of the events and of the thoughts of the other characters than Anne herself can know through direct observation and listening to conversations or through not always correct inference from what she sees or hears. We thus learn fully what has been going on in Wentworth's mind only after the resolution, in his long self-accusing narrative to Anne.

These were all technical decisions, but of a kind that were bound to have a significant effect on Jane Austen's conception of her subject and its emotional form, and hence bound to impose on her various particular problems of invention and treatment. The plot proper of a novel is not its story but the continuity of morally and emotionally determinate acts, thoughts, feelings we are expected to respond to in sequence as we read. And in *Persuasion*, by virtue of the manner in which Jane Austen chose to shape her novel, this is the succession of things which Anne Elliot undergoes and does with respect to Wentworth from the time of his return to the Kellynch country to her final reunion with him in Bath. The plot, in short, centers in her rather than in her and Wentworth conjointly: in what she does, unknowingly until just before the end, merely by being herself, to draw Wentworth gradually back to her; and in what she undergoes meanwhile in her private thoughts (there being no one to whom she can speak of them) as she moves from the state of 'desolate tranquillity' in which we first see her, through painful agitation (when she and Wentworth meet), more softened pain (when she thinks that he will surely marry Louisa but remembers his growing kindness to herself), then absorption in other interests (when she rejoins her family in Bath), then sudden hope only half believed in (when she hears of Louisa's engagement to Benwick), then full felicity (when she convinces herself at the concert that Wentworth has 'a heart returning to her at least'), then worry (when she discovers his jealousy of Mr. Elliot), to her final state when she enters her house after the reconciliation, 'happier than any one in that house could have conceived'. The plot is bounded by these extremes of feeling in Anne; and its emotional form is the pattern of pained suspense followed by ultimate gratification which her passage from the one extreme to the other creates in our minds. The moving cause of her changing feelings is of course the succession of Wentworth's actions after his return, as she interprets these from time to time. But she is our primary object of concern throughout; what Wentworth does or appears to be doing matters to us only as it matters to her.

There is one more thing to be said about Jane Austen's subject as thus narrowed down; namely, that Anne's breaking of the original engagement and her reasons for doing this are not parts of the plot or subject proper of *Persuasion*: they are necessary antecedent conditions only. The engagement had to be broken if it was to be restored, and it had to be broken for reasons which would naturally lead Wentworth with his 'decided, confident temper' to misconstrue Anne's character and in his young pride to resent what she had done. Hence Lady Russell and the nineteen-year-old Anne's sense of duty toward her. But the heroine of *Persuasion* is no longer a young girl but a mature woman approaching twenty-eight, who is both free to act and disposed to act as her own feelings and judgment dictate, independently of the friend whom she continues to love. Lady Russell is therefore the source of no suspense whatever (for the reader) in the plot: we know from the fourth chapter that Anne will surely marry Wentworth if he proposes again. The only source of suspense and delay is Wentworth himself – nothing else; certainly nothing in the respective social positions of the two or in any other external circumstance. For Wentworth, to be sure, Lady Russell and what happened eight years before *is* important, but only in his thoughts, as conditioning the state of mind in which he acts so coldly toward Anne on his return, a state of mind which pushes him into his entanglement with Louisa and which makes him fear, even toward the end, when he sees Lady Russell at the concert, that Anne may still be under her influence. But except thus subjectively for Wentworth (where it works as a 'retarding weight' in the action), the whole matter of Lady Russell and of Anne's persuadability is not an issue in the plot. There are no signs, for instance, that Anne's unhappiness is in any way colored by regret for what she had done (she would have suffered more, she tells Wentworth at the end, if she had gone against her friend's advice) or by any mental conflict, such as has been attributed to her, between the claims of prudence and the claims of love.

Of the many problems of invention and treatment which Jane Austen had to face as a result of her commitment to this general view of her novel, I will touch here on only a few of the more obvious ones – enough to suggest some of the various reasons of art that appear to have governed, whether consciously or not, her detailed working out of her subject.

Like any other novelist, she faced the elementary task of giving to the happenings of her plot enough of an illusion of probability to justify, for the reader, the degree of serious concern in the action her conception of it called for. It is important to observe that, because of the nature of her plot, this was really a double problem for her. What is essential to the plot of *Persuasion*, as we have seen, is what goes on in the minds of Anne and Wentworth; that is to say, it is primarily a plot of internal action, the only strictly external actions being the final communications to one another of their mutual feelings. But before this can take place, they have to meet after their long separation and they have to see enough of each other, in different situations, to enable them either to confirm their former opinions and feelings, as with Anne, or to form new ones, as with Wentworth. Now this could be effected only through the invention of incidents, and of characters to initiate or take part in them, over and above anything that the plot itself made necessary; and in fact the greater part of what happens from chapter to chapter in *Persuasion* consists of incidents of this kind – let me call them 'occasions' to distinguish them from the psychological 'events' of the plot proper. Unlike the latter, they form no continuous sequence but come about independently of one another as a result of immediate and, so to speak, accidental causes: someone, for example, suggests a walking party on which Anne and Wentworth, being present, go along; or Anne goes shopping with her family in Bath and chances to meet Wentworth; or the two happen to meet, without prearrangement, at a concert. Not any occasion, however, that one might think of will do in any given novel; quite as much as the events, the occasional incidents in *Persuasion* had to be made to seem probable as happenings in that novel; but the problem they presented to Jane Austen was quite distinct from the problem of conferring 'essential' probability, as it might be called, on Anne's persistence in her love for Wentworth and on Wentworth's reversal of opinion and feeling about Anne.

There are occasions of two kinds in *Persuasion*. One kind is illustrated by the examples I have just given – taking a walk, going shopping, attending the weekly concert. It is necessary that they should happen for reasons that go back to the nature of the plot and its representation; but their probability can in a sense be assumed, given the general definition of the social world in which the action takes place. We need no particularized preparation to make us accept the fact that people in the world of *Persuasion* do such things as I have mentioned – and that they also meet socially in the evening for conversation or cards, or pay visits to one another's houses, or sometimes at least, journey to places like Lyme Regis or Bath; and so on. The chief artistic problem with these ordinary occasions, I suppose, is one of variety – not inventing too many of the same kind, so that the reader fails to keep them distinct in his memory – and this was not a problem that gave Jane Austen much trouble in any of her novels.

But there are also occasional incidents in *Persuasion* of a rather more special kind. I am thinking of happenings such as Wentworth's return to Anne's neighborhood while Anne is there, Louisa's fall and concussion at Lyme Regis, and Anne's conversation with Captain Harville in the inn at Bath about constancy in men and women. These, again, are parts not of the novel's action properly speaking but merely of the external enabling circumstances in which it develops: the first is a necessary condition if this action is to begin where and when it does; the second and third help to precipitate changes in its course which would have come about in any case or might have been made to come about by other means. What distinguishes them from the other occasions I have spoken of is that they are all particular rather than customary happenings, which require, therefore, particular preparation if they are to seem to us artistically plausible.

I can consider only the first of the three. It has been objected that what brings about the new meeting of Anne and Wentworth is a series of quite shocking coincidences such as no good artist would indulge in: Sir Walter's extravagance; his acceptance of Wentworth's brother-in-law as his tenant; the sudden invitation to Anne to stay with Mary in Uppercross; Wentworth's choice of this moment to visit the Crofts, and so on. Coincidences, certainly; but are they really shocking? In any case, it is hard to see how Jane Austen could have managed the new meeting in any more tightly probable way. Given Wentworth's state of mind, she could not have made him seek the meeting deliberately; and given Anne's character and situation, she could not have made her invite him. But after all, there is nothing deeply sinful about such improbabilities in art provided our minds are diverted from dwelling on them as we read. And it seems to me that this condition is sufficiently met in the opening chapters of *Persuasion*, partly because of our ignorance until after the Crofts are introduced of what has happened in the past, partly because of the immediate interest we are made to take in Anne's relations with her father and Elizabeth and then with Mary and the Musgroves, and partly because of our hope that the coming of Wentworth may after all have happy results.

The problem of making sufficiently probable the essential internal action of the novel was inseparably bound up, for Jane Austen, with the problem of its emotional effect. What were the general conditions she had to fulfill if the reader was to respond with a maximum of appropriately serious pleasure to the happy reconciliation scenes at the end? And this in a novel of which the heroine was to be not merely the 'central consciousness' but the primary object of interest?

It is clear that we will respond all the more fully in proportion, first of all, to the strength of our attachment to Anne as an individual and hence of our wishes for her happiness, and in proportion, secondly, to the completeness of our conviction that it was natural and right, in terms of both her character and Wentworth's, that she should continue to love and esteem him – in short, that a marriage with him will be a good marriage for her. And it is also clear so far as Wentworth himself is concerned, that we must be convinced that his early misunderstanding of Anne was compatible, again in terms of both her character and his, with the ultimate revival of his love in greater force than ever. To fulfill these conditions was perhaps Jane Austen's major task in the detailed making of *Persuasion*, a task partly of poetic invention and partly of rhetorical representation; and it will be worthwhile to consider by what means, and to what extent, she achieved it.

The problem of achieving it for Anne was not an easy one for two main reasons. In the first place, if Wentworth's mistake about her was not to seem wholly implausible, she had to be a woman whose virtues all lay on the quiet side: a woman with strength of character indeed, but with markedly gentle and

self-effacing manners; sensible and intelligent, but not vivacious – almost the antithesis in temperament of Elizabeth
Bennet in *Pride and Prejudice* and a considerably more difficult
type of character to make vivid and appealing. And this
difficulty was compounded, in the second place, by another and
perhaps greater one. By virtue of her role in the plot, Anne had
to be, until the last few chapters of the novel, a completely
passive heroine and, more than that, for at least the first two-
thirds of the narrative, a heroine in constantly low spirits, with
nothing but cheerless prospects, as it seemed, before her;
pained, without being able to do anything about it, by her
family, still more deeply pained, of course, by Wentworth's real
or apparent indifference. About this last, moreover, she was
unable to speak to anyone, least of all to her only confidante
Lady Russell; she was thus cut off from the possibility of con-
soling sympathy; and she had no such external outlet as the
troubles of Marianne afforded Elinor Dashwood in *Sense and
Sensibility*, when Elinor was in a situation similar to Anne's. A
silent, solitary sufferer: how depict her so that she would not
seem merely dreary and insipid to the reader? It was an exacting problem, which Jane Austen had only recently faced with
Fanny Price in *Mansfield Park* and had solved with somewhat
less than perfect success, I think.

That she succeeded brilliantly with Anne in overcoming both
of these difficulties, there can be little question. We can surely
agree with John Bailey that 'there are few heroines in fiction
whom we love so much, feel for so much, as we love and feel for
Anne Elliot'. The reason lies ultimately of course in the clarity
and human warmth of Jane Austen's conception of her; but I
think we can point to at least some of the devices through
which she made this conception accessible and compelling for
the reader. I shall speak of them under three heads, beginning
with her handling of Anne's unspoken thought in the narrator's
discourse. It is thus that we get all our direct insights into
Anne's feelings until near the end, until, in fact, her conversation with Captain Harville at the White Hart inn. We are left
in no doubt about the painfulness of these throughout the

period of her estrangement from Wentworth; but the pain is, without becoming attenuated for us (which would be an error), kept from seeming excessive or monotonous by the manner of the rendering. The passages in which her suffering appears are all relatively brief; they recur at fairly long intervals only; and they represent her states of mind analytically rather than imitatively, in a fashion that suggests a certain amount of rational control and objectivity on her part, while keeping us aware that she is feeling as well as thinking. One example may serve – the summary of Anne's reflections as she is about to leave Uppercross after the episode at Lyme Regis:

Scenes had passed in Uppercross, which made it precious. It stood the record of many sensations of pain, once severe, but now softened; and of some instances of relenting feeling, some breathings of friendship and reconciliation, which could never be looked for again, and which could never cease to be dear. She left it all behind her; all but the recollection that such things had been.

A second main device for impressing Anne on us as we need to see her is Jane Austen's invention of happenings and conversations, most of them peripheral to the main business of the novel, that define and vivify for us her positive traits of personality and character: her serious principles, her superior standards, her sound judgments of people, her ability to look at herself and others (including Wentworth) objectively, her sense of what needs to be done in an emergency, her readiness to be at the service of her friends, her capacity for happiness, her personal charm, her quiet sense of the ridiculous (notice the frequency with which, even in her days of low spirits and anxiety, she is made to smile). On some of these occasions – as notably that of Louisa's injury at Lyme, when Anne is the only one who knows what to do – Wentworth is also present and draws his own conclusions; but mostly the incidents and conversations I am thinking of are in the novel for the sake of the reader rather than of the action; they are parts not so much of the 'subject' as of the 'treatment', to use Henry James's distinction.

The third principal device in the depiction of Anne involves the juxtaposition of her with other characters. We form very definite and favorable judgments of her, for instance, when we see her in company with Mary or Louisa, or follow her relations with Mrs. Smith, or compare her reactions to the Christmas visit to the Musgroves or to the prospect of spending the winter in Bath or to the character of Mr. Elliot with the reactions of Lady Russell. But there are two sets of characters that the author uses as means of rendering her with particular vividness and conviction: her immediate family and the Crofts. Neither group plays any role in the central action after the very beginning, where they function merely as part of the mechanism that brings Wentworth back to Somersetshire. Yet both are given much space in the narrative, and both are delineated with considerable fullness and particularity and by a variety of means, including much direct dramatization. It would be incorrect to say that all of this is for the sake of building up and vivifying our image of Anne; but much of it clearly has this as its raison d'être. What is being impressed upon us as we read is a radical contrariety in character and personality between two worlds, in both of which we see Anne in the course of the novel.

The contrariety, it should be emphasized, is a moral rather than a social one. It is not at all a question of a decaying feudal class on the one hand and a rising middle class on the other, as several recent critics in love with such abstractions have wanted us to believe. The contrast is between people – Sir Walter, Elizabeth, Mary, Mr. Elliot, Mrs. Clay – who are cold, self-regarding, proud, calculating; and other people – Admiral and Mrs. Croft and the Harvilles – who are conspicuously pleasant, warm-hearted, self-reliant, unpretentious. We see Anne at different points through the novel first with one group and then with the other; and we see her comparing the two in her mind and being more and more strongly drawn to the second, in whom she comes to see 'the frank, the open-hearted, the eager character', which she had prized beyond all others since her first meeting with Wentworth. When she goes with Lady Russell to call on the Crofts in her own home after her family have left it for Bath, she reflects that 'however sorry and ashamed for the necessity of the removal, she could not but in conscience feel that they were gone who deserved not to stay, and that Kellynch-hall had passed into better hands than its owners' '. Later on she sees the Crofts frequently on the streets of Bath, walking arm in arm and greeting their many friends.

Knowing their feelings as she did, it was a most attractive picture of happiness to her. She always watched them as long as she could; delighted to fancy she understood what they might be talking of, as they walked along in happy independence, or equally delighted to see the Admiral's hearty shake of the hand when he encountered an old friend, and observe their eagerness of conversation . . . , Mrs. Croft looking as intelligent and keen as any of the officers around her.

And the one thing that pains her after her marriage with Wentworth is her 'consciousness of having no relations to bestow on him which a man of sense could value . . .; nothing of respectability, of harmony, of good-will to offer in return for all the worth and all the prompt welcome which met her in his brothers and sisters'.

Now the function of all this in the novel, so far as Anne is concerned, is to constitute a kind of rhetorical argument from contraries, and a very effective one, I think, thanks to Jane Austen's success in convincing us artistically that the two sets of people do indeed have the qualities which Anne sees and estimates so contrastingly. We thus come to know more concretely than we otherwise could what kind of person she is, what standards she judges by, what ideal of happiness in life she cherishes, and, indirectly, what it is that has put Wentworth so high in her esteem. We are persuaded, moreover, in proportion as we are made to share her feelings about her family on the one hand and about the Crofts and Harvilles on the other, that it is with the latter rather than the former that she properly belongs. And this perception inevitably enhances our wishes for a reconciliation and our sympathetic pain so long as it seems not to be in prospect; as when, for instance, she first meets the Harvilles at Lyme. '"These would have been all my friends," was her thought; and she had to struggle against a great tendency to lowness.'

These were some of the means – but only some – which Jane Austen brought to bear on the difficult problem of Anne. The problems she faced with Wentworth were of a rather different order, but perhaps equally great, given her evident desire to write a love story that called for something more positive than merely 'sentimental' acquiescence in its dénouement. It was to be a novel the final effect of which, as we have seen, depended on our recognizing that the outcome was not merely happy but good, because of the value we set upon the lovers as moral individuals. Hence she had to convince us of the probability, in terms of Wentworth's intrinsic merits, that he should be loved as deeply and constantly as he is by a mature woman who is both discerning and strict in her judgments of characters. And the more she did to attach us to Anne, the more she had to do to vindicate Anne's attachment to Wentworth. There must at least be no obvious disproportion between the kind and degree of goodness Anne sees in him and the kind and degree of goodness we see in him. It will of course be to his favor, in our eyes, that Anne continues to feel about him as she does, for she is a person not given to illusions about others, whose affections must be grounded on esteem for intelligence and goodness of character; but we must be given some objective evidence that she is right.

The task of providing this was not an easy one on two accounts. The story, for one thing, was to be Anne's; and this committed Jane Austen, as she saw it, to giving us, with very few exceptions at any point in the narrative, only what Anne herself could see, hear, conjecture, and feel. There was no possibility of taking us at all fully within the mind of Wentworth as we are taken within Anne's mind, and of so giving us the kind of sympathetic apprehension of *his* thoughts and feelings, especially after these have turned decisively back to Anne, that

we get of Anne's thoughts and feelings throughout. We have to
wait for this until he can finally speak, in the next to the last
chapter; which is a great limitation on what Jane Austen could
do to recommend him to us. And, for another thing, the plot
of the novel required that he should act, for some time after his
return in the seventh chapter, in a manner painfully contrary
to both Anne's wishes and ours: treating her coolly as a mere
indifferent acquaintance whom he is forced to see with the
Musgroves, looking about in a somewhat cynical spirit for a
suitable girl to marry, accepting uncritically and irresponsibly
the attentions of Henrietta and Louisa, becoming entangled
with the obviously inferior Louisa without being really in love
with her. The plot also required that, after the great reversal
in his judgment and feelings, he should remain away from
Anne for a time and that, after his coming to Bath, he should
still, out of jealousy of Mr. Elliot, hold himself aloof until he
overhears her conversation with Captain Harville. All of which,
again, put difficulties in the way of so depicting him as to
convince us that he really possessed the high qualities of goodness and intelligence which Anne discerned in him.

How far Jane Austen overcame these difficulties, I will leave
it to others to decide; my own judgment is that Wentworth is
one of the best of her heroes: even better than Darcy; much
better than Edward Ferrars or Edmund Bertram; inferior,
perhaps, only to Knightley, who posed a much simpler problem.
But whatever the degree of her success, it is clear that she was
aware of what had to be done, and knew what kinds of devices
of 'treatment' would best help her, in the circumstances of the
novel, to do it. It is notable that, except for one brief statement
in the fourth chapter (where Wentworth is said to have been,
at the time of the first engagement, 'a remarkably fine young
man, with a great deal of intelligence, spirit and brilliancy'),
she avoided falling back on the authority of the narrator,
possibly judging that the testimony of Anne's clear-sighted
devotion would carry greater weight, as it undoubtedly does.
But she obviously felt that something more was needed by way
of proof; and in the novel as she finally constructed it, this

something more took two main forms – the first a kind of proof by sign, the second a kind of proof by analogy.

It would clearly help to set Wentworth right for us, particularly in the earlier part of the narrative, if we could see him acting, on various occasions, in a fashion that signified not his 'angry pride' but his innate kindness and intelligence. We are therefore given a series of little incidents, at Uppercross and Lyme, the main (though not always the only) function of which is to demonstrate dramatically his possession of these qualities. The first incident is the episode of the Musgroves' dead son, the worthless 'poor Dick', who had been a midshipman under Wentworth some years before, and who comes back into his mother's mind when she hears of Wentworth's impending visit to the Crofts at Kellynch-hall; she is more upset by thoughts of him now than she had ever been before, and mentions him to Wentworth at the party the Musgroves give for him shortly after his arrival. The episode (in chapters 6 and 8) has been attacked as a gratuitous intrusion into the novel of Jane Austen's alleged hatred of people like Dick and his mother. Dick's worthlessness and Mrs. Musgrove's sentimentality are perhaps overplayed; but the artistic function of the incident is clear enough: it is a device for emphasizing Wentworth's intelligence and goodness of heart at the moment when we most need to perceive these virtues in him – just before and just after his painful first meeting with Anne. It is made plain that he has no illusions about 'poor Dick' but has nevertheless treated him kindly at sea (before getting rid of him) and is now equally kind to Mrs. Musgrove, though he sees as clearly as Anne does the false pathos of her feelings: the boy and his mother had to be depreciated if the point about Wentworth was to come out. And much the same function of demonstrating the real Wentworth is served by other minor happenings in this early part of the novel: his conversation with the Crofts about women on shipboard (chapter 8); his quick intervention when Anne is beset by the little Musgrove boy (chapter 9); his silent rebuke of Mary's snobbishness about the Hayters (chapter 10); his thoughtfulness in putting Anne into the Admiral's gig (chapter

10); his appreciation of her helpfulness after Louisa's accident (chapter 12). All these are examples of what we would expect from him if he is the kind of man Anne believes he is: we therefore infer that she is probably right.

The inference, of course, is immediate; it carries us at once from a felt impression to an attitude; it is, in short, artistic rather than intellectual demonstration. And the same thing is true of the other line of proof with respect to Wentworth's qualities of mind and character that runs through the whole novel. We are continually seeing him in analogical relations, both negative and positive, to other characters. Part of the function in *Persuasion* of Sir Walter Elliot, Charles Musgrove, and Mr. Elliot is to set off for us, negatively, as they explicitly do for Anne, Wentworth's superiority: we can feel as well as understand why she has rejected Charles, why she can think for only a moment of marrying Mr. Elliot (and this before she really knows about him), why she is depressed when thoughts of her father and of Wentworth come together in her mind. But the positive analogies, I think, are still more effective: how much less assurance we would have of the rightness of Anne's belief in him if the Crofts and the Harvilles had been left out of the novel or rendered less vividly and fully than they are! They are all made to seem to us not only pleasant but admirable people – sensible and intelligent, open, easy, and decided; and they are Wentworth's closest friends. We therefore insensibly argue from them to him, on the basis of what might be called the principle of goodness by association; and the argument is reinforced by the fact that they feel as warmly toward him as he does toward them. The analogy begins to work very early in the narrative. There is a clear likeness between the impression we get of the Crofts in chapter 3, before we have heard of Wentworth, and the narrator's statement about him in chapter 4. We then learn (in chapter 6) that the Crofts are looking forward to his visit and (in chapter 9) that he is coming 'to Kellynch as to a home, to stay as long as he liked, being as thoroughly the object of the Admiral's fraternal kindness as of his wife's'. And then we get (in chapter 12) Captain Harville's story to Anne of how Wentworth had behaved at the time of Fanny Harville's death: 'You may think, Miss Elliot, whether he is dear to us!' Like can only feel thus for like; and hence we inevitably conclude that there must be something in Wentworth (which Anne has seen but which we so far cannot fully see) – some parity of good nature and good sense – that justifies these feelings for him. And so these characters – and more especially the Crofts – become stand-ins, so to speak, for Wentworth during all that long part of the novel in which he is unable to do justice to himself in our eyes, at the same time that they are continuing to attach us to Anne.

SOURCE: originally part of a lecture course on critical method presented by R. S. Crane in the University of Notre Dame in 1957; printed as 'Jane Austen: *Persuasion*' in his *The Idea of the Humanities and Other Essays, Critical and Historical* (1967) pp. 283–302.

D. W. Harding

THE DEXTERITY OF A PRACTISED WRITER (1965)

Chawton Cottage is one of the few places of literary pilgrimage that have relevance to an appreciation of the writer who lived there. At some little distance from the great house of the rich brother who provided it, respectable but rather cramped, with the small living room in which Jane Austen wrote – a room shared by her sister Cassandra and her ailing mother and used besides for receiving callers – the house speaks of the close pressure of a social milieu, and heightens our wonder at the work that emerged from it. The older idea that her novels simply offered amusing entertainment for people like those she lived amongst (and their successors down to our own time) has given way to the recognition in her work of a much stronger dislike of the society in which she seemed comfortably embedded, a dislike often implicit, often conveyed in passing and easily ignored, occasionally intense and bitter. In 1940 I published an essay called 'Regulated Hatred: an aspect of Jane Austen'; in 1964 a psychologist colleague who had never heard of that essay mentioned that she had recently tried in vain to recover the pleasure she took in the novels as a girl. 'They used to seem so light and amusing, but they're not like that at all. You know – she *hated* people.' Of course this is too extreme. The urbanity, the charm, the wit and lightness of touch, the good humour, are there as they always were, but the other aspect which readers nowadays notice means that for full enjoyment we have to appreciate a more complex flavour.

The situation of being a poor relation was one that Jane Austen could share with her sister and their widowed mother. The situation of being the most brilliant, the most sensitive and penetrating member of her family, while she filled the roles of affectionate spinster aunt and of dutiful daughter to a hypochondriac mother, was a situation she could share with no one. It is not surprising, therefore, that variants of the Cinderella story, as well as the psychologically allied story of the foundling princess, should be prominent among the basic themes of her novels.

Anne Elliot, the heroine of *Persuasion*, her last novel, is the most mature and profound of Cinderellas. Earlier, in *Mansfield Park*, she had tried an out-and-out foundling princess and Cinderella in Fanny Price – all moral perfection, thoroughly oppressed, rather ailing, priggish, but finally vindicated and rewarded with the hero – and few people can stomach her. The theme is inevitably difficult to handle. For one thing the fantasy of being mysteriously superior to one's parentage is rather common ('I refused to believe', remarks T. S. Eliot's Lady Elizabeth, 'that my father could have been an ordinary earl! And I couldn't believe that my mother *was* my mother') and commonly unjustified. And the crushed dejection (masking resentment) of the self-cast Cinderellas of real life always provokes a sneaking sympathy for the ugly sisters. The novelist's difficulty with this theme is to secure a lively enough interest in the heroine during the early stages, when the reality of her dejection has to be enforced, and to retain interest and sympathy during the necessarily long period before the *bouleversement*. Fairy tale and pantomime can resort to caricaturing the heroine's oppressors. The serious novelist whose heroine must be unappreciated and neglected by a credible social world faces a harder problem.

It is solved in *Persuasion* partly by the dexterity of a practised writer, and partly through more mature understanding of the basic situation and the forms it may take. The vanity and shallow self-importance of Sir Walter Elliot and his eldest daughter, their heartless worldliness, accompanied by ill-judgement even in worldly things, are handled scathingly but with only a little caricature. The situation used to exemplify the clash between their values and Anne's – the problem of extravagance, debt and retrenchment – is more convincing to modern minds than the episode of the private theatricals in

Mansfield Park. And the scales that were weighted too heavily against Fanny are here kept nearer level by the presence of Lady Russell, the influential friend, who not only sees Anne's worth (as Edmund did Fanny's) but is in many ways allied with her against the family and serves by her comments to indicate that people of good sense think as Anne does. Ill-health too is dealt with differently. Fanny's debility was presented almost as morally superior to the rude health of her companions. In *Persuasion*, which Jane Austen wrote when she was dying of a malady that gradually sapped her strength (resting on an arrangement of three chairs while her mother monopolized the sofa in the living room), it is the heroine's patience that has to be mustered to cope with the complaining hypochondria of her younger sister. Poor health is now as little a recommendation as it was in Miss De Bourgh in *Pride and Prejudice*. ('She looks sickly and cross – Yes, she will do for him him very well.')

Of even greater importance than these changes of treatment is a more mature interpretation of the theme, one no longer presenting the heroine as a passive sufferer of entirely un-merited wrongs. Anne has brought her chief misfortune on herself through a mistaken decision – to break her engagement with Wentworth – to which she was persuaded by Lady Russell. Her lapse from her own standard, in letting worldly prudence outweigh love and true esteem for personal qualities, is the error which has also to be excused in her mother, who in marrying Sir Walter was too much influenced by 'his good looks and his rank'. We start then with a much more mature Cinderella, more seriously tragic herself in having thrown away her own happiness, more complex in her relation to the loved mother, who not only made the same sort of mistake herself but now, brought back to life in Lady Russell, shares the heroine's responsibility for her disaster. Lady Russell is explicitly pre-sented as the equivalent of a greatly loved mother, more nearly ideal than any other living mother that Jane Austen gives a heroine. In fairy tales the baffling intermingling of the hateful and lovable attributes of all mothers is simplified into a dichotomy between the ideal mother – entirely lovable, dead and beyond the test of mature observation – and the stepmother, living, entirely detestable and doing her worst for the child. In the maturity of *Persuasion* Jane Austen puts her heroine into relation with a lovable but not perfect mother who, in doing her mistaken best for the girl, has caused what seems an irremediable misfortune.

It is Wentworth's hurt feelings and his belief that Anne was over-yielding in giving him up that create the barrier between them when he comes back prosperous, seeking a wife and attracted by the amiable, commonplace Musgrove girls. It is again Lady Russell, perceptive of Anne's worth though not of his, who provides a choric comment establishing the values. When Anne tells her about the apparent attachment between him and Louisa,

Lady Russell had only to listen composedly, and wish them happy; but internally her heart revelled in angry pleasure, in pleased contempt, that the man who at twenty-three had seemed to understand somewhat of the value of an Anne Elliot, should, eight years afterwards, be charmed by a Louisa Musgrove.

In fact, by the time this comment is made, the emotional barriers Wentworth had erected against Anne have been broken down in a graded sequence of incidents, mingling observation and action on his part, which Jane Austen manages with supremely delicate skill: at first, his comment on Anne's altered looks, 'his cold politeness, his ceremonious grace'; then his inquiry of the others whether she never danced (while she is playing for them to dance); later, his quite unceremoniously kind and understanding act in relieving her of the troublesome child, 'his degree of feeling and curiosity about her' when he is told of her having refused a more recent proposal of marriage, his realizing her tiredness and insisting on her going home in Admiral Croft's chaise ('a remainder of former sentiment,' Anne thinks, 'an impulse of pure, though unacknowledged friendship'); finally, his noticing the glance of admiration she receives from Mr Walter Elliot at Lyme, followed quickly by

the climax of the accident on the Cobb and the instant partner-
ship between him and Anne as the competent and responsible
people keeping their heads in a horrifying situation. From this
point onward the tables are turned; Captain Wentworth, in
the full return of his early love, has to face the anxieties of his
apparent commitment to Louisa and his jealousy at Mr Walter
Elliot's wooing of Anne. Although suspense and strong emotion
are maintained to the last pages, the visit to Lyme is the turning
point at which the earlier sadness – wasted opportunity, regret,
misunderstanding – has finally been modulated with infinite
skill into comedy.

It remains serious comedy. Captain Wentworth's release
from Louisa, it is true, has the arbitrariness of lighter comedy;
it recalls Edward Ferrars's release in *Sense and Sensibility*. The
serious problem lay in managing the psychological terms on
which the lovers came together again. In the foreshortened
ending of *Mansfield Park*, Fanny waits passively for Edmund to
recognize her full value and transfer his wounded affections to
her. Anne, who actively caused the breach with Wentworth,
must take more than a passive part in its healing if she is to
remain consistently more responsible than the simpler Cinderella. It is in this light that the cancelled chapter must be seen.
J. E. Austen-Leigh (*Memoir*, chapter 2) describes her dissatis-
faction with it; she had come with failing strength to the end of
the novel and had little resilience left for rewriting; yet she felt
that the chapter in which she brought the lovers together was
so unsatisfactory that the effort must be made. What was
wrong with it?

It is in the style of lighter comedy. In a rather artificially
contrived incident Admiral Croft compels Captain Wentworth
to give Anne a message which assumes that she is to marry
Mr Elliot. This obliges her to tell Wentworth that she is not
intending to marry Mr Elliot, and Wentworth does the rest.
Thus only an external event forces her to accept even the small
part she does play in clearing up the misunderstanding. She is
nearly as passive as Fanny. In the revised chapters (22 and 23)
her role is much more active. The problem for Jane Austen

was how to give her an active part in promoting the reconciliation without the impossible breach of decorum involved in
telling him of her love, in effect proposing to him. The same
problem had been met in *Pride and Prejudice* by Elizabeth's
refusal to assure Lady Catherine that she would *not* refuse Mr
Darcy. In the revised chapters of *Persuasion* the solution lies in
Anne's making an almost public avowal, easily overheard in the
crowded room, of her ideals of unchanging love and her belief
that women have the unenviable privilege 'of loving longest,
when existence or when hope is gone'. She could not have
spoken like this if she had accepted Mr Elliot, and it tells
Captain Wentworth enough. Like Elizabeth Bennet, she had
not deliberately spoken to convey a message to him, but by
standing up for her standards and openly avowing them she
had played her active part in bringing her lover back again.
The chapter goes on to emphasize still more the active responsibility she feels she must take: Wentworth having smuggled
his ardent letter to her and gone, she has to make absolutely
certain of giving him the word of encouragement he asks for.
Her struggles to ensure this, in face of her friends' kind mis-
understandings and ill-timed helpfulness, provide genial
comedy, but none the less form part of the serious theme that
distinguishes the revision from the cancelled chapter.

There is yet more of significance in the revision of the cancelled chapter, of significance for the central problem announced by the title of the novel – the rights and wrongs of
Lady Russell's persuasion and of Anne's yielding. For all its
general formulation the problem is embodied in the particular
form created by the conflict between elderly prudence and the
romantic love of two young people. The persuasion, or dis-
suasion, is exerted by an older person, disinterestedly concerned
for the younger – but not in love; and the younger has to make
up her mind. The novel was begun in 1815, and 150 years later
the problem, in spite of an easier economic situation, is not
unknown to girls of nineteen and their mothers.

In Jane Austen's time and in her social class, the ideal of
marriage for personal love rather than for an establishment or a

family alliance was in a transitional stage. The theme occurs in several of her novels, most centrally perhaps in *Mansfield Park* and *Persuasion*, and her attitude is consistent: marriage without love is wrong. In 1802 she herself suffered great agitation through accepting a proposal of marriage from a well-to-do man and then the next day withdrawing her acceptance. In *Mansfield Park* she expressed herself ironically on out-and-out worldliness in Mary's description of the Frasers:

'I look upon the Frasers to be about as unhappy as most other married people. And yet it was a most desirable match for Janet at the time. We were all delighted. She could not do otherwise than accept him, for he was rich, and she had nothing; but he turns out ill-tempered and *exigeant*; and wants a young woman, a beautiful young woman of five-and-twenty, to be as steady as himself . . . Poor Janet has been sadly taken in; and yet there was nothing improper on her side; she did not run into the match inconsiderately, there was no want of foresight. She took three days to consider of his proposals; and during those three days asked the advice of every body connected with her, whose opinion was worth having; and especially applied to my late dear aunt, whose knowledge of the world made her judgment very generally and deservedly looked up to by all the younger people of her acquaintance; and she was decidedly in favour of Mr Fraser. This seems as if nothing were a security for matrimonial comfort!'

But at the other extreme what of an engagement where there is love but poverty? She is no less clearsighted: 'Wait for his having a living!' exclaims Mrs Jennings in *Sense and Sensibility*,

'– aye, we all know how *that* will end; – they will wait a twelve-month, and finding no good comes of it, will set down upon a curacy of fifty pounds a year, with the interest of his two thousand pounds, and what little matter Mr Steele and Mr Pratt can give her. – Then they will have a child every year! and Lord help 'em! how poor they will be! – I must see what I can give them towards furnishing their house . . .'

These are extremes. In *Persuasion*, on the other hand, the problem is posed without exaggeration or caricature and therefore in its most intractable form:

'Anne Elliot,' thinks Lady Russell, 'with all her claims of birth, beauty, and mind, to throw herself away at nineteen; involve herself at nineteen in an engagement with a young man, who had nothing but himself to recommend him, and no hopes of attaining affluence, but in the chances of a most uncertain profession, and no connexions to secure even his farther rise in that profession; would be, indeed, a throwing away, which she grieved to think of! Anne Elliot, so young; known to so few, to be snatched off by a stranger without alliance or fortune,; or rather sunk by him into a state of most wearing, anxious, youth-killing dependance! It must not be, if by any fair interference of friendship, any representations from one who had almost a mother's love, and mother's right, it would be prevented.'

Some of the most interesting material in the revised chapters presents Jane Austen's attempt at an explicit answer to that problem, an enlargement and re-emphasis of what she had presented as Anne's opinion at the opening of the story. Here, however, in spite of some repetition (the extent of which she may possibly not have realized in this late revision), the answer is not without ambiguity. Once again, Anne is clear that she was right in yielding; it was a filial duty, and on that point there seems at first, as before, no question. Yet here she goes on immediately, in answer to Wentworth's question, to affirm that she would have renewed the engagement the following year if he had asked her when he returned to England 'with a few thousand pounds, and was posted into the Laconia'. His promotion to Captain, one profitable cruise in an old, worn-out sloop, and now a better posting, though it offered some promise would have been a weak answer to Lady Russell's full objections; and Jane Austen seems to imply that even a year's reflection and regret would have lessened the filial submissiveness of a girl like Anne. About Lady Russell's justification in the advice she gave there is a more decisive answer than that offered earlier. Then Anne did not blame her, though she felt now that she would never have given such advice herself. In the revised chapters, the adverse judgement is strengthened: 'I am not saying she did not err in her advice. It was, perhaps, one of those cases in which advice is good or bad only as the event decides; and for myself, I certainly never should, in any circumstance of tolerable similarity, give such advice.' Such an explicit and extended recurrence to the theme in her revised chapters brings out its importance to her conception of the novel.

This is not a problem that stands isolated, either in *Persuasion* or in her work as a whole; it is one outcome of the intense, highly organized pressures of a close-knit society. The functioning of individuals while they are hemmed in by others, all mutually controlled by the system of social forces, was one of her general preoccupations. The small country neighbourhood, with little travel, and no escape from the family by going to work in a large organization, precluded the individual from having the degree of anonymity we take for granted. He was, as Henry Tilney remarks in *Northanger Abbey*, 'surrounded by a neighbourhood of voluntary spies'. A characteristic feature, of which Jane Austen makes very frequent use, was the large party in the same drawing room, with the possibility of private conversations in an undertone, sometimes overheard, sometimes concealed by the conversation of others or the sound of the piano. Captain Wentworth and Anne manage to have their discussion of their broken engagement, and Lady Russell's part in it, during one of their short contacts at an evening party, 'each apparently occupied in admiring a fine display of greenhouse plants'. And Captain Wentworth listens contemptuously to Mary's remark after her snobbish sister has at last included him in her invitations: 'Only think of Elizabeth's including everybody!' whispered Mary very audibly. 'I do not wonder Captain Wentworth is delighted! You see he cannot put the card out of his hand.'

Whether so much semi-privacy and overhearing were really part of the drawing-room society of the period, they provide a constantly recurring device in Jane Austen's novels, almost as usual as the soliloquy on which the theatre of the period still relied. She was presumably exaggerating something that really went on. And her exploitation of it is not only a technical device for narrative and comment but a means of conveying her characteristic sense of the compressed social milieu, the criss-cross of unspoken awareness that marks a group of people in close contact and makes privacy, especially within the family, a precarious luxury.

Although these are the conditions of all that happens, Jane Austen's focus of interest is the survival and development of the private individual within them. The pressure of social contact may be escaped for brief intervals, as for instance when the heroine goes to her own room for 'reflection' – the half hour or so that allows her, after an agitating experience, to analyse her state of mind and bring order into her feelings before returning to the drawing room and playing her usual role. It is a way of life in which the more sensitive person can experience great isolation. Actual loneliness has its place in *Mansfield Park* and *Persuasion*, highlighted by the episode in each when, during the course of a walk, the heroine is left sitting alone while the others wander off. She remains involved with them (as spectator or overhearer) but left out of account by them, a figure of the Cinderella who turns novelist. Anne's detachment is presented again, within the framework of comedy, when she has to be confidante to both Mary and the Musgroves, sympathizing tactfully with the complaints of each about the others' household.

In such a society there are degrees of isolation. A high degree is created by the civil falsehood and polite evasion ('Emma denied none of it aloud and agreed to none of it in private') which break true social contact and leave the speaker in a position of tacit superiority but cut off from his hearers. So when Mary urges her sister to write home about the chance meeting with Mr Elliot, 'Anne avoided a direct reply, but it was just the circumstance which she considered as not merely unnecessary to be communicated, but as what ought to be suppressed'. And she deals similarly with the limitations of Admiral Croft, for whom she has real respect: 'Anne did not receive the perfect conviction which the Admiral meant to convey, but it would have been useless to press the enquiry farther. She, therefore satisfied herself with commonplace remarks, or quiet attention, and the Admiral had it all his own way.'

A second degree of social detachment, less complete, occurs when the heroine recognizes an obligation to try to communicate but, met by stupidity or stubbornness, feels exempt from farther effort and lets things take their course, as Anne does when she has failed to open Elizabeth's eyes to Mrs Clay's design to marry their father. When every man is surrounded by a neighbourhood of voluntary spies what should be told and what suppressed becomes a matter of careful thought; a mistake in that calculation – about Wickham's character – is a pivotal point of *Pride and Prejudice*, and in *Persuasion* a similar problem about Mr Elliot confronts Mrs Smith.

A third form of insulation in this close-pressing society, one implying less of superior detachment, is silently accepted reticence between equals. It creates the tension of confidence known to be withheld, but it remains social, since neither person breaks off the relation by resorting to deception or viewing the other clinically. In the much earlier *Sense and Sensibility* the withheld confidence, the 'reserve', although respected, is a source of some distress and mutual reproach for the sisters. In *Persuasion*, graver and much less effusive, there has been complete silence for several years between Anne and Lady Russell on the subject of the broken engagement: 'They knew not each other's opinion, either its constancy or its change, on the one leading point of Anne's conduct, for the subject was never alluded to.' The result is that Anne Elliot is presented as self-contained, controlled and with hidden power, in spite of her regrets and her real tenderness. She has the quiet maturity of a sensitive individual who is loyal to her own values without colliding needlessly and unprofitably with the social group she belongs to, or with people, like Lady Russell, to whom, in spite of seeing their limitations, she is deeply attached.

In so compact a civilized society, romantic love between individuals who freely choose each other for qualities not readily identified and categorized by those around them is a disruption. It seems to offer escape from that dependence on social support that discourages people from resisting the expectations of their immediate group. As Donne saw, the union of the two souls in love

> Defects of loneliness controules.

Lovers assuage their loneliness without paying the price of full conformity. Whether the ideals of romantic love are expressed in an attachment, like Anne's for Wentworth, or in a refusal to marry for anything other than attachment, like her resistance to the match with Mr Elliot, they simultaneously express and support the individual's partial nonconformity, his selection from the values ruling around him. This aspect of romantic love relates it closely to Jane Austen's concern with the survival of the sensitive and penetrating individual in a society of conforming mediocrity.

Although the nucleus of the fable – Cinderella, the foundling princess – has its universal significance, there would be no novel unless it were embodied in a particular time and place, something realized more substantially than the sketchy never-never land of fairy tale and once-upon-a-time. In Jane Austen's society – as indeed in fairy tale – the girl who made an individual romantic choice might well have to defy the standards of class and social position. And in *Persuasion* the story is embedded in a study of snobbery, snobbery displayed amidst the sharply realized detail, social and physical, of life in country houses and Bath at the end of the Napoleonic wars. Jane Austen created the perfect starting point for her satire by giving Sir Walter Elliot a baronetcy, thus putting the family in a twilit region between the nobility and the gentry – still no more than gentry but distinguished among them by the hereditary title. His scorn for those beneath him and his anxious toadying to 'our cousins, the Dalrymples' who are of the nobility (Irish), provide a good deal of the astringent comedy of the book. By making him, moreover, financially embarrassed, she contrasts

his pretensions, based on family and superficial elegance, with
the solid security of the Musgroves, undistinguished landowners
who look after their estates effectively, and of the families
rising into social consequence on naval prize money. The
querulous Mary, married into the Musgroves, carries on her
struggle for precedence and proper attentions as a baronet's
youngest daughter, and laments the impending disgrace of
being connected, through her sister-in-law's marriage, with a
family who actually farm. And Elizabeth, too, the eldest sister,
has to come to terms with social dilution when she finally
gives Captain Wentworth an invitation, realizing that in the
conditions of Bath society a man of such distinguished bearing,
whatever his forebears, will be an asset at her party. The
standards that Anne has to resist are brought as close to her as
possible by being shared in some degree even by Lady Russell,
who 'had a value for rank and consequence, which blinded her
a little to the faults of those who possessed them'.

Embodied and given life in the social realities of her own
period, Jane Austen's satire still has currency in ours. The sense
of the past which we need in reading it has two aspects, and
the more familiar – the ability to enter into her social world and
its outlook – counts for less than the other. The other is the
ability to notice the people and the institutions of our own time
on which her eye would have rested and her judgement been
passed, and this means recognizing contemporary equivalents
rather than seeking identities. We shall not look to Bath, then
the last word in the contemporary, for parallels to Elizabeth
Elliot's displaying, as part of her own distinction, the latest in
domestic architecture and fashionable décor for giving parties.
And if we look around us for Sir Walter Elliot, 'prepared', on
his departure from Kellynch Hall, 'with condescending bows
for all the afflicted tenantry and cottagers who might have had
a hint to shew themselves', we may not find him now in many
landed baronets. But we may be reminded of the story Lord
Woolton tells of Mr Gordon Selfridge, whose room at the store
was always filled with flowers on his birthday, contributed, as
he said, by 'those dear little girls' – meaning the sales assistants

and clerks: 'When, one day, I remarked on his good fortune, he asked whether my staff in Lewis's paid such testimony to me, and when I replied, "Never even a daisy", this naive character replied, "You ought to give them a hint".' (Lord Woolton, *Memoirs*, London, 1959.)

At some points Sir Walter Elliot is touched with caricature. His considered twofold objection to the navy, for instance, as an occupation that may be 'the means of bringing persons of obscure birth into undue distinction' and one that also ruins the appearance has the exaggeration that places him with such figures as Mr Collins and Lady Catherine De Bourgh. But there is none of the mercy of caricature in the measured severity of the final summing up:

Captain Wentworth, with five-and-twenty thousand pounds, and as high in his profession as merit and activity could place him, was no longer nobody. He was now esteemed quite worthy to address the daughter of a foolish, spendthrift baronet, who had not had principle or sense enough to maintain himself in the situation in which Providence had placed him . . .

And there is more than caricature in Elizabeth who 'felt her approach to the years of danger, and would have rejoiced to be certain of being properly solicited by baronet-blood within the next twelve-month or two'. Then she would be able to take up her father's favourite book, the Baronetage, 'with as much enjoyment as in her early youth; but now she liked it not. Always to be presented with the date of her own birth, and see no marriage follow but that of a youngest sister, made the book an evil; and more than once, when her father had left it open on the table near her, had she closed it with averted eyes, and pushed it away.' Although Elizabeth's conceit makes her ridiculous, in her relations with Mr Elliot and Mrs Clay for instance, she is not a figure of simple comedy. She is presented seriously, as a disappointed but cold-hearted and unlikeable young woman. Like Sir Walter, she is handled by Jane Austen with straightforward moral severity. When she faces the problem of entertaining the Musgroves on their unexpected visit to Bath:

Elizabeth was, for a short time, suffering a good deal. She felt that Mrs Musgrove and all her party ought to be asked to dine with them, but she could not bear to have the difference of style, the reduction of servants, which a dinner must betray, witnessed by those who had been always so inferior to the Elliots of Kellynch. It was a struggle between propriety and vanity; but vanity got the better, and then Elizabeth was happy again.

But the explicit moral comment is rare. Mainly the appraisal is implicit in the detail of setting and event: Elizabeth, once mistress of Kellynch Hall, exulting in the two drawing-rooms in Camden Place; the anxious renewal of acquaintance with the Dalrymples after the lapse occasioned by the accidental omission of a letter of condolence; the bustle and talking in Molland's, 'which must make all the little crowd in the shop understand that Lady Dalrymple was calling to convey Miss Elliot'.

A fable of profound human significance, embodied in people, time, place, and social setting acutely observed, vividly conveyed, justly appraised – but still *Persuasion* would not be the novel it is without that management of tone which was an essential part of Jane Austen's superb equipment, an integral characteristic of her writing at its best. The triumph in *Persuasion* is the harmonizing of several attitudes, which could have been distinct and even discordant, into a complex whole. Foremost among them is Anne's grave tone of regret in her reconsideration of the problems of personal relation that centred round her yielding to Lady Russell; and later her gradual emergence from resignation to hope. With this goes the regretful clearsightedness with which she condemns the vanity of her family, an attitude consistent both with her filial obligations and with the author's ruthless contempt for Sir Walter and his other children. Contempt is not an attitude Jane Austen shrank from; she gives it to Captain Wentworth, for instance, when he is the object of patronizing recognition by Anne's sisters. But in this novel it has to remain compatible with the good-humoured comedy found in the treatment of Admiral Croft, where genuine respect for his kindness and robust good sense is blended with amusement at his simplifications and lack of subtlety in matters of love and marriage. Recovering from his surprise at Captain Wentworth's not going to marry Louisa Musgrove, he laments that the Captain 'must begin all over again with somebody else. I think we must get him to Bath. . . . Here are pretty girls enough, I am sure. It would be of no use to go to Uppercross again, for that other Miss Musgrove, I find, is bespoke by her cousin, the young parson.' The tone is of good-humoured comedy. The robust simplifications are just exaggerated enough for every reader to be laughing a little at the Admiral, and yet there is an after-taste, for on reflection one notices that they exactly represent the level of personal and romantic discrimination that Jane Austen has shown to be characteristic of the Musgroves.

Appreciative as she is of their warmhearted family feeling, and sparing them the severity with which she treats the Elliots, she remains a detached observer of the limitations of such people as she represents in the Musgroves. One outcome of her detachment is the astringent handling of Mrs Musgrove's tearful laments about her dead son, Richard, a passage that has been criticized by people for whom Jane Austen's tough rationality in face of commonplace sentimentalism has been too much. Yet this passage is one of fine discrimination as well as toughness. The 'large fat sighings' of Mrs Musgrove are presented as ridiculous because her upsurge of lamentation is for 'a thick-headed, unfeeling, unprofitable Dick Musgrove' who 'had been very little cared for at any time by his family, though quite as much as he deserved; seldom heard of, and scarcely at all regretted, when the intelligence of his death abroad had worked its way to Uppercross, two years before'. The mother's lamentation now is sentimentalism. Even so, Captain Wentworth, who had once had the troublesome boy under his command, quickly controlled his scorn and entered into conversation with Mrs Musgrove 'in a low voice, about her son, doing it with so much sympathy and natural grace, as shewed the kindest consideration for all that was real and unabsurd in the parent's feelings'. The recognition that Captain Wentworth, more intelligent, more sensitive, and more mature than Mrs Musgrove, has the obligation of meeting her on whatever ground they genuinely share is balanced by the equally clear recognition that her emotion, though sincere, is based on delusions she has elaborated in a couple of days for the sake of having the emotion. The discriminations Jane Austen invites us to make allow her to claim our appreciation of the Musgroves' warm friendliness and delighted responsiveness to Captain Wentworth and at the same time to insist on our recognizing how commonplace and limited they are.

The mingling of tones is seen at its boldest in the climax, the accident on the Cobb, where elements of comedy are deliberately introduced into what is primarily a scene of shock and anxiety and family disaster. Some mis-readers have managed to ridicule the idea that a young woman could be seriously injured by slipping off a few steps, but in fact by impulsively jumping half a second before the reluctant Wentworth is ready to catch her Louisa launches herself on to her head on the stone quay and receives a severe concussion. There is nothing improbable about the seriousness of the accident or the consternation and terror of her friends. But although this gives the main note of the scene, the established character of her companions is used to bring in the overtones of comedy: Mary of course is hysterical and immobilizes her unfortunate husband, Henrietta faints and has to be supported by Anne and Captain Benwick, and Wentworth, desperate, is left with the real victim in his arms: '"Is there no one to help me?" were the first words which burst from Captain Wentworth, in a tone of despair, and as if all his own strength were gone.' The words are tragic but the tableau is comic, and after serious action has been taken and Benwick gone for a surgeon, the collapse of Mary and Henrietta is again used as a comic off-set to the real disaster:

As to the wretched party left behind, it could scarcely be said which of the three, who were completely rational, was suffering most, Captain Wentworth, Anne, or Charles, who, really a very affectionate brother, hung over Louisa with sobs of grief, and could only turn his eyes from one sister, to see the other in a state as insensible, or to witness the hysterical agitations of his wife, calling on him for help which he could not give.

And then, when the isolated group of friends has to be brought back into contact with the wider world, Jane Austen allows herself for a moment her characteristic note of banter: 'By this time the report of the accident had spread among the workmen and boatmen about the Cobb, and many were collected near them, to be useful if wanted, at any rate, to enjoy the sight of a dead young lady, nay, two dead young ladies, for it proved twice as fine as the first report.'

After this the high stress of the accident is eased off into the warmhearted care and generosity of the Harvilles, with the note of comedy sounding easily in their eager plans for somehow or other accommodating two or three more of the party in their tiny house.

For all its gravity and tenderness, *Persuasion* works within the convention of high comedy, like *Emma* and *Pride and Prejudice*. The inter-penetration of the various tones – severe satire, good-humoured comedy, appreciation of domestic affection, moral seriousness about personal relations and especially about love – is not merely a high development of skill in writing but reflects unity of conception and coherence of underlying values.

How far and in what ways *Persuasion* falls short of the novel Jane Austen would have written if she had been in full health can only be guessed at. It is not an unfinished novel, but by her standards it is short and there are hints towards the end of possible elaborations that were never carried out. It is about as long as the early *Northanger Abbey*, only about two thirds the length of *Sense and Sensibility* or *Pride and Prejudice*, and little more than half as long as *Mansfield Park* or *Emma*, the two novels which immediately preceded it.

The cancelled chapter indicates one way in which there might have been extensions. Had it stood, the novel would still have been complete, the outline unbroken, the story told, the characters and their pattern of interaction established. The revision brought not only the improvements that have already been discussed but substantial enlargement too, by the additional episode of the Musgroves' visit to Bath and the patterns of personal interchange which that allowed her to create. The Elliot snobbery, with Elizabeth's modified attitude to Captain Wentworth, is more fully exhibited, the good-natured confusion of a Musgrove gathering exemplified again, and Charles Musgrove's relations with his Elliot wife further illustrated. These enlargements repair no omission and correct no error of balance but, besides being entertaining in themselves, they enrich and strengthen the structure which has in essentials already been built. The same vitality and inventiveness, controlled within the main pattern, might presumably have amplified much of the latter part of the novel.

Possibly the revelation of Mr Elliot's character and past history is a problem that Jane Austen, given her earlier resources of physical energy, might have handled more enterprisingly (though Shakespeare found no better solution in *The Tempest*). But this is only one way in which the parts of the novel centring on Mr Elliot give an impression of something contemplated but not fully worked out. Though he is more villainous (a blacker villain than any other of Jane Austen's), his role is similar to Henry Crawford's in *Mansfield Park*: his charm is resisted by the morally perceptive Cinderella in spite of the attempted persuasion of her guardian figure, and the vanity of one of the Ugly Sisters allows him to lead her up the garden path. The two themes are given a much smaller part in this novel than in the earlier, and in particular Anne is not exposed to any persistent effort of persuasion from Lady Russell, who bides her time partly from caution and partly because Mr Elliot is still in mourning for his first wife. It may be that no more serious attempt at persuasion and no call for farther resistance by Anne would have formed part of a longer version, though it might well have done. What is much clearer, however, is that the tale of Mr Elliot's machinations is handled very cursorily and was never worked out in detail.

His main object was to prevent Sir Walter's remarriage and obviate the consequent threat to his own succession to the title. At the same time his attraction to Anne is shown as genuine, something quite other than the pretence with which he pays his attentions to her elder sister in order to gain admission to the household and keep an eye on the designing Mrs Clay. There are elements of conflict here. For although in her winding-up of the loose threads Jane Austen suggests that as a son-in-law he would have had his best chance of keeping Sir Walter single, his marrying Anne would have so angered the deceived Elizabeth who controlled the household that his admission would have been on sufferance and his antagonism to Mrs Clay would have confirmed Elizabeth in keeping her there. In any case it is never clear what he could do to prevent Sir Walter's marrying her, beyond encouraging the snobbery that might oppose a 'degrading' connexion. Her chances are as prosperous as ever up to the last, and her throwing them up in order to become Mr Elliot's mistress (with the very slender chance of eventual marriage) is left exceedingly improbable.

That Jane Austen realized how poorly she had prepared for this last disentanglement is evident from two features of her revision of the cancelled chapter. One is the overseen meeting of Mrs Clay and Mr Elliot when he is supposed to be away from Bath, the first clear indication of anything between them (though a very subtle hint has been dropped earlier when Lady Dalrymple takes Miss Elliot home from the shop in Milsom-street). The second relevant feature of the revision is a little more puzzling – the repeated and carefully emphasized postponements of Anne's revelation to Lady Russell of Mr Elliot's deplorable character. She meant to tell her at once – and had she in fact done so it would have made no difference at all to the novel as it now stands. And yet the importance of the disclosure is stressed, and so is the fact of its being twice delayed, first by the Musgroves' arrival ('but Anne convinced herself that a day's delay of the intended communication could be of no consequence'), and then by her preoccupation with Captain Wentworth ('it became a matter of course the next morning, still to defer her explanatory visit . . . and Mr Elliot's character, like the Sultaness Scheherazade's head, must live another day'). This has all the air of preparing us for some development in the story of Mr Elliot's scheming for which the continued ignorance of Lady Russell as well as of Sir Walter and Elizabeth was essential. Possibly she was feeling her way towards the sort of sub-plot she had used in *Emma*, the immediately preceding novel, where she had presented full-blown the modern detective story technique of giving the reader all the clues and still misleading him. Whatever she had in mind would have meant elaborating much more carefully Mr Elliot's part in the plot, and that evidently involved a greater enlargement or revision of the novel than she could feel was worth undertaking, especially as earlier chapters would also need revision if the extended sub-plot were to be fully integrated with the main theme.

We are left with a slight puzzle, of the fascinating kind that creative work not quite completed will always offer. Not that *Persuasion* is an unfinished novel, as Henry James's *The Sense of the Past* is, for instance, or *The Last Tycoon* of Scott Fitzgerald. After all, she had told the story that essentially interested her and told it with all the richness of social setting and personal relation that make it a self-sustaining complex structure. She rightly judged that in *Persuasion* she had, as she wrote to her favourite niece four months before she died, 'a something ready for Publication'.

SOURCE: Introduction to Penguin edition of *Persuasion* (1965) pp. 7–26.

Malcolm Bradbury

'PERSUASION AGAIN' (1968)

Persuasion may indeed be, as Professor Daiches has said, 'the novel which in the end the experienced reader of Jane Austen puts at the head of the list', but if this is so it has never really had the kind of critical analysis commensurate with that status. Indeed, Andor Gomme's complaints against the novel in 'On Not Being Persuaded'[1] seem a good deal more typical of critical opinion. Undergraduates generally seem not to like the novel in comparison with Jane Austen's other books, and commonly on the sort of grounds that Andor Gomme invokes: its movement is largely mechanical or haphazard; 'character is frozen on each first appearance, and human relations [are] either perfectly predictable or quite arbitrary'; the whole action takes place under conditions of nearly complete moral stasis, and of the characters only Wentworth (and in an oddly played down way) is more than momentarily affected by what he sees and learns. Thus, it is complained, the central character, Anne Elliot, does not change, and nor really does the hero, Captain Wentworth; this makes it less interesting and genuinely exploratory than, say, *Emma*, where the heroine changes in her moral attitude, or *Pride and Prejudice*, where she is rewarded for her moral quality by changing socially, rising in rank. The result of this absence of change is (at least according to many of my students) that a large part of the book seems simply diversionary, a succession of delaying events holding back the incident we too predictably expect, the marriage of Wentworth and Anne. Further, since the characters develop very little in moral or psychological terms, this conclusion is not brought about by any discovery at any internalized, psychological level – by, say, an inner revelation – but simply by externally artificial means that do no more than provide each party with the real information they need about the feelings of the other. In short, the novel seems to lack the structure which they and other critics in some way suppose necessary to sustain interest in a novel of this sort; certain features of the logical requirements of this kind of structure appear to be missing. Further, *Persuasion* is a book often said to be less convincing than the others in another respect – a novelist whose field is domestic attempts mistakenly to deal with scenes more violent (the scene at Lyme) and more dramatic (Mrs. Smith's story) than is appropriate, and comes off very badly at it. And so if we take as our measure of the worth of a novel of this sort the degree to which the characters alter in attitude or sentiments, discover themselves or suffer radical changes of fortune, or if we regard the full rendering of every event as the measure of a book's interest, *Persuasion* would in each case appear to have something missing.

What happens? An engagement and a love-relationship that has existed in the past has been broken, by interference from outside. It is finally renewed, by luck. A mature heroine grows, perhaps, a few faint gradations in maturity; but we are mostly concerned with misapprehension and suffering that could easily be resolved at almost any point in the action. The very fact that Anne is so stable and sensible means that the incidents that happen to her seem to have little import. She is not upset by losing the family home; why, then, that incident? She is not even upset or changed by the accident at Lyme; it seems to be an unnecessarily violent incident composed by the author to convince us that a person who is strong willed is liable to get into more trouble than one who is, like Anne, persuadable and held within right proportions and limits. She *is* attracted to a dishonest man, but this does not take the action very far, since she is so cautious. Jane Austen's description of Anne as a heroine almost too good for her may itself suggest why the book seems, by this view, thin, since there are few grounds for positive conflict and this tends in turn to create an abstractness of rendering and cause the action to appear as a collection of chance incidents stretching out until all the various mechanical confusions have been put right, and the predictable can happen. Andor

Gomme's article, and the discussion of *Persuasion* in Mark
Schorer's 'Fiction and the "Analogical Matrix"', which suggests that there is in the very rhetorical base of the book an
attitude and manner of discourse mechanical and calculated
(he argues that *Persuasion* has a discourse derived from com-
merce and property: 'Time is divided, troubles multiply,
weeks are calculated, and even a woman's prettiness is reck-
oned'), thus tend to crystallize a significant order of objection
to the book.

In short, the book can be seen as having a compositional
structure that is deficient, the standard of success here deriving
from a notion either about what kind of fictional development
is most effective and convincing for this kind of novel, or, more
pragmatically, about what constitutes success in Jane Austen's
other novels. But it is clearly possible to propose – and I believe
this to be true – that Jane Austen is here trying to create effects
that differ from those other novels. Certainly, as in most of the
previous novels, she is quite evidently seeking to persuade us
that marriage is in various terms the ideal reward for two
persons whose maturity as people, whose capacity to act and
value, has been shown to us at length and, in this case, over a
considerable period of time. Here, as before, marriage is
regarded both as an affectionate relationship involving the
moral regard of both partners for the other, a recognition of
some difference in function and sensibility between male and
female, and as a form of stewardship, involving the tending of
a household or estate. In previous novels, this view is developed
by distinguishing the heroine in numerous details from others
who fail to show the appropriate maturity, or else by showing
her growing toward that maturity through a succession of
events in which she reveals relative success or failure; the events
and incidents seem largely to be selected by the novelist with
such ends in view. Often, though not necessarily, marriage
involves the heroine, who is often, though not necessarily, the
point of consciousness from which we survey a considerable part
of the action, rising in class. One reason why the choice of
events in *Persuasion* seems to us less controlled and consistent

seems therefore to be, first, that the heroine does not learn very much or alter in character, so that her 'maturity' can appear rather a species of old age, and, second, that the marriage involves what the sociologists would call downward mobility, so that the fascination of the movement toward social steward-ship seems diminished. These two aspects are very much connected, and the connection lies, I think, in Jane Austen's desire to explore two salient forces in her society, two classes in interaction, in a way that she has never chosen to do before. She does this, throughout, within the framework of the domestic novel of marriage, but as each of her novels differs from one another, so this one differs from the rest and moves into dimensions much more elaborate than those we usually associate with her work. This, in turn, leads her into striking differences of narrative method and moral implication, and I think it is only if we grant this that we can effectively question the kind of critique that Andor Gomme makes.

Some of the differences can be suggested by briefly describing the action of *Persuasion*. A young sea-captain, Wentworth, who has no ship and no fortune, and a girl of nineteen, Anne Elliot, from an aristocratic family which has in fact little fortune either, fall in love and wish to get engaged. Anne is dissuaded from this by her father, a man vain and self-conscious about his class, on the grounds that the marriage is degrading; and, more influentially, by a friend of the family, indeed a mother-substitute, Lady Russell, on the grounds that her suitor's expectations are based primarily on his confidence in his future (which seems to her excessive). The suitor departs, and Anne remains at home for six years, somewhat regretting her pru-dence in being so persuaded, and fading in her looks. The family fortunes deteriorate and Anne's sensible suggestions about retrenchment are ignored. After six years – at a point which coincides with Jane Austen's opening of the 'narrative present', earlier events being told as recollection – the suitor returns at the moment when the family has to let its house and estate to an Admiral who has become wealthy from his profes-sion, though he is without inherited social rank. And Anne's suitor's confidence has been justified; his luck has been good; he is now a Captain in the Navy – and rich. The two move together through a society interlinked both by family connection and by the letting of the house; they meet from time to time, though without seeking to do so. But both have retained their original love, though neither knows that the other has, and Wentworth does not entirely know that he has; so they become more and more divided. But at the same time Anne is growing further and further away from her own family, because of its extravagance in poverty. When Wentworth is drawn towards another woman whose striking characteristic is her strong will, Anne is drawn towards another man who is one of the family and can solve its problems. But circumstances enable Anne and Wentworth to discover that they are still in love, and the action concludes with their marriage and Anne's effective severance from the bonds of her family. So described, with the emphases I have given it, the action seems coherent; it also has elements strikingly different from the other novels, elements which involve Jane Austen as a conscious artist in all sorts of differences of treatment. These differences are, I think, clearly involved in the entire conception of the book, being fundamental to the structure (as one describes it in this abstract way) and in the kind of presentational choices she has in communicating it to us. I will list some of the most important features; Andrew Wright has observed that the book is marked by a faith in society, and that in Jane Austen's world the measure of a man is not isolation but integration; more recently Richard Poirier has developed a similar point, though with regard primarily to *Emma*. But this is only true of *Persuasion* in a certain sense. For the landowning virtues and responsibilities are not to be had among the class that should embody them, that is, among the Elliots themselves. They are not, however, to be had in a direct sense among the second main group of agents in the novel, the seafarers, with their luck and pluck. Andrew Wright says that Jane Austen is untouched by any awareness of radical social transformation; about this novel, the remark is wrong. For the tension that Anne embodies is, in my view, precisely that of a 'revolutionary' situation, or rather a situation of social transformation. It is in accommodating the new complex of values raised by that – raised by, to put it at its grandest, the question of who shall inherit England – that Anne is the necessary focus of the action (hence, I think, Andor Gomme's well-put argument that the focus of any process of growth and discovery lies in Wentworth, and it might therefore be more apposite for us to see the action through his eyes, is probably finally incorrect).

What I am suggesting, then, is that in this book Jane Austen seems to want to persuade us that the moral life and the life of the classes are intimately connected, and in a way that she has not so regarded the matter before. For here she is interested in exploring the ways in which the co-existence of two quite carefully defined social groupings – the world of the inherited aristocracy and the world of the seafarers – extends our notion of what the moral life is, and creates contrasting areas of value. In order to engage our interest in this, I would propose, she has employed certain new methods of deploying her materials to make these connections urgent, and has in fact altered her actual scope. She creates, as she always does, a very full social world, with its elaborate conventions of manners, a world whose probabilities we are led into with elaborate caution, through ironical tones of narrative voice and overt statements and a kind of implicit recognition of the constituted barriers – methods familiar enough in her work. But the ironies, statements, and conventions are always ordered somewhat differently from novel to novel, and there are numerous new intonations here. They are perhaps most evident of all in the larger blocks of presentation, the structural elements of the novel. For instance, she chooses to show us several representatives of each of the two groupings I have mentioned, and to do this, by comment and less direct methods of presentation, in such a way as to make the groupings significant. Because she does it here on this scale, there seems a strong case for our supposing that there is something more crucial to these differences than just to provide a division of background and therefore of values between the hero and the heroine, which at first separate them but which can finally be overcome. It is not just that Wentworth has insufficient appreciation of the role of caution and prudence, and that Anne has not sufficient of Wentworth's confidence to take a risk in marrying. We are also persuaded that there is a significant set of moral and social relationships and implications to be found in the way the other characters are socially and morally grouped. The grouping we see first is that of the Elliot family, which is aristocratic, land-owning, ancient and respectable, of distinction and service in the past but now in different ways inclined to vanity, extravagance and social irresponsibility. The other group is composed around Admiral Croft, who becomes the tenant of Kellynch, and consists of a number of high-ranking professional sailors and their wives and friends. They are not, by Sir Walter Elliot's view, gentlemen; they are represented as a varied, intelligent and up to a point cultured group of people, who have risen rapidly in society as a result of having served it and defended it; their wealth comes from capturing sea-prizes, particularly in their battles with the French. Certain effective distinctions are made by the author between the two groups as groups; one instance is when Mrs. Clay, to flatter Sir Walter, comments on the value of not having a profession, and he finds himself making a double complaint against the seafarers:

'The profession has its utility, but I should be sorry to see any friend of mine belonging to it . . . it is in two points offensive to me: I have strong grounds of objection to it. First, as being the means of bringing persons of obscure birth into undue distinction, and raising men to honours which their fathers and grandfathers never dreamt of; and secondly, as it cuts up a man's youth and vigour most horribly; a sailor grows old sooner than any other man . . .'.

Equally for Anne, who is effectively the central consciousness in the story, the sailors are a force of change, and she sees the difference between the two groups in social and moral terms. Not only are they freer and easier, but they can actually keep up estates better; and Anne's severance from her family is conducted by means largely of this sort of insight and her realization that here, in this group, there are much more supportable values, values basic to the moral level of persuasion in the book. The significant movement in the moral action is therefore the moment when Anne returns from Lyme Regis to see the Crofts at Kellynch, having already learned more about the lives and attitudes of the sailors, and realizes that they have more right to be there than her own family:

She could have said more on the subject; for she had in fact so high an opinion of the Crofts, and considered her father so very fortunate in his tenants, felt the parish to be so sure of a good example, and the poor of the best attention and relief, that however sorry and ashamed for the necessity of the removal, she could not but in conscience feel that they were gone who deserved not to stay; and that Kellynch had passed into better hands than its owners.

And since one of the things that the novel persuades us towards is that, in this social world she has introduced to us and mediated for us, the social pattern is squirearchical, a world of rural gentry in which the administration of estates is a social and a moral duty, the Crofts now represent values for which her own family once stood but in which they have now failed. Hence Jane Austen's pattern here, as in the other novels, is to bestow the favours she can bestow in a domestic rural universe – a good marriage, a good home – on those who have deserved them.

And there are other moral reasons why the sailors deserve the favour of history which the action of the novel rewards them with. For if we go on to examine the moral values toward which the action persuades us, we must then see that these have sufficiently close analogies with this theme of supersession, of reappraising the relationship between the classes and the way in which the aristocratic duty can well devolve elsewhere. The sailors are carefully shown to have a more open, freer set of values, a demonstration which is encompassed within the moral stretch of the novel and given an important, in some ways a conclusive, place in the moral equilibrium of the ending. The difference between the two groupings is presented in many ways; in Captain Benwick, with his romantic reading, and Captain Harvill with his fitted-up house at Lyme, showing both the effect of his profession and his own labours. Generally the sailors are presented to us as members of a profession shaped by their life of duty and yet making the most of their chances. 'These would have been all my friends', thinks Anne; finally they are. The play given to values associated with energy, steadfastness, and even luck (when it takes the form of 'honourable toils and just rewards') is here crucial. Because the action is about mistaken persuasion, we find a stress on the will (but not wilfulness). Because it is about status unearned, it is about the importance of luck that has been earned. But, though the testing place of these values is rural-domestic and genteel, they are also seen as in some sense heroic virtues and are given a place in the broader world, so suggesting, in a way unusual in Jane Austen, that there are other fields of action than the country and Bath; there is the question of social and national importance, the question of the very claims that the professions have on society, the sense, indeed, of an evolving need for moral virtue in an evolving society. This touch is of the greatest importance, and it is enforced right to the end; the concluding sentences enforce it again:

His profession was all that could ever make her friends wish that tenderness [which Anne and Wentworth, married, have for each other] less; the dread of a future war all that could dim her sunshine. She gloried in being a sailor's wife, but she must pay the tax of quick alarm for belonging to that profession which is, if possible, more distinguished in its domestic virtues than in its national importance.

Anne now belongs in effect to the profession: it is, for Jane Austen, an unusual ending; and she associates herself with and so vindicates its domestic in addition to its heroic virtues. In consequence the moral universe, the scale of approved and unvalidated values, is in this novel different from the others (though in this matter all differ one from another) and answers to broader social necessities.

To say that in some sense the moral values of the novel are affected by a concern with the values of a new and emergent class is not, of course, to say that in this book they yield to a more primary interest; this is hardly a novel of social symbolism in the manner of, say, *Howards End*. The point is rather that Anne, originally persuaded towards a caution appropriate to rank and security, comes to question the values associated with these for those of energetic uncertainty and promise. Security proves to be false, morally and financially; the promise justifies itself, morally and financially. Anne's development in the novel is more substantial than most critics allow. She accepts as a given standard of her social world the dangers of lowering herself, and it is necessary that we realize this if the persuasion of Lady Russell is to seem to us rightly accepted by her. It is the subsequent events which show Lady Russell wrong, not the grounds on which she persuaded Anne; Anne comes to an understanding more radical than even a good woman like her can conceive of. If those events do have any order and meaning for a novelist with the controlling exactness that we know Jane Austen to have had, then surely their pattern takes its order from her development in her understanding of her situation. Anne's essential temptation is Kellynch, and it is a meaningful temptation. In the early part of the novel she shows, by her concern, her worthiness for it; in the latter part it is shown to be unworthy of her, for it is to be inherited by Walter Elliot; by the end of the action therefore Anne has moved out of the world of stewardship we are familiar with in Jane Austen ('Anne had no Uppercross-Hall before her, no landed estate, no headship of a family . . .'), and the reader is now persuaded that this is to the good. But substantively this must be a moral rather than a social good, since it is in marriage and really in marriage alone that it is to be realised. Two essential lines of possible development of a sort that we are familiar with in the novels – the progress of a heroine towards social status and to self-awareness – must diverge in such a way as to show that self-awareness is incompatible with a social inheritance. The rewards that time can bring are thus, in this novel, of an unusual kind, and the real effort of literary management must be toward persuading us that Anne does, significantly, grow – does extend in moral and social awareness, does advance from a biddable acceptance of duty and 'persuasion exerted on the side of safety' to a conscientious appreciation of the proper obligations of risk-taking, this movement being justified by a revelation about the nature of the social and family world to which she belongs, and by an increased understanding not so much of Wentworth's character as of the environment in which it takes on its moral force.

This is, I think, the thread that takes us through *Persuasion*, and despite certain local failures (on which Andor Gomme pounces very effectively) it seems in general a triumph of management. One of the most obvious ways in which this theme is handled is the way in which the narrative present of the book is employed. A large part of the action, including the original engagement and the act of persuasion, is told to us in short compass and in retrospect. This leaves the present of the novel to deal with a relatively short period of time in which the complications deriving from that earlier action are worked out with close attention, in such a way as to follow out a real growth in Anne. These complications take us two ways – first, towards the theme of the separation of the lovers and their final reconciliation, and, second, towards the theme of the divorcing of Anne from her family. The novel begins at a point where the latter can only be the primary point of attention, since there are few direct grounds for supposing that she can regain Wentworth. At this point the real significance of the persuasion is that it has committed Anne to exploring life from within the family, and it is only when the moral and social weaknesses here have been fully exposed that she can have real grounds for judging Lady Russell to have been wrong. In fact, then, the main action is concerned not with Anne falling in love or feeling new emotions, but with recreating old emotions under the stimulus of Wentworth's presence and with showing how Anne, with no expectation whatever of getting back Wentworth's love, is growing away from her family. Hence, too, the meaning of presenting most of the action 'through' Anne, for if we were to know at just what point after the occasion in chapter 7 when the author intervenes to indicate that Anne's power with Wentworth has gone forever the situation changes, we should not continue to regard Anne's discarding of her family as a disinterested moral progression. Nor would we appreciate in the same way those crucial virtues of steadfastness and constancy which are part of the moral meaning of the final alliance. The steadfastness, the constancy, the evident maturity of Anne are, of course, elements of her character when the action commences and give meaning to Wentworth's final sense that she has not altered, but the restoration of her energies and spirits through making mature free choices do form an essential advance. In the later scenes at Bath, Anne's capacities are severely tested, not only through the complications of the Walter Elliot episode, but through numerous other choices; and here we have a refiguring of the initial act of persuasion in a situation in which Anne is now capable of realizing all her actions and values and so of regaining the final 'warmth of heart' with which the novel ends.

Clearly, the ending of the novel complies with Richard Poirier's description of Jane Austen's culminating marriages – they are not only meaningful acts of choice but unions of 'social and natural inclinations' – and, as I have said, the direction of the literary persuasion is towards convincing us that two people have made a good marriage, in terms of a complex of social and moral discoveries, illuminating experiences of persons and events. But the nature of the persuasion, as we witness it and appreciate it through the basic dispositions of the action and the working decisions about what is to be told and how to tell it, is surely one that has a full development best defined through the way in which Anne's constancy enforces discoveries she could not have made had she sustained the engagement at the beginning (and hence can be measured by the distance Anne moves from her initial view of Lady Russell's assessment). The novel is a good deal more than a demonstration of the triumph of constancy, then, as the scene where Wentworth and Anne restore their engagement indicates:

There they exchanged again those feelings and those promises which had once before seemed to secure every thing, but which had been followed by so many, many years of division and estrangement. There they returned again into the past, more exquisitely happy, perhaps, in their re-union, than when it had been first projected; more tender, more tried, more fixed in a knowledge of each other's character, truth, and attachment; more equal to act, more justified in acting.

And because there is, through the action as given, a demonstrable meaning in the claim that both are 'more equal to act, more justified in acting', and since this is very specifically true of Anne, from whose point of view most of the significant perceptions are realized, there are real grounds for judging the passage where Anne justifies her previous yielding to persuasion ('You should have distinguished. . . . You should not have suspected me now: the case so different, and my age so different') as other than what Mr. Gomme says it is – 'disingenuous'. For only now, and because she has altered in a way that makes her more equal to act, more justified in acting, can the limitations of the persuasion be seen; and we are surely meant to perceive that there have been real benefits in it, since through it we have an Anne now who is not the original Anne. Jane Austen's proper qualifications ('. . . more exquisitely happy, *perhaps*, in their re-union . . .') shouldn't, surely, be taken as lessening the point; they are emotionally logical in view of the initial joy felt by Anne in her first love. Equally, the way in which Wentworth varies between suggesting that Anne has altered and that Anne has remained the same should not be mistaken; for one thing, his judgments refer now to personal appearance, now to character, now to her attitude toward him, her constancy, and for another they are in any case offered with a mild and amused irony, in which Anne partakes, with regard to what can now be regarded as his own mild inconstancy, which he now plays down. But the significant fact is that he does realize that Anne has acquired new extensions of character, as well as re-realizing her virtues, which are now thrown before him in a new light (mainly through the comparison with Louisa), and this explains his long pursuit of Anne, which is his real reason for being in Bath. Anne has acquired a new conception of duty, a new species of moral energy derived from social independence, which is associated, in turn, with the restoration of her looks and the new resources of her tenderness.

Far, then, from having created a novel in which the two major characters do not see and learn, Jane Austen has, in my view, created one in which a remarkable growth in moral resource and energy does occur in a heroine already distinguished from other Austen heroines by her relative maturity when the action of the book commences, a growth which occurs through the exploration of values having to do with luck, spirited energy and emotional resource that are made available to men by changes in society and by new conceptions of 'national importance'. Without wanting to overstate this element, I think we shall not see the moral radicalism of *Persuasion* without taking account of it and of the degree of interest Jane Austen exerts in it. And so, far from regarding the novel as one in which the action takes place under conditions of 'nearly complete moral statis', I would hold it to cover moral and social dimensions on a scale that justifies our seeing it as a classic of its author's maturity; on a scale, in fact, that might let us put it near 'the head of the list'.

SOURCE: '*Persuasion* Again', in *Essays in Criticism*, XVIII (1968) 383–96.

NOTE

1. [*Essays in Criticism*, XVI (1966) – Ed.]

A. Walton Litz

'PERSUASION: FORMS OF ESTRANGEMENT' (1975)

Virginia Woolf, in her essay on Jane Austen in *The Common Reader* (1925), found that *Persuasion* was characterized by 'a peculiar beauty and a peculiar dullness'. [Quotes passage reproduced on page 151 above – Ed.] Most readers will agree with Virginia Woolf's response, whether or not they care to use the term 'dullness': Jane Austen has her eye on new effects in *Persuasion*, and situations or characters which yielded such rich comic pleasures in previous novels are given summary treatment. Most readers would also agree that there is a 'peculiar' beauty in *Persuasion*, that it has to do with a new allegiance to feeling rather than prudence, to poetry rather than prose, and that it springs from a deep sense of personal loss. As Virginia Woolf phrases it, Jane Austen

is beginning to discover that the world is larger, more mysterious, and more romantic than she had supposed. We feel it to be true of herself when she says of Anne: 'She had been forced into prudence in her youth, she learned romance as she grew older – the natural sequel of an unnatural beginning'. . . . There is an expressed emotion in the scene at the concert and in the famous talk about woman's constancy which proves not merely the biographical fact that Jane Austen had loved, but the aesthetic fact that she was no longer afraid to say so. [For the whole of this passage, see page 152 above – Ed.]

Persuasion has received highly intelligent criticism in recent years, after a long period of comparative neglect, and the lines of investigation have followed Virginia Woolf's suggestive comments. Critics have been concerned with the 'personal' quality of the novel and the problems it poses for biographical interpretation; with the obvious unevenness in narrative structure; with the 'poetic' use of landscape, and the hovering influence of Romantic poetry; with the pervasive presence of Anne Elliot's consciousness; with new effects in style and syntax; with the 'modernity' of Anne Elliot, an isolated personality in a rapidly changing society. Many of these problems were discussed in my own earlier study,[1] but I would like to consider them again, I hope with greater tact and particularity. Of all Jane Austen's major works, *Persuasion* suffers the most from easy generalizations, and requires the most minute discriminations. For example, my own remark that 'more than has been generally realized or acknowledged, [Jane Austen] was influenced by the Romantic poetry of the early nineteenth century'[2] has been frequently quoted with approval, but I now feel that it needs severe definition: What are the qualities of Romantic poetry reflected in Jane Austen's new attitudes toward nature and 'feeling'? How do these new effects in *Persuasion* differ from those in the earlier novels? The following pages offer no startlingly new perspectives, but rather a refinement of several familiar points of view.

In spite of Jane Austen's warning to a friend 'that it was her desire to create, not to reproduce',[3] readers from her own day to the present have delighted in identifying Anne Elliot with Jane Austen. Anne is twenty-seven years old, a dangerous age for Jane Austen's young women; Charlotte Lucas is 'about twenty-seven' when she accepts the foolish Mr Collins, and Marianne in *Sense and Sensibility* laments that a 'woman of seven and twenty . . . can never hope to feel or inspire affection again'.[4] Jane Austen's own broken 'romance', the details of which are hopelessly obscure, seems to have taken place around 1802, when she was twenty-seven, and Virginia Woolf was probably justified in her belief that *Persuasion* confirms 'the biographical fact that Jane Austen had loved'. Other passages from Jane Austen's life are obviously driven deep into the life of the novel: the careers of her sailor brothers, and the pleasant days at Lyme Regis in the summer of 1804, when she explored the area with Cassandra and her brother Henry. These facts give a certain sanction to biographical speculation, if one cares for that sort of thing, but they do not explain the intensity with which readers have pursued the 'personal' element in *Persuasion*. That intensity comes from the fiction, not from a curiosity about the writer's life, and has to do with the lost 'bloom' of Anne Elliot.

If asked to summarize Jane Austen's last three novels in three phrases, one might say that *Mansfield Park* is about the loss and return of principles, *Emma* about the loss and return of reason, *Persuasion* about the loss and return of 'bloom'. To make these formulations, however crude they may be, is to appreciate the deeply *physical* impact of *Persuasion*. The motif words of the earlier novels are the value terms of the eighteenth century – sense, taste, genius, judgment, understanding, and so forth – and their constant repetition is a sign of Jane Austen's rational vision. But there is something idiosyncratic and almost obsessive about the recurrence of 'bloom' in the first volume of *Persuasion*. 'Anne Elliot had been a very pretty girl, but her bloom had vanished early', while Elizabeth and Sir Walter remained 'as blooming as ever', at least in their own eyes (p. 6). The word occurs six times in the first volume, culminating in the scene on the steps at Lyme where Anne, 'the bloom and freshness of youth restored by the fine wind', attracts the admiration of Wentworth and Mr Elliot (p. 104). It then disappears from the novel, only to return in the 'blushes' which mark Anne's repossession of her lost love: 'Glowing and lovely in sensibility and happiness, and more generally admired than she thought about or cared for, she had cheerful or forebearing feelings for every creature around her' (p. 245).

But 'bloom' is only one of many physical metaphors which make the first half of *Persuasion* Jane Austen's most deeply felt fiction. A sense of the earth's unchanging rhythms, confined in earlier works to an occasional scene and usually presented in the 'picturesque' manner, provides a ground-rhythm for the first half of *Persuasion*.

Thirteen years had seen [Elizabeth] the mistress of Kellynch Hall, presiding and directing with a self-possession and decision which could never have given the idea of her being younger than she was. For thirteen years had she been doing the honours, and laying down the domestic law at home, and leading the way to the chaise and four, and walking immediately after Lady Russell out of all the drawing-rooms and dining-rooms in the country. Thirteen winters' revolving frosts had seen her opening every ball of credit which a scanty neighbourhood afforded; and thirteen springs shewn their blossom, as she travelled up to London with her father, for a few weeks annual enjoyment of the great world. (pp. 6–7)

This marvellous passage, which acts out the progress of time and exposes the static lives of Kellynch Hall, would have been cast in a very different form in the earlier fictions. Narrative summary and authorial commentary have given way to a poetic sense of time's changes that commands the first volume of *Persuasion*. The chapters set in Somerset are pervaded with references to the autumnal landscape, which dominates Anne's emotions as she waits with little hope for 'a second spring of youth and beauty' (p. 124); while the scenes at Lyme are softened by the romantic landscape and the freshening 'flow of the tide' (pp. 95–6, 102). This poetic use of nature as a structure of feeling, which not only offers metaphors for our emotions but controls them with its unchanging rhythms and changing moods, comes to a climax in the scene where Anne's mind, depressed by the recent events at Lyme and her imminent departure for Bath, becomes part of the dark November landscape.

An hour's complete leisure for such reflections as these, on a dark November day, a small thick rain almost blotting out the very few objects ever to be discerned from the windows, was enough to make the sound of Lady Russell's carriage exceedingly welcome; and yet, though desirous to be gone, she could not quit the mansion-house, or look an adieu to the cottage, with its black, dripping, and comfortless veranda, or even notice through the misty glasses the last humble tenements of the village, without a saddened heart. – Scenes had passed in Uppercross, which made it precious. It stood the record of many sensations of pain, once severe, but now softened . . . She left it all behind her; all but the recollection that such things had been. (p. 123)

Such a passage fully justifies Angus Wilson's reply to those who say 'that there is no poetry in Jane Austen'. The poetry is there in 'the essential atmosphere of her novels – an instinctive response to those basic realities of nature, the weather and the seasons'. All of Jane Austen's heroines, whether declining like Fanny and Anne, or flourishing like Emma and Elizabeth, are acutely conscious of their physical lives. The fact of 'being alive', as Wilson says, 'is never absent from the texture of the thoughts of her heroines'.[5]

Most readers of Jane Austen would agree with Wilson's claims, and would also agree that *Persuasion* represents her most successful effort to build this sense of physical life into the language and structure of a novel. If asked for proof, they would point to the frequent allusions to the Romantic poets, especially Byron and Scott, and to the famous passage (pp. 84–5) where Anne's autumnal walk is permeated with poetic 'musings and quotations'. But here they would be, I think, demonstrably wrong. Most of Jane Austen's direct references to the Romantic poets in *Persuasion* are associated with Captain Benwick, and have the same satiric intent – although they are gentler in manner – as the references to contemporary poetry in *Sanditon*. When Anne and Captain Benwick talk of 'poetry, the richness of the present age', his enthusiasm for Scott and Byron is so emotional that Anne ventures to 'recommend a larger allowance of prose in his daily study' (p. 101), and her caution is confirmed when Benwick's raptures on Byron's *The Corsair* are interrupted by Louisa's rash jump to the Lower Cobb. Jane Austen has no place in her world for the Byronic hero, and Wentworth is not – as one recent critic has claimed – a successful recreation of Byron's Corsair.

Surely Angus Wilson is right in implying that Jane Austen's assimilation of the new poetry is most profound when least obtrusive. 'If we seek for any conscious concern for nature, we get either the Gilpin textbook stuff of *Northanger Abbey* or the "thoughts from the poets" of Fanny or Anne Elliot.'[6] A good example of Jane Austen's conscious concern for nature would be the scene in *Mansfield Park* where Edmund joins Fanny at the window to view the stars:

his eyes soon turned like her's towards the scene without, where all
that was solemn and soothing, and lovely, appeared in the brilliancy
of an unclouded night, and the contrast of the deep shade of the
woods. Fanny spoke her feelings 'Here's harmony!' said she, 'Here's
repose! Here's what may leave all painting and all music behind,
and what poetry only can attempt to describe. Here's what may
tranquillize every care, and lift the heart to rapture! When I look
out on such a night as this, I feel as if there could be neither wickedness nor sorrow in the world; and there certainly would be less of
both if the sublimity of Nature were more attended to, and people
were carried more out of themselves by contemplating such a
scene'. (p. 113)

This is a set-piece out of eighteenth-century aesthetics, in which
Fanny responds to the natural landscape with appropriate
emotions of 'sublimity' and transport. Even the descriptive
details are heavily literary, drawn from Shakespeare and Ann
Radcliffe.[7] A different and more intimate sense of landscape is
displayed by the famous autumnal walk in *Persuasion*:

Her *pleasure* in the walk must arise from the exercise and the day,
from the view of the last smiles of the year upon the tawny leaves
and withered hedges, and from repeating to herself some few of the
thousand poetical descriptions extant of autumn, that season of
peculiar and inexhaustible influence on the mind of taste and
tenderness . . . After one of the many praises of the day, which were
continually bursting forth, Captain Wentworth added:
'What glorious weather for the Admiral and my sister! They
meant to take a long drive this morning; perhaps we may hail them
from some of these hills. They talked of coming into this side of the
country. I wonder whereabouts they will upset to-day. Oh! it does
happen very often, I assure you – but my sister makes nothing of it –
she would as lieve be tossed out as not.'
'Ah! You make the most of it, I know,' cried Louisa 'but if it
were really so, I should do just the same in her place. If I loved a
man as she loves the Admiral, I would be always with him, nothing
should ever separate us, and I would rather be overturned by him,
than driven safely by anybody else.'
. . . Anne could not immediately fall into a quotation again. The
sweet scenes of autumn were for a while put by – unless some tender
sonnet, fraught with the apt analogy of the declining year, with

declining happiness, and the images of youth and hope, and spring, all gone together, blessed her memory. She roused herself to say, as they struck by order into another path, 'Is not this one of the ways to Winthrop?' But nobody heard, or, at least, nobody answered her.

Winthrop . . . was their destination; and after another half mile of gradual ascent through large enclosures, where the ploughs at work, and the fresh-made path spoke the farmer, counteracting the sweets of poetical despondence, and meaning to have spring again, they gained the summit of the most considerable hill, which parted Uppercross and Winthrop, and soon commanded a full view of the latter, at the foot of the hill on the other side. (pp. 84–5)

Fanny Price has three transparencies on the panes of her window, depicting Tintern Abbey, a cave in Italy, and a moonlit lake in Cumberland; the subjects may suggest Wordsworth, but her tastes are strictly for the picturesque and the academic sublime. The presentation of Anne Elliot's autumnal walk is much closer to a Wordsworthian view of nature, emphasizing as it does the responsive ego, yet it would be a mistake to identify Anne's thoughts on autumn with the powerful reactions of the great Romantic poets. Her 'poetical descriptions' are, most likely, culled from the popular magazine poets, and her literary taste is not necessarily superior to that of Fanny Price. What is different in *Persuasion* is the way in which two views of nature, both conventional, have been internalized to provide a complex and original impression. Whereas in *Sense and Sensibility* Marianne's sentimental effusions on nature are dramatically counterpointed to Edward's practical view, her sense of the picturesque set against his sense of the ordinary, the autumnal scene from *Persuasion* locates both responses within Anne's mind. After she has fallen sentimentally and self-indulgently into quotation, the sight of the farmer ploughing, 'meaning to have spring again', rescues Anne from 'poetical despondence', and restores her emotional composure. This passage is infused with a sense of immediate feeling absent from the description of Fanny's rapture, but it remains a consciously 'literary' construction, closer to Cowper than to Wordsworth. In the final scene at Uppercross already quoted, however, the effects are truly Wordsworthian. The cottage viewed on a 'dark November day' is a stock-piece of the picturesque, with its irregular shape and misty appearance, yet it is transformed by memory, by 'reflection' and 'recollection', into a complex symbol of what 'had been'. In the opening chapters of *Persuasion* Jane Austen is most 'poetic', most Wordsworthian, when she is willing to abandon the literary allusion and give herself to a direct passionate rendering of nature's changing face.

Our discussion of the romantic dimensions of *Persuasion* has been confined to the first half of the novel, the opening twelve chapters, and for good reason: the latter half of the novel is radically different in style and narrative method. Any census of the metaphors of natural change will find that they are concentrated in the first half, suggesting that *Persuasion* has a deliberate two-part structure that has been often overlooked. *Northanger Abbey*, its companion in the posthumous four-volume edition, was always intended as a two-part romance: the original version sold to the publisher Crosby in 1803 was described as 'a MS. Novel in 2 vol. entitled Susan'. All of Jane Austen's other novels were published in three parts, and designed to fit that pattern. Thus the three-part division of *Pride and Prejudice* follows the three-act structure of a stage comedy, and the three parts of *Emma* correspond to three successive stages in a process of self-discovery. But Jane Austen deliberately chose to construct *Persuasion* in two parts (the numbering of the cancelled last chapters proves this), and much of the apparent unevenness or 'dullness' of the novel is explained by this artistic decision.

The first half of *Persuasion* portrays Anne Elliot against a natural landscape, and it is there that Jane Austen's new-found Romanticism is concentrated. Once the action has moved to Bath a claustrophobic atmosphere descends, and the external world becomes insubstantial: Anne, without a human confidante but sustained by nature in the first volume, is left terribly alone in the second volume – only the reconciliation with Wentworth can save her from anonymity. The language of the second volume, although less satisfying to our modern taste, is deliberately fashioned to express this sense of personalities moving in a vacuum. The rich metaphors of Volume One are replaced by the eighteenth-century value terms of earlier novels, but – as Virginia Woolf noted – with a sense of perfunctory ritual. It is as if Jane Austen, hurrying to the final reunion, were at long last impatient with those weighty terms of judgment and admonition that had served her so well in earlier years. In a space of seven pages (pp. 140–7) the word 'sensible' occurs six times along with 'pride', 'understanding', 'decorum', 'candid', 'amiable', 'sensibility', and 'imaginations'. This is an aggressive return to the abstract language of the earlier fictions, but it is difficult to tell whether Jane Austen does so out of boredom – as Virginia Woolf seems to imply – or out of a desire to convey the eighteenth-century stasis of Bath. In any case, the contrast between the first and second volumes of *Persuasion* is profound in the realm of language and metaphor, reflecting the radical dislocation of Anne Elliot. And there are differences in narrative method as well. The first half of the novel presents Anne as the commanding center. As Norman Page has shown, the 'slanting of the narrative through the mental life of the principal character', already developed in *Emma*, is the dominant mode in *Persuasion*; narrative, authorial comment, dialogue, and interior monologue merge into one another.[8] 'Free indirect speech', in which lengthy dialogue is compressed and located within the central consciousness, is combined with more conventional narrative methods to give a sense of the entire novel taking place within the mind of the heroine. But this complex method of internalized presentation is most evident in the first volume, and in Volume Two – as Anne Elliot enters the alien environment of Bath – Jane Austen reverts to earlier and more objective methods. It is a sign of Anne's isolation that the revelation of William Elliot's true nature, and even of Wentworth's love, must come to her through letters, one of the most 'external' of fictional devices.

Another aspect of style in *Persuasion*, present in both volumes but more characteristic of the first, is a rapid and nervous syntax designed to imitate the bombardment of impressions upon the mind. A fine example occurs when Anne, a victim of the rambunctious child Walter, is rescued by Captain Wentworth.

> In another moment, however, she found herself in the state of being released from him; some one was taking him from her, though he had bent down her head so much, that his little sturdy hands were unfastened from around her neck, and he was resolutely borne away before she knew that Captain Wentworth had done it. (p. 80)

Here the passive construction, the indefinite pronouns, and the staccato syntax all imitate the effect of the incident upon Anne's mind. Page is certainly right when he says that such passages, common in *Persuasion*, do not make statements about an emotional situation but suggest the quality of the experience through the movement of the prose.[9]

When we examine these details of sentence structure and punctuation, however, a certain caution is necessary. The sentences of *Persuasion* do, for the most part, move away from the Johnsonian norm, and in the revisions of the cancelled chapters one can see Jane Austen struggling toward a more expressive form. But one should remember that all of Jane Austen's manuscripts display a greater flexibility of sentence structure than her printed works, and although the cancelled chapters of *Persuasion* and the manuscript of *Sanditon* exhibit an extraordinary freedom, many of the same qualities are present in the manuscript of 'The Watsons' (c. 1803-4). The printer of Jane Austen's day had great license with punctuation, paragraphing, and even sentence structure, and part of the 'flowing' quality of *Persuasion* may derive from a printer (T. Davison) whose standards and tastes differed from those of the printers who handled the earlier manuscripts. This does not affect the general import of Page's argument, but the dangers of relying too heavily on details of punctuation and sentence structure are evident in Page's comparison of a passage in the cancelled chapter 10 with the revised version:[10]

> He found that he was considered by his friend Harville an engaged man. The Harvilles entertained not a doubt of a mutual attachment

between him and Louisa; and though this to a degree was contradicted instantly, it yet made him feel that perhaps by *her* family, by everybody, by *herself* even, the same idea might be held, and that he was not *free* in honour, though if such were to be the conclusion, too free alas! in heart. He had never thought justly on this subject before, and he had not sufficiently considered that his excessive intimacy at Uppercross must offer its danger of ill consequence in many ways; and that while trying whether he could attach himself to either of the girls, he might be exciting unpleasant reports if not raising unrequited regard.

He found too late that he had entangled himself [cancelled version, p. 260 of Chapman's edition].

'I found', said he, 'that I was considered by Harville an engaged man! That neither Harville nor his wife entertained a doubt of our mutual attachment. I was startled and shocked. To a degree, I could contradict this instantly; but, when I began to reflect that others might have felt the same – her own family, nay, perhaps herself, I was no longer at my own disposal. I was hers in honour if she wished it. I had been unguarded. I had not thought seriously on this subject before. I had not considered that my excessive intimacy must have its danger of ill consequence in many ways; and that I had no right to be trying whether I could attach myself to either of the girls at the risk of raising even an unpleasant report, were there no other ill effects. I had been grossly wrong, and must abide the consequences.'

He found too late, in short, that he had entangled himself . . . [final version, pp. 242–3].

Page's comments upon the improved 'personal and dramatic form' of the revised version are just, but his observation that three long sentences have been broken up into nine shorter sentences falls away when we realize that the cancelled version, as Page quotes it, is actually reprinted from the 1870 *Memoir*, where Jane Austen's lively manuscript had been 'regularized' by the Victorian editor and printer. The actual passage from the manuscript, reproduced below, shows the nervous energy of Jane Austen's first draft, and reminds us that the relationship between Jane Austen's first drafts and the printed texts must often have been that of sketch to varnished canvas.

He found that he was considered by his friend, Harville, as an engaged Man. The Harvilles entertained not a doubt of a mutual attachment between him & Louisa – and though this to *a degree*, was contradicted instantly – it yet made him feel that perhaps by *her* family, by everybody, by *herself* even, the same idea might be held – and that he was not *free* in honour – though, if such were to be the conclusion, too free alas! in Heart. – He had never thought justly on this subject before – he had not, sufficiently, considered that his excessive Intimacy at Uppercross must have it's danger of ill consequence in many ways and that while trying whether he cd attach himself to either of the Girls, he might be exciting unpleasant reports, if not, raising unrequited regard! – He found, too late, that he had entangled himself –[11]

Persuasion reveals an author who is unusually sensitive to the forces of her time. Of all the novels, it is the only one where the action is precisely dated, and that date is 'the present' (1814–15). The other novels are slightly retrospective in their treatment of manners and events, but *Persuasion* is filled with references to contemporary history ('This peace will be turning all our rich Navy Officers ashore') and the most recent publications of the Romantic poets. These topical references are matched by certain passages in the novel which seem to reflect the events of 1815–16, when *Persuasion* was a work-in-progress. The description of the 'green chasms between romantic rocks' near Lyme may echo *Kubla Khan*, first published in 1816, although the chronology is doubtful and the whole passage strikes me as more picturesque than Coleridgean;[12] more likely is the influence of Scott's famous review in the *Quarterly* upon Jane Austen's retreat from 'prudence'. In Scott's review, which Jane Austen had read by 1 April 1816 (*Persuasion* was not completed until the summer), Jane Austen was characterized as anti-sentimental and anti-romantic, her novels bearing the same relation to those of the 'sentimental and romantic cast, that cornfields and cottages and meadows bear to . . . the rugged sublimities of a mountain landscape'. Scott then went on to deplore the neglect of Cupid and romantic feelings, implying that Jane Austen coupled 'Cupid indivisibly with

calculating prudence'.[13] This must have stung the creator of
Anne Elliot, and we may take her passionate statement on
'romance' as a covert reply.

How eloquent could Anne Elliot have been, – how eloquent, at
least, were her wishes on the side of early warm attachment, and a
cheerful confidence in futurity, against that over-anxious caution
which seems to insult exertion and distrust Providence! – She had
been forced into prudence in her youth, she learned romance as she
grew older – the natural sequel of an unnatural beginning. (p. 30)

Unlike Jane Austen's other major works, *Persuasion* is filled
with a sense of the moment – both historical and personal – at
which it was written.

It is not these particular signs of contemporaneity, however,
but Jane Austen's powerful response to a changing relationship
between society and the self that gives *Persuasion* its hold on the
modern reader. In *Pride and Prejudice* the old order of Darcy
and Pemberley can be accommodated to the new forces represented by the middle-class Gardiners; in *Persuasion* there seems
little hope of accommodation between statis and unpredictable
change. 'The Musgroves, like their houses, were in a state of
alteration, perhaps of improvement' (p. 40), and this tension
between old ways and 'more modern minds and manners'
divides the novel. Sir Walter has retreated into a wilderness of
mirrors, the Baronetage his favorite looking-glass, and Jane
Austen's sympathies are firmly on the side of the new natural
aristocracy represented by the Navy; but in giving her allegiance to them Jane Austen knows that Anne must 'pay the
tax of quick alarm' (p. 252). The ending of *Persuasion*, unlike
that of the other novels, is open and problematic. One could
glean from *Persuasion* a list of terms which would make it
sound like a textbook in a modern sociology: 'estrangement',
'imprisonment', 'alienations', 'removals'. The heroine is 'only
Anne' (pp. 5–6), and the word 'alone' echoes through the
novel. *Persuasion* is filled with a sense of what time can do, with
its 'changes, alienations, removals': it can lead to 'oblivion of
the past' (p. 60) and even annihilation of the self. Anne has

painfully learned 'the art of knowing our own nothingness beyond our own circle' (p. 42), and at the end of the novel that circle, so lovingly restored and enlarged, has no permanence beyond the moment. Virginia Woolf might have said that *Persuasion* is marked by a peculiar terror as well as a peculiar beauty.

SOURCE: '*Persuasion*: Forms of Estrangement', in *Jane Austen: Bicentary Essays*, ed. John Halperin (1975) pp. 221–32.

NOTES

1. *Jane Austen: A Study of Her Artistic Development* (New York, 1965).
2. Ibid., p. 153.
3. J. E. Austen-Leigh, *Memoir of Jane Austen*, ed. R. W. Chapman (Oxford, 1926) p. 157.
4. *Sense and Sensibility*, p. 38. All page references for the novels are to *The Novels of Jane Austen*, ed. R. W. Chapman, 3rd ed. (London: Oxford University Press, 1933).
5. Angus Wilson, 'The Neighbourhood of Timbuctoo', in *Critical Essays on Jane Austen*, ed. B. C. Southam (London, 1968) p. 191.
6. Ibid.
7. In *Jane Austen and Her Predecessors* (Cambridge, 1966) pp. 78 and 107–8, Frank W. Bradbrook points out the allusions to *The Merchant of Venice* and *The Mysteries of Udolpho*.
8. Norman Page, *The Language of Jane Austen* (Oxford, 1972) pp. 48–53 and 127–36.
9. Ibid. p. 50.
10. Ibid. pp. 51–2.
11. *Two Chapters of Persuasion*, ed. R. W. Chapman (Oxford, 1926) pp. 20–1.
12. See Alethea Hayter, 'Xanadu at Lyme Regis', *Ariel*, 1 (1970) 61–4.
13. *Jane Austen: The Critical Heritage*, ed. B. C. Southam (London, 1968) p. 68. Jane Austen refers to Scott's review in a letter of 1 April 1816.

SELECT BIBLIOGRAPHY

The following books and articles, not included in this volume, are of special interest in the criticism of these two novels.

H. S. Babb, *Jane Austen's Novels: The Fabric of Dialogue* (Ohio University Press, 1963). Provides a detailed analysis and discussion of the style and function of dialogue in each of the novels.

J. H. Duffy, 'Structure and Idea in *Persuasion*', *Nineteenth Century Fiction*, VIII (1954).

A. W. Litz, *Jane Austen: A Study of her Artistic Development* (London & New York, 1965). An excellent and scholarly treatment of the novelist's development.

A. D. McKillop, 'Critical Realism in *Northanger Abbey*', in R. C. Rathburn and M. Steinmann Jr (eds), *From Jane Austen to Joseph Conrad* (Minneapolis, 1958).

G. Ryle, 'Jane Austen and the Moralists', in B. C. Southam (ed.), *Critical Essays on Jane Austen* (London, 1968).

M. Schorer, 'Fiction and the "Analogical Matrix"', *Kenyon Review*, XI (1949). A stimulating and controversial interpretation of a level of metaphorical meaning in the language of *Persuasion*.

B. C. Southam, '*Sanditon* – the seventh novel', in Juliet McMaster (ed.), *Essays on Jane Austen* (London, 1976). Explores the relationship between *Northanger Abbey*, *Persuasion* and *Sanditon*.

D. P. Varma, *The Gothic Flame* (London, 1957). A sound account of the Gothic fashion in literature.

ADDENDUM 1982

David Cecil, *A Portrait of Jane Austen* (London, 1978).

NOTES ON CONTRIBUTORS

ELIZABETH BOWEN (1899–1973), novelist and essayist.

MALCOLM BRADBURY is Professor of English Literature, University of East Anglia, and author of several novels as well as of much literary criticism.

MARILYN BUTLER is University Lecturer in English and a Fellow of St Hugh's College, Oxford.

The late R. S. CRANE was for many years Professor of English in the University of Chicago, and editor of the *Philological Quarterly*.

D. W. HARDING is Emeritus Professor of Psychology in the University of London, and was a member of the editorial board of *Scrutiny* from 1933 to 1947. In addition to works on psychology, his publications include *Experience into Words: Essays on Poetry* (1963) and articles on literary criticism.

ELIZABETH HARDWICK, American novelist and critic. Her publications include *The Simple Truth* (1955) and *A View of My Own* (1962).

W. D. HOWELLS (1837–1920), American novelist, playwright, essayist and critic; editor of the *Atlantic Monthly* from 1866 to 1881.

MARY M. LASCELLES is an Honorary Fellow of Somerville College, Oxford, and was formerly Reader in English Literature at Oxford. In addition to *Jane Austen and Her Art* (1939), her publications include books on Shakespeare and Samuel Johnson.

A. WALTON LITZ is Chairman of the Department of English in Princeton University, and author of studies of Jane Austen, James Joyce and Wallace Stevens.

MARVIN MUDRICK is Professor of English in the University of California at Santa Barbara. In addition to *Jane Austen: Irony as Defense and Discovery* (1952), his publications include *On Culture and Literature* (1968) and studies of Conrad.

B .C. SOUTHAM formerly lectured in English at Westfield College, University of London. He has subsequently become prominent in academic publishing. For several years he was General Editor of the 'Critical Heritage' series, and in 1980 he became proprietor and manager of The Athlone Press. In addition to books on Jane Austen, his publications include studies on Tennyson and T. S. Eliot.

VIRGINIA WOOLF (died 1941), novelist and literary critic.

INDEX